Organizational Conflict - New Insights

Edited by Josiane Fahed-Sreih

Published in London, United Kingdom

IntechOpen

Supporting open minds since 2005

Organizational Conflict - New Insights
http://dx.doi.org/10.5772/intechopen.78825
Edited by Josiane Fahed-Sreih

Contributors
Norman Chivasa, Mitashree Tripathy, Louise Kiernan, Ann Ledwith, Raymond Lynch, Nanche Billa Robert, Kyriaki Fousiani, Antony Tebitendwa, Ngoni Chikwanha

First published in London, United Kingdom, 2022 by IntechOpen
IntechOpen is the global imprint of INTECHOPEN LIMITED, registered in England and Wales, registration number: 11086078, 5 Princes Gate Court, London, SW7 2QJ, United Kingdom
Printed in Croatia

British Library Cataloguing-in-Publication Data
A catalogue record for this book is available from the British Library

Additional hard and PDF copies can be obtained from orders@intechopen.com

Organizational Conflict - New Insights
Edited by Josiane Fahed-Sreih
p. cm.
Print ISBN 978-1-83880-579-1
Online ISBN 978-1-83880-592-0
eBook (PDF) ISBN 978-1-83880-890-7

Meet the editor

Dr. Josiane Fahed-Sreih is a full-time associate professor of Management in the School of Business, Lebanese American University. She is the founder and director of the Institute of Family and Entrepreneurial Business and a chairperson in the Department of Management at the same university. She was previously the assistant dean. She obtained a Ph.D. from Sorbonne University, Paris, France. Dr. Fahed-Sreih is the Middle East Coordinator for the Family Firm Institute (FFI), the USA, and a family wealth and family business consultant. She received the 2007 FFI International Award for outstanding achievement in furthering the understanding of family business issues that occur between two or more countries. She has participated in and organized international conferences, workshops, and seminars. She has presented at major conferences locally and internationally and consulted on management issues in many countries, including Saudi Arabia, Dubai, Jordan, Qatar, Kuwait, Syria, Bahrain, Oman, France, Cyprus, and Lebanon. She currently sits on five boards of directors as a shareholder, two as a chairman of the board, and one as an independent director in the private sector. She is also an advisor on boards of community service organizations. She speaks regularly to trade and professional groups and presents her research at academic conferences worldwide. She is frequently invited as a keynote speaker to the recognized family business and corporate governance conferences. Her research interests are in management, family business, the functioning of boards of directors, and corporate governance. She has published three books, several book chapters, and academic articles in international journals. She is on the editorial board of the *Journal of Family Business Management* and is a reviewer for *Family Business Review, Corporate Governance*, and *Journal of Management.*

Contents

Preface

Workplace conflict is a state of disagreement or misunderstanding between members of the same organization. Conflict is normal and can arise in any workplace where people interact and have opinions that are contradictory.

Conflict arises when one person in any given organization sees that their goal, attitude, or values are different from those of other members of the organization. Conflict can occur between two members of the same organization or between one member and a group of members.

This book is a collection of chapters that deal with conflict in organizations from different perspectives. Whenever there are two persons exchanging relationships or tasks, there is a chance that conflict may occur. In the traditional perspective, conflict is viewed as something bad and negative. The human behaviorist perspective on conflict stipulates that conflict is normal whenever two persons are in contact, and the interactionist perspective on conflict stipulates that conflict can have a positive influence in organizations up to a certain level, below which conflict is functional and above which conflict becomes dysfunctional. When conflict is functional, it creates competitiveness, which can bring positive results in an organizational setting.

There are three types of organizational conflict: relationship conflict, task conflict, and process conflict. Two persons in an organization might have conflict about the way to perform a certain task, or they may have conflict about a process. The most difficult type of conflict to handle is relationship conflict, which can be very harmful because it affects the individual on a personal level.

Conflict can take place if there is **unclear responsibility** and there is a lack of clarity about who is responsible for a certain project or task. To avoid organizational conflict, roles and responsibilities of team members should be explicitly stated and agreed upon ahead of time. **Scarcity of resources**, such as money, time, and materials, is another factor influencing organizational conflict. **Conflict of interest** is when there is a distortion between the personal goals of the individual and the goals of the organization. Fighting for one's own goals may hinder the overall success of the organization. Interpersonal relationships can influence conflict as well. Different people have different personalities, and this can affect their relationships. Conflicts in the workplace can arise due to both individual and inter-individual factors. Individual causes are attitudes, personalities, beliefs, and norms. Inter-individual conflict arises when there is a breach of the organization's norms by a manager.

This book sheds light on the different types of conflicts that may arise in organizational settings and how to go about solving them.

Josiane Fahed-Sreih, Ph.D.
Lebanese American University,
Lebanon

Section 1

Conflict and Creative Problem Solving

Chapter 1

Power Asymmetry, Negotiations and Conflict Management in Organizations

Kyriaki Fousiani

Abstract

Relationships are seldom equal. In fact, social interactions involve most of the times power asymmetric relationships. Especially in organizations people are daily faced with situations where they are either in a powerful or in a powerless position compared to others. Power stems from various sources and takes several forms. For instance, people are powerful when they can administer punishments or rewards, when they are in a hierarchically higher position than others, when they have knowledge and expertise, when they are admired and respected, and when they have alternative options which enable them to make choices. Importantly, power determines the way people interact with each other and subsequently, the way they engage in conflicts and conflict resolution. Power-holders are best able to asymmetrically enforce their will and therefore, they have the capability to determine the process and the outcome of a conflict. In this chapter, I present the major sources of power and the main differences between them. Consequently, I elaborate on the impact of power on conflict management based on the negotiation literature. I conclude by touching on the necessity to distinguish between two contradictory faces of power: power as opportunity and power as responsibility.

Keywords: power, negotiation, conflict management, power as opportunity vs. responsibility

1. Introduction

Imagine that you are a manager in a large organization. You ask your subordinate employee for her help with a new project, but she refuses to help out because she has been working on a tight deadline and currently, she does not have any time for extra tasks. You are annoyed by the employee's reaction and there has been tension between you two ever since. You ask her to meet up and discuss... How do you think the meeting will go? How will you react to the employee and how do you think that the employee will respond?

A key element to take into account before trying to think of possible answers to these questions is that between the two persons, you and the subordinate employee, there is one big difference: power asymmetry. You, manager, have power over the employee, which enables you to punish, reward, or enforce your will to her, whereas the employee does not have power over you. Power asymmetry is a decisive factor in how all kinds of relationships develop and how conflicts are handled and resolved.

IntechOpen

Power makes the world go round. Power enables people to enforce their will over others and as such, it determines people's attitude towards a conflict and the way they choose to resolve it. In this chapter, I will delineate the role of power in conflict management focusing on conflicts in organizations in particular. First, I will explain how power is defined and which are the main sources of power. Consequently, I will present research-based evidence on the role of power in conflict management. Finally, I will touch on the importance of distinguishing power that is construed by the power-holder as opportunity from power that is construed as responsibility.

2. What is power and what are its sources?

Power is pervasive and as such, it is difficult to give it an accurate and clear-cut definition. For instance, power can be seen as the access to valuable material (food, money) or social (knowledge, information, decision-making opportunities) resources [1, 2], as the capability to achieve personal goals and influence other people's outcomes, as the capability to administer punishments and rewards, or as the potential to influence others and modify their attitude and behavior [3].

Power may stem from various sources. For example, a senior manager may rely on their ability to punish or reward others to get things done. A renowned expert in a field may rely on their knowledge and expertise, and a person who is admired by others for their skills or achievements may rely on personal qualities to influence others.

Social psychologists John French and Bertram Raven [4] studied power more than half a century ago and suggested that power can arise from various sources. French and Raven have grouped the forms of power into two broad categories, namely *positional* (or structural) and *personal* power. Positional power refers to the type of power that people have because of their status or position in an organization or society. This type of power aims to ensure that individuals and teams conform and work together towards predetermined outcomes and common goals set out for the group. Positional power includes the following three sub-types:

Legitimate power is derived from holding a formal title in some organization or in society and using the power that comes with that title. A country president, a senior manager, a CEO, or a prime minister have legitimate power. However, this type of power is unstable because when the title or position is lost, power instantly evaporates.

Coercive power is derived from one's ability to punish others for not complying with the rules and regulations or for not doing what needs to be done. Threats and punishment are standard coercive tools. For instance, when people imply that someone will be denied privileges or will get demoted or fired, they use coercive power.

Finally, *reward* power is derived from one's ability to reward others for doing positive things or for doing what needs to be done. Some examples of reward power include salary raises, promotions, compliments, and desirable assignments.

Although positional power enables power-holders to get things done and ensure that everyone works towards the same goal, it is not the type of power that inspires people. It is personal power that wins the hearts and minds of people, inspires them, and prompts them to commit to tasks. In other words, personal power inspires people to rise to greater heights, set the bars high, and perform as well as possible. Personal power includes the following two types:

Expert power is derived from having unique, in-depth information, expertise, or knowledge about a subject or a topic. When one has knowledge and skills that enable them to understand a situation, use solid judgment, and suggest useful or practical solutions, people trust them and eventually do what they say or want.

Finally, *referent* power is derived from the respect or admiration a person commands because of their personality traits and personal qualities. For instance, celebrities have referent power, which is why they exert such an influence on how laypeople think, feel, or behave. Actors, singers, and famous artists can influence everything from what people like or buy to which politician they vote. In the workplace, a person with referent power is a person who often makes everyone feel good and inspired, so that person has a lot of influence on their colleagues.

Apart from the above sources of power, which stem from either one's position or one's personal qualities, people may possess a different type of power, the so-called *Best Alternative To a Negotiated Agreement* (BATNA). The term BATNA was originally used by Roger Fisher and William Ury in 1981 in their book "Getting to Yes: Negotiating Without Giving In" and it involves a type of power that is inherent in conflict management and negotiation situations in particular. BATNA is defined as the most attractive alternative that a person can take if conflict management (i.e., negotiation) with a partner fails and an agreement cannot be made. In other words, one's BATNA is what one's best alternative is if negotiations do not succeed. In fact, having an attractive alternative enables people to be less dependent on others, which is translated into increased (sense of) power [5, 6]. For example, "*think for a moment about how you would feel walking into a job interview with no other job offers — only some uncertain leads. Think about how the talk about salary would go. Now contrast that with how you would feel walking in with two other job offers. How would that salary negotiation proceed?*" ([7], p. 52) In the first situation, your BATNA is unattractive (you have no other job offers

Source of power	Description and examples
Positional power	
Legitimate power	*Description:* Holding a formal title in some organization or in society and using the power that comes with that title. People are influenced by the power-holder's position rather than by the power-holder as a person. *Example:* A president, a CEO, a prime minister, a king.
Coercive power	*Description:* Ability to punish others for not doing what needs to be done. People comply out of fear. *Example:* Use of threats and punishments.
Reward power	*Description:* Ability to reward others for doing what needs to be done. People comply in order to get rewarded. *Example:* Raises, promotions, desirable assignments, training opportunities, compliments.
Personal power	
Expert power	*Description:* Possession of in-depth information or knowledge about a subject. People are actually influenced by the power-holder's claims and change their attitude and behavior based on the power-holder's attitude and behavior. *Example:* Suggestion of effective solutions, use of solid judgment, outperforming others.
Referent power	*Description:* Respect or admiration of a person based on his/her personality traits and personal qualities. People "follow" (oftentimes uncritically) the power-holder no matter whether they agree with him/her or not. *Example:* Celebrities and people with a "charismatic" and inspiring personality and attitude.
Contextual power	
Best Alternative To a Negotiated Agreement	*Description:* The most attractive alternative that a person can take if negotiation or conflict management with a partner fails and an agreement cannot be made. People comply with the will of others more if they have no other attractive alternatives. *Example:* Going to a job interview while having already another attractive job offer.

Table 1.
Major sources of power.

and thus no other good alternatives), which increases the likelihood that you accept a low salary in case you are offered the job. In the second situation, however, you have a strong BATNA (you have two other job offers), making you less dependent on your prospective employer and enabling you to negotiate a higher salary. The difference between the two examples is "power" (see **Table 1** for a brief description of all sources of power) (for a review of types of power, see also [8]).

3. Why is power important in conflict management?

Research suggests that besides their content-based differences, all kinds of power have a main characteristic in common: "dependence". Regardless of the specific sources of power that are involved, it is the level of *dependence* between individuals that allows power to occur [9]. Accordingly, the less one is dependent on the other, the more powerful one is, and the more one is dependent, the more powerless one is. As such, whether it is positional, personal, or contextual (e.g., BATNA), power should influence the direction of a conflict and conflict management process in the same way.

To test this hypothesis, Van Kleef, De Dreu, Pietroni, and Manstead [10] conducted five studies. In Study 1, power was operationalized as one's possession of an attractive alternative (BATNA). Participants were recruited in the lab and were assigned into one of the two experimental groups: high or low-power groups. All participants were assigned to the role of a phone seller and were told that two buyers were interested in the phones they were selling. The first buyer had already made an offer and participants had to negotiate the price with the second buyer. Participants in the high-power group were given an attractive offer (alternative) by the first buyer (the first buyer's offer would give them 570 points, while the maximum points they could reach were 760 points). However, participants in the low-power group were given an unattractive offer (alternative) (the first buyer's offer would only yield 190 points). Subsequently, participants had to negotiate the phone price with the second buyer and make a counteroffer. Importantly, participants got informed about the buyer's (opponent) emotional reaction to their counteroffer. More specifically, buyers were presented as having reacted happily or angrily to the participants' counteroffer. Results showed that low-power participants made more concessions than high-power participants, and also, the buyer's emotions (angry or happy) influenced them to a greater extent. Specifically, low-power negotiators conceded more to an angry buyer than to a happy one, whereas high-power negotiators were immune to the buyer's emotional state.

Van Kleef et al. [10] replicated these findings in four additional studies, where power was operationalized differently. For instance, in one study, high-power participants had a managerial position in an organization (legitimate power). In contrast, low-power participants had a junior-trainee position. In another study, high-power participants had the full support of the top management for the negotiation to come. In contrast, low-power participants did not (i.e., note that in conflicts in organizations), the availability of support increases individuals' sense of power because it enables them to form coalitions with others in order to get their way and assures them that they do not stand alone in the conflict [11]. These findings suggest that regardless of the power source, the mere existence of power asymmetry between negotiators determines the negotiation outcome: The low-power negotiators are more likely to concede to their powerful opponent than the other way around. It is noteworthy, however, that in none of these studies did the researchers operationalize personal power. All five studies used positional power or BATNA to operationalize power and therefore, there is no evidence about how referent or expert power of power-holders influences an opponent's reaction in the conflict.

An important reason for which power is such a determinant factor of conflict management is that power directs people's willingness to search for information about their partner [12, 13]. Information gathering involves questioning one's partner and "asking for information" to test one's beliefs and assumptions [14, 15] and as such, it is central to conflict management. Importantly, questions can be diagnostic or leading. Diagnostic questions aim at providing evidence for or against one's beliefs or assumptions, whereas leading questions have the purpose to yield answers that confirm one's beliefs or assumptions, regardless of whether those beliefs and assumptions are valid or not [16]. Subsequently, diagnostic questions allow negotiators to better understand their partners and their wishes than leading questions [17–19]. In three experiments, De Dreu and Van Kleef [20] investigated the effects of power on people's willingness to search for information about their negotiation partner. Participants were placed in a high or low-power position (relatively to their partners) and were also told that their partners had competitive or cooperative personalities. Just before negotiations began, participants were given the opportunity to write down questions they would like to ask their partners. Participants' questions were then content-coded as diagnostic or leading.

In line with their predictions, De Dreu and Van Kleef [20] found that low-power participants indicated a stronger drive to understand their partner, which prompted them to ask more diagnostic than leading questions, especially when their partner was described as competitive. These findings provide evidence that low-power individuals, especially when faced with a competitive partner, feel less comfortable and are more likely to develop an accurate impression and opinion about their partner. However, high-power participants did not indicate such motivation regardless of their partner's (competitive or cooperative) personality. These results might also shed light on why low-power negotiators are more influenced by powerful people's emotions and why they concede more (as was shown by [10]).

Besides the differential outcomes that powerful and powerless individuals can achieve in conflicts and negotiations (e.g., more or less concessions of the opponent), power can also shape people's emotional expression during a conflict. For instance, Petkanopoulou, Rodríguez-Bailón, Willis, & Van Kleef [21] carried out three studies to investigate how power shapes anger expression and what are the motives of high- versus low-power individuals to express anger at others. In line with their predictions, researchers found that high-power individuals are more prone to express their anger directly at their target as compared to low-power individuals, who are more likely to express their anger indirectly (e.g., by sharing it with other people rather than with the target of the anger). Moreover, low-power individuals expected that expressing their anger directly would elicit reciprocal anger in the powerful and would cause negative consequences to them. In contrast, high-power participants expected that both direct and indirect anger expressions would elicit fear rather than reciprocal anger in the powerless.

Based on the above, one would conclude that holding power, no matter what the source of power is, makes people appear tougher in conflict management processes, more immune to the others' emotions, and more focused on self-interested goals. A fundamental question that arises here is: "Is power inherently "selfish", and what is its functionality in organizations?" This is a very interesting question as power is inherent in organizations, in human interactions and relationships, and of course, in all kinds of conflict.

In real-life, we see that the effects of power on people's behavior are not uniform. For instance, laypeople frequently rely on powerful others, seek advice, or count on their help whenever they need it. In the following, I present two contradictory functions of power in order to illuminate this issue: power as opportunity versus power as responsibility.

4. Is power an opportunity or a responsibility?

In the above, we defined and examined power as one's capability to influence one's outcomes, as one's access to valuable material and social resources, as one's capability to administer rewards or punishments to others, and as one's potential to influence others. As such, power prompts power-holders to view their advantage over the powerless as an opportunity to achieve personal goals instead of taking care of the powerless. Indeed, power-holders frequently show less caring and affection towards the powerless and treat them as a means for goal attainment [22, 23]. The opportunistic propensity of power-holders is nicely depicted in the activation/ inhibition system theory [2]. which suggests that possessing power frees people up from external constraints as power makes them feel that their resources approach or even exceed the demands of a situation. Therefore, power-holders have the luxury to experience situations predominantly as opportunities to achieve their own goals and therefore, construe others through a lens of self-interest [2]. In contrast, low power activates an "alarm system" that makes people experience situations and social interactions as a threat. Accordingly, low-power people are more sensitive to powerful others' potential constraints and become more attentive to the interests, desires, and goals of the powerful. Subsequently, powerless people often become easier targets of power-holders' aggression, dominance, and self-interested behavior [24, 25].

Based on the above, one would conclude that some paranoia about the powerful seems to be reasonable. There is evidence, however, that the effects of power are not uniform. In fact, we often observe that in real-life (e.g., within an organization) powerful people are more benevolent than they are thought to be, attentive to the others' needs, and show concern about other people's goals and interests [26, 27]. Indeed, rather than being careless or selfish, power-holders often see their power as responsibility towards others and as an inner obligation to take care of things that need to happen (e.g., ensuring that important goals are met [28]). For instance, we frequently see in organizations that leaders do show concern for their followers' outcomes and use their power not only to serve their own goals but also the needs and desires of their followers [29, 30]. All in all, power, apart from giving power-holders the opportunity to act upon will and behave self-servingly, it also entails responsibility towards the powerless [29, 31].

A fundamental and interesting question is "when do power-holders see their power as responsibility or opportunity and how does the differential perception of power influence conflict management"? To the best of my knowledge, there is no empirical evidence to test this hypothesis directly. However, recent research shows that power-holders do not behave opportunistically when their power is stable and safe, that is when they do not fear that they might lose it. In contrast, when their power is unstable, power-holders are more susceptible to act self-servingly [32]. Indeed, prior research in the field of leadership suggests that when leaders are threatened by the prospect of losing power, which goes together with losing access to valuable resources, they react negatively to the prospective loss (see [33]). In a similar vein, research in the field of conflict management revealed that power-holders show more concern for their low-power partners' needs when their power is not in jeopardy.

Fousiani et al. [34] conducted two studies to come to this conclusion. In the first study, participants were put in dyads and were told that they would negotiate some issues/disagreements with their partner. Participants were split into two groups: high and low-power groups. Participants in the high power group were assigned to the role of a powerful manager who had the ability to make decisions that affect employees. Participants in the low power group were assigned to the role of a powerless employee who had to follow the managers' decisions. Most importantly, the issues or disagreements that participants were invited to negotiate with each other were not always the same. Dyads were invited to negotiate (in random order) power-related disagreements, that is disagreements about power possession in the decision-making processes, and task-related disagreements, that is disagreements regarding the coordination of work activities. Researchers found that high-power negotiators accommodated (gave in) their low power negotiating partner especially when the disagreements at hand touched on task-related but not power-related disagreements. According to the researchers' interpretation, these findings point out power-holders' motivation to accommodate the powerless when their powerful position was safe, and theis inclination to maintain the status quo and keep their power position intact [35–37]. In other words, high-power negotiators do not mind using their power in favor of the powerless and accommodating them as long as their power position is safe, but they do mind if their power position is in jeopardy.

Overall, these findings reveal that power-holders are not as opportunistic or competitive as they are believed to be. In fact, whether power-holders collaborate, accommodate or compete with the powerless in conflict situations seems to depend on how stable and safe their power is perceived to be. Based on the above, one would expect that power not only is it not inherently "selfish" but it is used responsibly and benevolently, especially when power-holders perceive their position as safe.

5. Concluding remarks

This chapter presented the impact of power on organizational conflict and conflict management in organizations based on the negotiation literature. Power is pervasive and as such, it has a great impact on conflicts in organizations. People usually associate power with unethicality and immorality, self-interested attitude and behavior, and win-lose outcomes [34, 38]. Indeed, empirical evidence supports this postulation and shows that power-holders are less empathic to the powerless and unaffected by their low-power partners' emotions, less willing to search for the beliefs, needs, and desires of the powerless, and they always demand the larger piece of a pie.

However, we should be careful with overgeneralizing these findings as power is also associated with providing help and support to the powerless, taking care of things that others cannot take care of, and treating those in need with responsibility and benevolence. As such, power asymmetry in organizations is desirable and functional and may promote win-win outcomes for the involved members, especially when power-holders feel that their powerful position is safe and not subject to changes. This suggests that organizations should encourage interventions geared at fostering power-holders' (e.g., leaders) sense of safety regarding their positions (see also, [39, 40]) in order to enable them to see their power as responsibility towards others rather than as opportunity and pay more attention to the needs and goals of the powerless (e.g., subordinate employees). Although power as responsibility is less attractive to power-holders and power as opportunity is particularly alluring [31], organizations might consider fostering the positive sides of being responsible for the outcomes and achievements of the powerless. This is the best way to ensure fairer outcomes and effective conflict management between those involved in asymmetric power relationships.

Conflict of interest

"The author declares no conflict of interest."

Author details

Kyriaki Fousiani
Faculty of Behavioural and Social Sciences, Department of Organizational Psychology, University of Groningen, Groningen, The Netherlands

*Address all correspondence to: k.fousiani@rug.nl

References

[1] Fiske, S. T. (2010). *Interpersonal stratification: Status, power, and subordination*. In S. T. Fiske, D. T. Gilbert, & G. Lindzey (Eds.), Handbook of social psychology (p. 941-982). John Wiley & Sons, Inc.. Doi: 10.1002/9780470561119.socpsy002026

[2] Keltner, D., Gruenfeld, D. H. & Anderson, C. (2003). Power, approach, and inhibition. Psychological Review, 110, 265-284. Doi: 10.1037/0033-295X.110.2.265

[3] Sturm, R. E., & Antonakis, J. (2015). Interpersonal power: A review, critique, and research agenda. Journal of Management, *41,* 136-163.

[4] French, J. R. P., & Raven, B. (1959). The bases of social power. In D. Cartwright (Ed.), *Studies in social power*. Oxford, United Kingdom: Univer, pp. 150-167.

[5] Lee, F., & Tiedens, L. Z. (2002). Is it lonely at the top? The independence and interdependence of power holders. In B. M. Staw, & R. I. Sutton (Eds.), *Research in organizational behavior (Vol. 23*, pp. 43-92). New York: JAI Press.

[6] Pinkley, R. L. (1995). Impact of knowledge regarding alternatives to settlement in dyadic negotiations: Whose knowledge counts? Journal of Applied Psychology, *80,* 403-417.

[7] Fisher, R. & Ury, W. (1981). *Getting to YES: Negotiating agreement without giving in*. New York, NY: Penguin.

[8] Lewicki, R. J., Barry, B. and Saunders, D. M. (2020), *Negotiation*. Boston, MA: McGraw-Hill.

[9] Emerson, R. M. (1962). Power-dependence relations. American Sociological Review, 27, 31-41. Doi: 10.2307/2089716

[10] Van Kleef, G.A., De Dreu, C. K. W., Pietroni, D., & Manstead, A. S. R. (2006). Power and emotion in negotiation: power moderates the interpersonal effects of anger and happiness on concession making. European Journal of Social Psychology, *36:* 557-581. Doi:10.1002/ejsp.320

[11] Beersma, B., & De Dreu, C. K. W. (2002). Integrative and distributive negotiation in small groups: Effects of task structure, decision rule, and social motive. Organizational Behavior and Human Decision Processes, *87,* 227-252.

[12] Fiske, S. T. (1993). Controlling other people: The impact of power on stereotyping. American Psychologist, *48,* 621-628.

[13] Fiske, S. T., & Dépret, E. (1996). Control, interdependence, and power: Understanding social cognition in its social context. In W. Stroebe & M. Hewstone (Eds.), *European Review of Social Psychology, 7,* 31-61. Chichester, UK: Wiley.

[14] Pruitt, D. G., & Lewis, S. A. (1975). Development of integrative solutions in bilateral negotiation. Journal of Personality and Social Psychology, *31,* 621-630.

[15] Thompson, L. L. (1991). Information exchange in negotiation. Journal of Experimental Social Psychology, *26,* 82-90.

[16] Snyder, M. (1992). Motivational foundations of behavioral confirmation. In L. Berkowitz (Ed*.), Advances in Experimental Social Psychology* (Vol. 25, pp. 67-114). New York: Academic Press.

[17] Klayman, J., & Ha, Y.-W. (1987). Confirmation, disconfirmation, and information in hypothesis-testing. Psychological Review, *94*, 211-228.

[18] Skov, R. B., & Sherman, S. J. (1986). Information-gathering processes: Diagnosticity, hypothesis confirmatory strategies, and perceived hypothesis confirmation. Journal of Experimental Social Psychology, *22*, 93-121.

[19] Trope, Y., & Bassok, M. (1983). Information gathering strategies in hypothesis testing. Journal of Experimental Social Psychology, *19*, 560-576.

[20] De Dreu, C. K. W., & Van Kleef, G. A. (2004). The influence of power on the information search, impression formation, and demands in negotiation. Journal of Experimental Social Psychology, *40*, 303-319.

[21] Petkanopoulou, K., Rodríguez-Bailón, R., Willis, G.B. & Van Kleef, G.A. (2019), Powerless people don't yell but tell: The effects of social power on direct and indirect expression of anger. European Journal of Social Psychology, *49*, 533-547. Doi:10.1002/ejsp.2521

[22] Gruenfeld, D. H., Inesi, M. E., Magee, J. C. & Galinsky, A. D. (2008). Power and the objectification of social targets". Journal of Personality and Social Psychology,. 95, 111-127. Doi: 10.1037/0022-3514.95.1.111.

[23] Lammers J., & Stapel D. A. (2011). Power increases dehumanization. Group Processes & Intergroup Relations. 14, 113-126. Doi:10.1177/1368430210370042

[24] Sidanius, J. (1993). The psychology of group conflict and the dynamics of oppression: A social dominance perspective. In S. Iyengar & W. McGuire (Eds.), *Explorations in Political Psychology*. Durham, NC: Duke University Press, pp. 183-219

[25] Wisse, B., & Rus, D. (2012). Leader self-concept and self-interested behavior: The moderating role of power. Journal of Personnel Psychology, *11*, 40-48.

[26] Overbeck, J. R., & Park, B. (2001). When power does not corrupt: Superior individuation processes among powerful perceivers. Journal of Personality and Social Psychology, 8, 549-565. Doi:10.1037/0022-3514.81.4.549

[27] Overbeck, J. R., & Park, B. (2006). Powerful perceivers, powerless objects: Flexibility of power-holders' social attention. Organizational Behavior and Human Decision Processes, 99, 227-243. Doi:10.1016/j.obhdp.2005.10.003

[28] Sassenberg, K., Ellemers, N., Scheepers, D. & Scholl, A. (2014). Power corrupts revisited: The role of construal of power as opportunity or responsibility. In J-W. van Prooijen & P. A. M. van Lange (Eds.), *Power, politics, and paranoia: Why people are suspicious of their leaders*. Cambridge, UK: Cambridge University Press. pp. 73-87

[29] De Wit, F. D., Scheepers, D. T., Ellemers, N., Sassenberg, K. & Scholl, A. (2017). Whether power holders construe their power as responsibility or opportunity influences their tendency to take advice from others. Journal of Organizational Behavior, 38, 923-949. Doi: 10.1002/JOB.2171

[30] Scholl, A., De Wit, F., Ellemers, N., Fetterman, A. K., Sassenberg, K., & Scheepers, D. (2018). The burden of power: Construing power as responsibility (rather than as opportunity) alters threat-challenge responses. Personality and Social Psychology Bulletin, 44, 1024-1038. Doi:10.1177/0146167218757452

[31] Sassenberg, K., Ellemers, N. & Scheepers, D. (2012). The attraction of social power: The influence of construing power as opportunity versus responsibility. Journal of Experimental Social Psychology, 48, 550-555. Doi: 10.1016/j.jesp.2011.11.008

[32] Wisse, B., Rus, D., Keller, A. C., & Sleebos, E. (2019). Fear of losing

power corrupts those who wield it: The combined effects of leader fear of losing power and competitive climate on leader self-serving behavior. European Journal of Work and Organizational Psychology, 35, 28, 742-755. Doi: 10.1080/1359432X.2019.1635584

[33] Deng, M., Zheng, M., & Guinote, A. (2018). When does power trigger approach motivation? Threats and the role of perceived control in the power domain. Social and Personality Psychology Compass, *12*, e12390.

[34] Fousiani, K., Steinel, W., & Minnigh, P. A. (2020). Power asymmetry in negotiations: A comparison of cooperative versus competitive accounts. *International Journal of Conflict Management*. Vol. ahead-of-print, No. ahead-of-print. Doi: 10.1108/IJCMA-05-2020-0081

[35] Fehr, E., Herz, H., & Wilkening, T. (2013). The lure of authority: Motivation and incentive effects of power. American Economic Review, 103, 1325-1359. Doi: 10.1257/aer.103.4.1325

[36] Kteily, N., Saguy, T., Sidanius, J., & Taylor, D. M. (2013). Negotiating power: Agenda ordering and the willingness to negotiate in asymmetric intergroup conflicts. Journal of Personality and Social Psychology, 105, 978-995. Doi: 10.1037/a0034095

[37] Saguy, T., & Kteily, N. (2014). Power, negotiations, and the anticipation of intergroup Encounters. European Review of Social Psychology, 25, 107-141. Doi: 10.1080/10463283.2014.957579

[38] Fousiani, K., & Van Prooijen, J.W. (in press). Punishment reactions to powerful suspects: Comparing a corrupt" versus a "leniency" approach of power [Special Issue on What drives second- and third-party punishment? Conceptual replications of the 'intuitive retributivism' hypothesis?]. *Zeitschrift für Psychologie, Vol. 4,* No. ahead-of-print. Doi: 10.23668/psycharchives.3159

[39] Greer, L. L., van Bunderen, L., & Yu, S. (2017). The dysfunctions of power in teams: A review and emergent conflict perspective. *Research in Organizational Behavior, 37,* 103-124. Doi: doi.org/10.1016/j.riob.2017.10.005

[40] Kong, C. (2018, August 9). Demoted at work. Retrieved from www.roberthalf.com/blog/salaries-and-skills/demoted-at-work.

Chapter 2

How Task Conflict Can Support Creative Problem Solving in Teams by Stimulating Knowledge Sharing, Critical and Creative Thinking and Meta-Cognition

Louise Kiernan, Ann Ledwith and Raymond Lynch

Abstract

This study explores how task conflict can support creative problem solving in teams and the cognitive processes applied. As multidisciplinary teams can be diverse in nature, they may not always partake competently in the pooling of information, and as a result task conflict may arise due to differences in mental models. Under certain conditions task conflict is considered to be beneficial to creative problem solving because it stimulates knowledge exchange and integration and constructive criticism to reach co-created decisions and solutions. Four case studies were conducted to analyse the discourse of teams carrying out design and innovation projects. Task conflict was found to have a positive impact on creative problem solving in the application of four cognitive processes: knowledge processing, critical and creative thinking and metacognition (team self-reflection). Task conflict was positively related to creativity in the proposal of solution alternatives. The successful application of the cognitive processes was dependent on an awareness of when task conflict is appropriate and high level social skills. The findings have implications for managers of teams solving complex problems. They highlight how the cognitive processes can be constructively used to stimulate and manage conflict to effectively solve problems in teams.

Keywords: creative problem solving, task conflict, knowledge sharing, critical thinking, creative thinking, meta-cognition, cognitive processes

1. Introduction

Institutions and businesses are increasingly reliant on multidisciplinary teams to develop innovative solutions. Creative problem solving can occur in a variety of settings such as entrepreneurship, new venture research and development, and science [1, 2]. Many problems in organisations are complex and ill-defined and therefore orchestrate the need for the methods and processes of multidisciplinary teams which is now common place [3–5]. Team, creative problem solving is considered to be a key contributor to a company's competitiveness [6, 7]. Successful team cognition is when knowledge is distributed, shared and integrated within a team to make informed evaluations, judgements and decisions, during problem solving [8].

Alternative views and opinions when solving complex and ill-defined problems can result in the consideration of a wider array of perspectives and relevant information, which can ultimately result in more informed decision making [8–10]. The sharing and elaboration of diverse perspectives can steer group members to avoid early agreements and snap decisions by encouraging divergent thinking to explore alternative requirements and solutions [2, 11]. However the cognitive processes necessary for creative problem solving have had limited study, in the literature [12]. It has also been shown that the formation of functionally diverse teams does not automatically lead to knowledge sharing and subsequent creative problem solving and disciplinary differences may cause disagreements [13–15]. Alternatively teams may form an early consensus in the form of groupthink, where team members opt for team cohesion at the expense of the further examination of the problem elements [16]. Team creativity and performance has been shown to benefit from task conflict [17–19].

Task conflict is believed to support the exchange and integration of distributed information held by each team member, making for more informed judgements, decisions and solutions [14, 20]. The benefits of task conflict are associated with the constructive challenging of other's opinions and ideas; the encouragement of assertive, independent and unbiased thinking, to balance opposing arguments [21, 22]. These benefits are however subject to strong social, communication and collaboration skills [20, 23]. While conflict can be viewed as communication through dialogue, the components of communication that determine how conflict may support teams has not been significantly addressed [20, 24].

From the perspective of a discourse study around conflict, this study builds on the discussion that views conflicts as episodes of social interaction that are constructed between team members [24, 25]. Therefore, the objective of this study is to explore how through dialogue teams manage task conflict and the cognitive processes applied during creative problem solving.

2. Team cognition in creative problem solving

Previous research on creative problem solving has focused on individual, rather than on team cognition but there is now increased recognition of the importance of understanding team cognition [1]. Team creativity relates to the processes that integrate diverse views to create useful and novel solutions [26]. Studies have found task conflict to relate positively to creativity [27]. Task conflict is considered to promote divergent thinking to explore the problem area and broaden the scope of ideas [2]. The process of creative problem solving involves a number of steps. The first step is the identification of the problem scope and problem elements in order to provide some structure to the problem [28]. Ideation then occurs where one or more ideas are developed. The next step is concept development where selected ideas from the previous stage are further developed, critiqued and evaluated to identify difficulties with the solution. The final step is the refinement of solutions and their implementation [6]. Although numerous forms of team cognition may facilitate team creative problem solving, we focus on four forms of thinking that have a strong influence.

The following cognitive processes are instrumental to creative problem solving [29]. Firstly, as creative problem solving is focused on generating multiple solution options it has mainly been associated with creative thinking. Creative thinking is divergent with the purpose of creating a range of novel ideas [30–32]. It is linked to ideation and brainstorming [33, 34]. In many creative industries such as design and innovation, the solution space can be large in the iteration of multiple ideas which calls for creative thinking [35]. Design and Innovation studies have linked heightened levels of creative thinking to creative performance

[32, 36]. Individuals with advanced creative thinking skills, are deemed to have more originality, and novelty in their outcomes. Tests to determine levels of divergent and creative thinking measure fluency, flexibility and originality [37, 38]. Team creativity concerns the production of novel and useful ideas to produce products, processes and procedures by a team of people working together [39]. Team work is beneficial to creativity as groups are able to produce novel, creative outputs due to quality interactions and diverse cognitive inputs of the team members [40]. The working definition of creative thinking for this study is defined as:

Divergent thinking to explore and generate alternative ideas and options [41].

Secondly, while creative thinking is intrinsic to creative problem solving it is not sufficient in addressing the scope of many complex problems. Creative problems, such as design and innovation problems are ill-defined [42] and un-structured [43]. These problems often have multiple ways to represent the problem, multiple solution paths, emergent sub problems, goals that conflict, requiring distributed knowledge to solve them [42, 43]. Therefore many work place problems require convergent as well as creative and divergent thinking [44], which has not been extensively studied [45]. In creative fields like design, concept generation involves alternating between convergent and divergent thinking [46]. This has been attributed to a co-evolution process where the solution and problem space are explored and constructed in parallel [47, 48]. This entails alternating between the creation of solutions and then the further structuring of the problem as solution generation surfaces a need for further information. Convergent thinking is deductive and logical, involving evaluation, judgement and analysis. Convergent thinking can support the creative process. As alternative options are created through divergent thinking, convergent thinking is applied in a sense making process in order to select the more viable solutions for further development where divergent thinking is applied once again [49, 50]. These alternating cycles are thought to be so frequent that cognitively they occur concurrently in the ideation process [45]. Critical thinking is associated with convergent thinking as it is deductive and logical and includes the skills of analysis, interpretation, inference and evaluation [51, 52]. It involves questioning the reliability of knowledge and sources, and converging on answers and decisions [52, 53]. It involves being able to provide rational arguments to defend a position taken [54, 55]. The working definition of critical thinking for this study is defined as:

Convergent, logical and deductive thinking to interpret, analyse and judge information [41].

Thirdly, Along with the application of critical and creative thinking, functioning communication is essential for teams to create and share information, make decisions and coordinate their efforts [56, 57]. Mol et al. [8] define team cognition as "an emergent state that refers to the manner in which knowledge is mentally organized, represented and distributed within the team" (p. 243). Teams do not always pool distributed knowledge successfully due to difficulties in understanding other team members, the task, and a tendency to agree rather than look for clarifications or elaborations [58]. Therefore, communication and knowledge processing are key aspects of the collaboration process [8, 56]. The presentation of information clearly during creative problem solving can improve creative outcomes [32]. Knowledge processing relates to the collaborative process of the co-construction of knowledge where team members interact with each other to build shared new knowledge [59, 60]. Activities include active discussions such as asking for feedback and clarifications [61]. The working definition of knowledge processing for this study is defined as:

The process of elaborating, explaining, clarifying and exchanging information [41].

Lastly, Reflective thinking or meta-cognition is identified as one of the essential creative problem solving skills to control and monitor the process [51]. The literature has shown that metacognitive skill is synonymous with creativity and open ended problem solving [62, 63]. The ability to switch between divergent and convergent thinking requires metacognitive knowledge about when, how, and why to alternate between these processes [64, 65] Meta-cognitive activities are around planning the management of the problem solving process, monitoring the progress and ability of the team, and evaluating the success of the methods used [62, 66, 67]. The main elements of meta-cognition are: planning, monitoring and evaluating one's problem solving strategies [62, 68, 69]. The working definition of meta-cognition for this study is defined as:

Self-reflection through planning, monitoring and evaluating oneself or the team [41].

While these are the main cognitive processes involved in creative problem solving, multi-disciplinary teams can fail to collaborate and disagreements may occur due to differences in views and opinions [13, 14, 58].

3. Task conflict

Teams engage in discussions and negotiations to integrate diverse perspectives and ideas and this can cause conflict [70, 71]. Task conflict relates to disagreements about the task, including differences in judgements, opinions and alterative directions [72, 73]. Four meta-analyses have been carried out to understand the effect of conflict on team performance, including [17, 70, 74, 75]. The findings from these studies is incomplete but some of the findings show that task conflict can improve creative problem solving when certain conditions prevail. While the findings unanimously found process and relationship conflict to negatively influence team interactions task conflict can enhance team interaction through debate to consider a greater amount of information, opinions and ideas to create an in-depth understanding of the task [19, 76].

Task conflict has been associated with enhanced creativity in inter-organisational teams [77, 78]. Task related disagreements among team members are a key driver for rich collective knowledge structures emerging from knowledge exchange, which has a positive influence on team creativity [40]. Task conflict is considered to aid creative problem solving and group decision making because it defers decision making and triggers critical thinking and constructive criticism to evaluate solutions [17, 79, 80]. During the negotiation of conflict several opinions can be shared and integrated to support solutions and decisions [9, 81] As groups participate in task conflict they acquire a deeper learning and more knowledge of the problem elements. As individuals are willing to hear other perspectives they can then examines their own position and adjust [73] to reach common ground [82]. Task conflict can provide the team with the opportunity for further thinking to broaden the problem and promote novel and creative problem-solving solutions [20]. Micro conflicts for teams solving complex unstructured and ill-defined problems can be beneficial by decreasing uncertainty [14]. The benefits of task conflict are not automatic, Teams must be willing to communication in order to mitigate against the potentially negative influence that task conflict can create [20, 72].

The discussions of the team members during episodes of conflict can determine if conflict has a positive influence on teams. Gheorghe et al. [40] argue that the ability of teams to process information rests on the cognitive processes and individual representations, as well as on the quality of interactions that take place among group members. It can take team members several turns of speech to negotiate and resolve task conflict [25]. Task conflict can instigate collaboration, and social skills are necessary for effective collaboration to resolve conflicts [23]. A collaborative approach with the application of social skills can reduce task conflict transforming to dysfunctional forms of conflict like relationship conflict. [23, 83]. There are two approaches to resolving conflict, either through degenerative and competitive dialogue or through generative and collaborative dialogue [24, 84]. In degenerative discussions, the focus is not on forming a shared understanding, and the competitive nature of this approach often ends in a win or lose outcome [84]. In a generative dialogue the conflict is used as a vehicle to promote discussion and debate with the ultimate aim of arriving at a shared understanding. Collaboration, means focusing on shared goals, accommodating and integrating the positions of others [24].

While a number of studies have addressed the social skills necessary for collaborative problem solving such as [23, 85] there have been limited studies that have explored the cognitive processes involved in managing task conflict during creative problem solving. Many studies on conflict involve retrospective studies e.g. [70] and researchers have proposed that studies on conflict processes, require observational studies to understand the micro conflicts in the course of discussions [14]. They argue that examining the social-cognitive processes during the back and forth exchanges during conflict in creative problem solving, can provide insights into why task conflict can benefit team performance.

We propose that limited levels of task conflict can have a beneficial impact on creative problem solving by stimulating certain cognitive processes to encourage information exchange and negotiation, to build constructed knowledge within the team. Producing a creative output involves finding connections among seemingly unrelated concepts, requiring a complex knowledge structure facilitating groups to shift between perspectives [40]. In turn this will stimulate iterative episodes of idea exploration and evaluation to arrive at considered solutions. The purpose of this study is to understand how task conflict can support creative problem solving in teams and the cognitive processes used in the process.

4. Method

Case studies were used to investigate design teams working in context at the front end of innovation projects and explores the dialogue of the participants to understand their cognitive processing. The research methodology was chosen to understand the context dependent and complex interconnected processes of creative problem solving. An important part of team creative problem solving is verbal communication and conversation.

5. Data collection

There were four cases in the study. Two of the cases involved two teams within each case, this is summarised in **Table 1**. A case was determined by the context and the project. Therefore, if two teams worked on the same project within the same environment this made up one case. The first case consisted of a bio-medical fellowship program (MedDev1), the second an undergraduate project (Students), the third a professional practice case (Consultants) and the fourth an additional bio-medical case (MedDev2). All data collected was from the front end of the design and innovation process.

Observations were carried out during meetings and work sessions. The raw data was audio recorded and transcribed. Field notes were taken during and shortly after observations episodes to correctly record the activity (Cohen et al. 2007). The research data analysed for each case is summarised in **Table 2**.

Teams	Project	Team Type	Expertise
Med-Dev 1 (2 teams of 4)	Medical device innovation	Interdisciplinary: engineering, medicine, business and law.	Fellows, experienced /post-doctoral level
Undergraduate (2 teams of 7)	Design of a user-centered crew rest for flight attendants.	Interdisciplinary: product design and digital communication	Undergraduate design students, novice
Consultants (1 team of 4)	User experience software interface design.	Interdisciplinary: interaction design, software engineering and business.	Industry consultants, experienced
Med-Dev 2 (1 team of 4)	Medical device innovation	Interdisciplinary: engineering, medicine and design.	Fellows experienced /post-doctoral level

Table 1.
Case study profile.

	MedDev1	Students	Consultants	MedDev2
Analysed data	4 hrs of conversation recorded and analysed	5 hrs of conversation recorded and analysed	1.5 hrs of conversation recorded and analysed	5.5 hrs of conversation recorded and analysed
Meeting durations	*Problem definition:* Team A: 1 hr. 40 min Team B: 1 hr. 52 min	*Problem definition:* Team A: 40 min Team B: 46 min. *Ideation:* Team B: 1 hr. *Concept development:* Team A: 30 min	*Problem definition & Ideation:* 1.5 hrs	*Problem definition:* 3 hrs *Ideation:* 1 hr. 25 min *Concept development:* 1 hr

Table 2.
Details of data collection.

6. Data analysis

The analysis followed protocol and conversation analysis studies in creative research [86, 87]. The turn taking during conversations was analysed during meetings, e.g. [87]. The team dialogue was audio recorded, transcribed and imported to NVIVO and organised per case study. Analysis was both manual, in reviewing the data and digital, in the use of NVivo to theme the codes. The data was first divided into manageable chunks of topic segments. Topic shifts or changes were considered to be a suitable means to define topic segments as, topic shifts and changes start and finish through cooperation and consensus [88]. How a topic shift, or change occurred was assessed to determine if the participants reached agreement or if they changed topic without agreement. Expressions of agreement came in the form of utterances such as: uh, yeah, yes, mm, and Ok (ibid). Content analysis was applied in the deductive analysis of text data from the team discussions, through a systematic classification process of coding and identifying themes or patterns [89]. The four cognitive processes selected from the literature (knowledge processing, critical thinking, creative thinking and meta-cognition) were allocated to the utterances of each participants. **Table 3** shows the cognitive processes explored and descriptors for each [41]. There was some overlap for example where an utterance could overlap two cognitive processes.

Cognitive processes	Primitives
Knowledge processing	The process of elaborating, explaining, clarifying and exchanging information.
Critical thinking	Convergent, logical and deductive thinking to interpret, analyse and judge information.
Creative thinking	Divergent thinking to explore and generate alternative ideas and options.
Meta-cognition	Self-reflection through planning, monitoring and evaluating oneself or the team.

Table 3.
Descriptor of each cognitive process.

Reliability is about the degree to which findings can be repeated in subsequent studies, even by other researchers. An inter-rater reliability study was performed with a second coder, to code a portion of the data according to the descriptions of the themes provided by the researcher. The results showed a Kappa coefficient of: 0.718.

7. Findings

The findings have confirmed that during creative problem solving teams will alternate between the four cognitive process of: critical thinking, knowledge processing, metacognition and creative thinking to different degrees to instigate conflict and use it to support creative problem solving. The level of use across the four cases was:

1. Critical Thinking (40%)

2. Knowledge Processing (34%)

3. Meta-Cognition (27%)

4. Creative Thinking (7%)

Table 4 outlines the number of topics segments per team at each phase with task conflict. While the teams were solution orientated and proposed several solutions to problems they engaged in limited creative thinking. As teams shared knowledge this surfaced a diversity in opinions and views which triggered task conflict. To resolve the conflict and arrive at a united position the teams iteratively alternated through the cognitive processes outlined, in a cycle of information sharing and elaboration, solution generation, solution evaluation and reflection (**Figure 1**).

	Med-Dev1 Team A	Med-Dev1 Team B	Under-graduate Team A	Under-graduate Team B	Consultants	MedDev2
Problem Definition	0 of 40	1 of 56	0 of 13	0 of 11	0 of 44	3 of 40
Ideation	—		—	3 of 34		0 of 37
Concept development	—		3 of 15	—		3 of 34

Table 4.
Number of topic segments per team at each phase with task conflict.

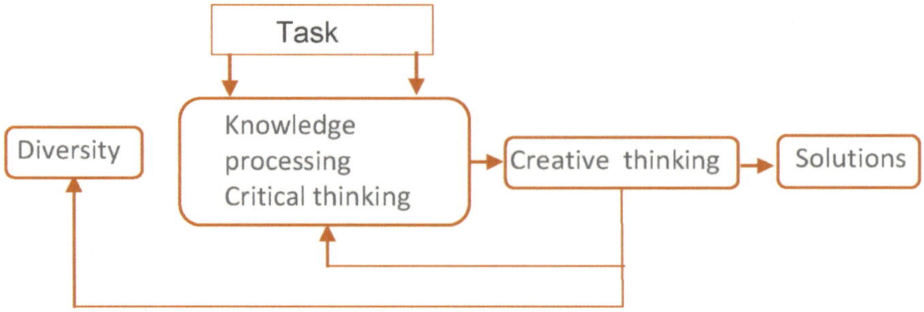

Figure 1.
Team creative problem solving cognitive processes.

Table 5 provides an example of four topic segments from the Med Dev 2 case. The team were at the stage of developing and selecting solution directions for their project. Their aim was to develop an:

"easier way to manage faecal matter from an Ileostomy[1] *in a way that reduces the risks of skin complications and improves security in its management."*

The team were trying to reach a conclusion on the selection of a final solution. Agreement was slow to reach, as solutions were evaluated, critiqued and judged by the team members before reaching a decision. Task conflict prompted the evaluation of solutions put forward by team members and strong negotiations ensued before any common ground was reached. There were a number of options that the team were considering which were around removing the risks of skin complications that can occur when using ileostomy bags. The purpose of the meeting was to discuss the viability of the options. The example in **Table 5** is a proposal put forward by L suggesting that users would cut the proposed solution to their size. He uses knowledge processing to share this information and critical thinking in providing a rational for the proposal. Team member R instigates task conflict by disagreeing with the proposal and uses critical thinking to argue that it allows too much room for error. While L accepts R's argument he counter argues to justify his solution with a material that would stretch to size with an undersized hole. The team members continue to share information and then L picks up the argument again to propose that it is acceptable for users to cut a hole in the product. While this is accepted by K it is not accepted by RS who argues that the solution may not be any better than the original product which leaks. L provides a further argument to justify his proposal over the existing solution. While the team have not reached an agreement the task conflict that has ensued has forced the elaboration of information between the team members and an evaluation of the potential risks associated with the proposed solution.

The discussion continues and a new line of argument is introduced by L in **Table 6** around the requirement for a solution to adhere to manufacturing requirements. He argues against a proposal that had been put forward earlier by R arguing that it complicates the manufacturing process. A number of counter arguments proceed further. There is still no agreement between the team members in reaching a solution path but a further analysis of proposed solutions have been put forward through the exchange of knowledge processing and critical thinking brought about by task conflict.

As consensus did not occur in the previous topic, K shifts the topic to propose a different solution. The response to this is more positive, as *creative thinking* is used to develop the solution instead of critiquing it. K proposes how the idea could work.

---

[1] An ileostomy is an opening in the abdominal wall that's made during surgery. The end of the ileum (the lowest part of the small intestine) is brought through this opening to form a stoma.

	Cognitive processes
L: You could go with the guideline that if your stoma is an inch in diameter you cut it at ¾ of an inch.	KP, CT
R: I would not have anyone cut anything. Just the cutting thing L. if you allow them to cut it gives someone the room for error.	CT
L: Yeah you are right, but again this is cut and if you look at the difference between this material and that one. There is no real stretch in this one. They cut it and it leaves gaps. Do not worry if it's not disposable then you can pick a size. Whereas if it is that type of material you cut it smaller and you get a seal.	KP, CT
K: If you could get these bags.	KP
R: If they get it, there is a top on it that is completely closed over and they come along with their scissors and cut it.	KP
L: I'm actually speaking about creating the hole in that.	KP
K: Alright (agreement).	
L: Let us say for arguments sake that that is a flat at the moment .	KP
K: It's flat and there is no hole and you get your cutter and cut it to the size of the stoma. That's ideal.	KP, CT
RS: Are you not back to square one then, as the original?	CT
L: There would be two differences one slightly more than the other. One difference is that there is no adhesive. This is touching the skin. Ordinarily there is an adhesive there and that is causing a problem. You do not have any adhesive and you do not have to change it. If you have to change the bag ten times a day this stays on. The second thing is if you cut a hole in that it does not stretch around the stoma. It's just placed around it and there are gaps. Whereas with this one let us say you make a hole in that you have got that element of stretch around it.	KP, CT

KP: knowledge processing, CT: Critical thinking, CRT: Creative thinking, MC: meta-cognition.

Table 5.
Concept development discussion.

Examples	Cognitive process
L: I'm trying to think of it from a manufacturing point of view, as soon as you put this protrusion on it you have a different mode of selection, like what size is your stoma? It's almost like you have to buy these as customised. I'm just thinking production line.	CT
R: It's three different moulds.	CT
L: If it's three different moulds it becomes more expensive very fast.	CT
RS: But if they have to cut it to size would it be accurate enough?	CT
R: I would not allow them cut it at all. I think if we made it flat and this gives you your accommodation that might be enough, we might prove that you need two different sizes within the range.	CT
RS: would it not just stretch on to any size?	CT
K: I would not be worried about manufacturing that, versus a flat in terms of a mould. This stuff is very easy to mould.	KP, CT
L: The question is are you manufacturing ten different sizes or can you customise it?	CT
RS: That looks like it would stretch to any size	CT

KP: knowledge processing, CT: Critical thinking, CRT: Creative thinking, MC: meta-cognition.

Table 6.
Concept development discussion 2.

Both R and K then build on the idea and establish an agreement on the solution path. Another observation is that when solutions were rejected in the previous topic segments and critiqued in the course of conflict episodes the team members were forced to consider alternatives or adjustments to solutions. This shows a clear relationship between task conflict and creativity (**Table 7**).

The discussion continues with further back and forth exchanges of critical thinking which then results in an agreement on a solution direction and a conclusion of the topic (**Table 8**).

Examples	Cognitive processes
K: The way I was thinking, this part could be stiffer and smaller or bigger but if you could get bags with a standard shape cut out that slots into that perfectly every time.	CRT
R: A snap fit.	CRT
K: And your inner flowery type opening always guides the fluid in, they still stick on to each other, then you are sure that there is no contact with the skin. The problem there probably is this hole. Maybe you have to sell exclusively H. bags with a standard hole size.	CRT, CT
R: There is two different options of bags, you can get ones that are cut to size and ones that are pre-cut, so they can sell a pre-cut.	KP
K: So they can do that.	KP
R: So maybe just to further that, if this was to go in you would nearly snap fit it in or that once it's in, there is a rim that goes out this way and it hooks into it. It might be harder to get it in, but once it's in there is a lock on it.	CRT, CT
L: Like vacuum cleaners.	CT
Kev: That's a clever mechanical lock all right but I would still be hoping that the adhesive we currently use in bags and manufacture would suffice to stick the bag onto whatever we have so that there is no leak. But it would be a nice addition.	CT
R: I just thought that if you were getting direct contact between here and here that it is not touching the skin at all is that not it?	CT
K: yeah that's it.	

KP: knowledge processing, CT: Critical thinking, CRT: Creative thinking, MC: meta-cognition.

Table 7.
Concept development discussion 4.

Examples	Cognitive processing
L: Let us say for argument sake that this was your size and it goes into the bag and that's your stoma. There is the risk if you have a smaller stoma that it comes out and leaks back and gets held in here, I mean.	CT
R: Unless this stretches on. Try it on that and see.	CT
L: I'm just saying that in the worst case scenario if that happens you may still be in a much better position than you are if it happens without this ring because as you have seen from the pictures it can spread out whereas it might just be limiting the problem to a few millimetres around it. So you might still be off to a pretty good start.	CT
R: You might get 95% cover.	CT
L: 95% effectiveness. **CONSENSUS**	
R: Yeah that would be great. **CONSENSUS**	CT

KP: knowledge processing, CT: Critical thinking, CRT: Creative thinking, MC: meta-cognition.

Table 8.
Concept development discussion 4 continued.

A final observation as witnessed in the data presented was that at no stage did the task conflict head towards relationship conflict which has been shown to be a risk and a reason why some researchers do not support the benefits of task conflict [70]. The teams showed an advanced level of social skills in recognising how to benefit from the conflict. For example, in **Table 8** L actively argues against his own solution to ensure that all risk associated with the solution are uncovered. In **Table 7** the teams avoided conflict during episodes of idea generation in order to suspend judgement to let ideas flow.

8. Discussion

Our findings have a number of implications. Firstly, the significant contribution of this paper to the literature on conflict management is in showing how task conflict can stimulate cognitive processes that facilitate teams to partake in creative problem solving. The topic segments depicting conflict as presented here are representative of discursive social interactions, illuminating the cognitive processes and results of the conflicts [24, 90]. They present an understanding of the generative dialogues that are used in instances of task conflict during creative problem solving. The findings highlight that the negotiation of conflict can prompt teams to share diverse information and perspectives, negotiate and elaborate on that information to arriving at co-created solutions as shown in **Figure 1**. Task conflict prevented premature agreement by challenging the status quo and instigating new lines of thinking. As team members shared diverse knowledge and perspectives with knowledge processing this triggered task conflict. To negotiate the conflict and arrive at a united goal, the teams iteratively cycled through episodes of creative thinking in the proposal of ideas, critical thinking to judge and evaluate the ideas and the perspective of others and metacognition to reflect on the suitability of the strategies engaged with by the team.

Secondly, another finding was that task conflict is indirectly and positively connected to team creativity [78]. The findings show however that conflict was not associated with creative thinking and that the topic segments that displayed creative thinking were not topics that had instances of task conflict. Team members appeared to recognise where and when to use conflict and did not critique early ideas. However, there was evidence to show that the task conflict that occurred in preceding topics often forced a rethink in terms of solution directions and it was this, that prompted the teams to use creative thinking to come up with alternative solutions. This required a balance in the management of the conflict in that, while task conflict led to a creative rethink on solution paths, it was important that task conflict did not stifle creative thinking in the flow of alternative ideas. This supports Kiernan et al. [91] who showed that task conflict impacts positively only at certain stages of the creative process, the problem definition and concept development phases. While they recommend moderate levels of conflict at these phases they argue that conflict has the potential to have a damaging impact at the ideation phase by stifling the fluency of ideas. Therefore the focus for teams at the ideation phase should be on producing a breath of ideas which is desirable for creative problem solving [92].

The third contribution points for a need to have advanced social skills [23] and a heightened awareness of when and how to apply these skills. It is about understanding when the introduction and the continuation of task conflict can benefit the progress of the team. It has been shown that enhanced communication, [20] social skills, [23] and generative dialogues [24] are necessary to support the negotiation and beneficial impact of task conflict. This study provides empirical evidence that the use of the cognitive processes of knowledge processing, critical thinking, creative thinking and meta-cognition were linked to advanced social, communication and collaboration skills that supported the teams to partake in, control and gain from the conflict. Many team members demonstrated this with being able to build strong arguments but also in knowing when not to argue. Team members also regularly built on the arguments of others in order to build on a position being advocated to the group. This concurs with the literature which shows that this is a differentiating factor between experts and novices during episodes of conflict in design problem solving [91].

With respect to the inconclusive findings in the literature with regard to the benefits of task conflict, this research has made a fourth contribution to show that task conflict can benefit creative problem solving and should be encouraged. This study has highlighted the cognitive processes that are verbally uttered and how they are used to both instill and resolve task conflict. These findings have implications for how creative problem solving teams are managed. This study proposes that while task conflict can support creative problem solving it needs to be managed carefully. Advanced social, communication and collaboration skills need to be developed. This can be reached by facilitating the application of the cognitive processes outlined. These cognitive processes can serve as an aid to support teams to start and then negotiate the conflict. The levels of collaboration and social skills applied will determine how well teams function and an experienced facilitator may be necessary to both instigate and manage the negotiation of task conflict to ensure that the level of conflict does not escalate to unmanageable levels. This may be even more necessary when facilitating more novice and inexperienced teams. The level of conflict observed in this research was moderate. Higher levels of conflict could have a counterproductive impact on team interaction resulting in prolonged delays in decision making. This supports the literature which stresses that heightened and prolonged episodes of task conflict could be detrimental to a team's ability to move forward [17, 79].

9. Conclusions

The findings highlight how task conflict can benefit creative problem solving in teams by prompting team members to engage in a social exchange by applying cycles of the cognitive processes of; knowledge processing, critical thinking, creative thinking and meta-cognition. These cognitive processes were instrumental in supporting both divergent and convergent thinking and suspending decision making to process additional information and explore alternative ideas. While conflict was positively related to creativity it was not associated with creative thinking, however previous episodes of conflict often resulted in subsequent topic segments of creative thinking. The ability to apply the cognitive processes appeared to depend on advanced social and collaborative skills pointing to a possible difference between how experts and novices might compare in managing conflict.

Author details

Louise Kiernan*, Ann Ledwith and Raymond Lynch
University of Limerick, Limerick, Ireland

*Address all correspondence to: louise.kiernan@ul.ie

References

[1] Thayer, A.L., A. Petruzzelli, and C.E. McClurg, *Addressing the paradox of the team innovation process: A review and practical considerations.* American Psychologist, 2018. **73**(4): p. 363.

[2] Chen, X., et al., *Cognitive diversity and innovative work behaviour: The mediating roles of task reflexivity and relationship conflict and the moderating role of perceived support.* Journal of Occupational and Organizational Psychology, 2019. **92**(3): p. 671-694.

[3] Cross, N., *Designerly Ways of Knowing* 2006, London: Springer.

[4] De Vere, I., G. Melles, and A. Kapoor, *Product design engineering–a global education trend in multidisciplinary training for creative product design.* European journal of engineering education, 2010. **35**(1): p. 33-43.

[5] Jonassen, D.H. and W. Hung, *All problems are not equal: Implications for problem-based learning.* Interdisciplinary Journal of Problem-Based Learning, 2008. **2**(2): p. 4.

[6] Basadur, M., G. Gelade, and T. Basadur, *Creative problem-solving process styles, cognitive work demands, and organizational adaptability.* The Journal of Applied Behavioral Science, 2014. **50**(1): p. 80-115.

[7] Hirst, G., D. Van Knippenberg, and J. Zhou, *A cross-level perspective on employee creativity: Goal orientation, team learning behavior, and individual creativity.* Academy of management journal, 2009. **52**(2): p. 280-293.

[8] Mol, E., S.N. Khapova, and T. Elfring, *Entrepreneurial team cognition: A review.* International Journal of Management Reviews, 2015. **17**(2): p. 232-255.

[9] Parayitam, S., B.J. Olson, and Y. Bao, *Task conflict, relationship conflict and agreement-seeking behavior in Chinese top management teams.* International Journal of conflict management, 2010. **21**(1): p. 94-116.

[10] Talke, K., S. Salomo, and K. Rost, *How top management team diversity affects innovativeness and performance via the strategic choice to focus on innovation fields.* Research Policy, 2010. **39**(7): p. 907-918.

[11] Hoever, I.J., et al., *Fostering team creativity: perspective taking as key to unlocking diversity's potential.* Journal of applied psychology, 2012. **97**(5): p. 982.

[12] Dumas, D., L.C. Schmidt, and P.A. Alexander, *Predicting creative problem solving in engineering design.* Thinking Skills and Creativity, 2016. **21**: p. 50-66.

[13] Cheung, S.Y., et al., *When and how does functional diversity influence team innovation? The mediating role of knowledge sharing and the moderation role of affect-based trust in a team.* Human Relations, 2016. **69**(7): p. 1507-1531.

[14] Paletz, S.B., J. Chan, and C.D. Schunn, *The dynamics of micro-conflicts and uncertainty in successful and unsuccessful design teams.* Design Studies, 2017. **50**: p. 39-69.

[15] Salazar, M.R. and T.K. Lant, *Facilitating Innovation in Interdisciplinary Teams: The Role of Leaders and Integrative Communication.* Informing Science, 2018. **21**.

[16] Janis, I.L., *Groupthink: Psychological Studies of Policy Decisions and Fiascoes*. 2nd ed. 1982, Boston: Houghton Mifflin

[17] de Wit, F.R., L.L. Greer, and K.A. Jehn, *The paradox of intragroup conflict: a meta-analysis.* Journal of Applied Psychology, 2012. **97**(2): p. 360-390.

[18] Bradley, B.H., et al., *When conflict helps: Integrating evidence for beneficial*

conflict in groups and teams under three perspectives. Group Dynamics: Theory, Research, and Practice, 2015. **19**(4): p. 243.

[19] O'Neill, T.A. and M.J. McLarnon, *Optimizing team conflict dynamics for high performance teamwork.* Human Resource Management Review, 2018. **28**(4): p. 378-394.

[20] Wu, G., et al., *Investigating the relationship between communication-conflict interaction and project success among construction project teams.* International Journal of Project Management, 2017. **35**(8): p. 1466-1482.

[21] Nemeth, C.J., et al., *Improving decision making by means of dissent* Journal of Applied Social Psychology, 2001. **31**(1): p. 48-58.

[22] Yong, K., S.J. Sauer, and E.A. Mannix, *Conflict and creativity in interdisciplinary teams.* Small group research, 2014. **45**(3): p. 266-289.

[23] Lee, D., Y. Huh, and C.M. Reigeluth, *Collaboration, intragroup conflict, and social skills in project-based learning.* Instructional Science, 2015. **43**(5): p. 561-590.

[24] Hirvonen, P., *Positioning, conflict, and dialogue in management teams.* Qualitative Research in Organizations and Management: An International Journal, 2019. **ahead-of-print**(ahead-of-print).

[25] Holmes, J. and M. Marra, *Leadership and managing conflict in meetings.* Pragmatics, 2004. **14**(4): p. 439-462.

[26] Amabile, T., *Creativity in context: Update to.* 1996.

[27] Farh, J.-L., C. Lee, and C.I. Farh, *Task conflict and team creativity: a question of how much and when.* Journal of Applied Psychology, 2010. **95**(6): p. 1173.

[28] Reiter-Palmon, R. and V. Murugavel, *The effect of problem construction on team process and creativity.* Frontiers in psychology, 2018. **9**: p. 2098.

[29] Kiernan, L., A. Ledwith, and R. Lynch, *Comparing the dialogue of experts and novices in interdisciplinary teams to inform design education.* International Journal of Technology and Design Education, 2020. **30**(1): p. 187-206.

[30] Casakin, H., N. Davidovitch, and R.M. Milgram, *Creative thinking as a predictor of creative problem solving in architectural design students.* Psychology of aesthetics, creativity, and the arts, 2010. **4**(1): p. 31.

[31] Goldschmidt, G. and D. Tatsa, *How good are good ideas? Correlates of design creativity.* Design studies, 2005. **26**(6): p. 593-611.

[32] Montag-Smit, T. and C.P. Maertz Jr, *Searching outside the box in creative problem solving: The role of creative thinking skills and domain knowledge.* Journal of Business Research, 2017. **81**: p. 1-10.

[33] Runco, M.A. and G.J. Jaeger, *The standard definition of creativity.* Creativity Research Journal, 2012. **24**(1): p. 92-96.

[34] Ritter, S.M. and N.M. Mostert, *How to facilitate a brainstorming session: The effect of idea generation techniques and of group brainstorm after individual brainstorm.* Creative Industries Journal, 2018. **11**(3): p. 263-277.

[35] Stempfle, J. and P. Badke-Schaub, *Thinking in design teams-an analysis of team communication.* Design Studies, 2002. **23**(5): p. 473-496.

[36] Badke Schaub, P., G. Goldschmidt, and M. Meijer, *How does cognitive conflict in design teams support the development of creative ideas?* Creativity and Innovation Management, 2010. **19**(2): p. 119-133.

[37] Paulus, P., *Groups, teams, and creativity: The creative potential of idea-generating groups.* Applied psychology, 2000. **49**(2): p. 237-262.

[38] Runco, M.A. and S. Acar, *Divergent thinking as an indicator of creative potential.* Creativity Research Journal, 2012. **24**(1): p. 66-75.

[39] Gilson, L.L. and C.E. Shalley, *A little creativity goes a long way: An examination of teams' engagement in creative processes.* Journal of management, 2004. **30**(4): p. 453-470.

[40] Gheorghe, A., O. Fodor, and A. Pavelea, *Ups and downs on the roller coaster of task conflict: the role of group cognitive complexity, collective emotional intelligence and team creativity.* Psihologia Resurselor Umane, 2020. **18**(1): p. 23-37.

[41] Kiernan, L.l., A Lynch, R, *Does creativity rely on creative thinking? An exploration of the cognitive processes of design teams [Unpublished manuscript].* 2020, University of Limerick.

[42] Jonassen, D.H., *Instructional design models for well-structured and III-structured problem-solving learning outcomes.* Educational Technology Research and Development, 1997. **45**(1): p. 65-94.

[43] Goel, V. and P. Pirolli, *Motivating the notion of generic design within information-processing theory: The design problem space.* AI Magazine, 1989. **10**(1): p. 19.

[44] Cortes, R.A., et al., *Re-examining prominent measures of divergent and convergent creativity.* Current Opinion in Behavioral Sciences, 2019. **27**: p. 90-93.

[45] Goldschmidt, G., *Linkographic evidence for concurrent divergent and convergent thinking in creative design.* Creativity Research Journal, 2016. **28**(2): p. 115-122.

[46] Dong, A., *The enactment of design through language.* Design Studies, 2007. **28**(1): p. 5-21.

[47] Dorst, K. and N. Cross, *Creativity in the design process: co-evolution of problem–solution.* Design Studies, 2001. **22**(5): p. 425-437.

[48] Maher, M. and H.-H. Tang, *Co-evolution as a computational and cognitive model of design.* Research in Engineering design, 2003. **14**(1): p. 47-64.

[49] Ferreira, D.J. and G. Lacerda dos Santos, *Scaffolding online discourse in collaborative ill-structured problem-solving for innovation.* Informatics in Education-An International Journal, 2009(Vol 8_2): p. 173-190.

[50] Dorst, K., *The core of 'design thinking'and its application.* Design Studies, 2011. **32**(6): p. 521-532.

[51] Hong, Y.C. and I. Choi, *Assessing reflective thinking in solving design problems: The development of a questionnaire.* British Journal of Educational Technology, 2015. **46**(4): p. 848-863.

[52] Choi, I. and K. Lee, *Designing and implementing a case-based learning environment for enhancing ill-structured problem solving: Classroom management problems for prospective teachers.* Educational Technology Research and Development, 2009. **57**(1): p. 99-129.

[53] Wechsler, S.M., et al., *Creative and critical thinking: Independent or overlapping components?* Thinking Skills and Creativity, 2018. **27**: p. 114-122.

[54] Jonassen, D.H., *Instructional design as design problem solving: An iterative process.* Educational Technology, 2008. **48**(3): p. 21-26.

[55] Hung, W., D.H. Jonassen, and R. Liu, *Problem-based learning,* in

Handbook of research on educational communications and technology, J.G.v. J. M. Spector and M.D. Merriënboer, Merrill, & M. Driscoll Editors. 2008, Erlbaum.: Mahwah, NJ. p. 485-506.

[56] Détienne, F., M. Baker, and J.-M. Burkhardt, *Quality of collaboration in design meetings: methodological reflexions.* CoDesign, 2012. **8**(4): p. 247-261.

[57] Chiu, M.-L., *An organizational view of design communication in design collaboration.* Design Studies, 2002. **23**(2): p. 187-210.

[58] van Ginkel, W. and D. van Knippenberg, *Group information elaboration and group decision making: The role of shared task representations.* Organizational Behavior and Human Decision Processes, 2008. **105**(1): p. 82-97.

[59] Vuopala, E., et al., *Knowledge co-construction activities and task-related monitoring in scripted collaborative learning.* Learning, Culture and Social Interaction, 2019. **21**: p. 234-249.

[60] Janssen, J., et al., *Influence of group member familiarity on online collaborative learning.* Computers in Human Behavior, 2009. **25**(1): p. 161-170.

[61] Baker, M., *Argumentative interactions and the social construction of knowledge*, in *Argumentation and Education: Theoretical Foundations and Practices*, N.M.M.A.-N. Perret-Clermont, Editor. 2009, Springer: Berlin. p. 127-144.

[62] Hong, E., H.F. O'Neil, and Y. Peng, *Effects of explicit instructions, metacognition, and motivation on creative performance.* Creativity Research Journal, 2016. **28**(1): p. 33-45.

[63] Jaušovec, N., *Metacognition in creative problem solving*. 1994: Ablex Publishing.

[64] Van de Kamp, M.T., et al., *Enhancing divergent thinking in visual arts education: Effects of explicit instruction of meta-cognition.* British Journal of Educational Psychology, 2015. **85**(1): p. 47-58.

[65] Nijstad, B.A., et al., *The dual pathway to creativity model: Creative ideation as a function of flexibility and persistence.* European Review of Social Psychology, 2010. **21**(1): p. 34-77.

[66] van Ginkel, W., R.S. Tindale, and D. van Knippenberg, *Team reflexivity, development of shared task representations, and the use of distributed information in group decision making.* Group Dynamics: Theory, Research, and Practice, 2009. **13**(4): p. 265.

[67] Andres, H.P., *Team cognition using collaborative technology: a behavioral analysis.* Journal of Managerial Psychology, 2013. **28**(1): p. 38-54.

[68] Flavell, J.H., *Metacognition and cognitive monitoring.* American Psychologist, 1979. **34**(10): p. 906-911.

[69] Schraw, G. and D. Moshman, *Metacognitive theories.* Educational Psychology Review, 1995. 7(4): p. 351-371.

[70] De Dreu, C.K. and L.R. Weingart, *Task versus relationship conflict, team performance, and team member satisfaction: a meta-analysis.* Journal of Applied Psychology, 2003. **88**(4): p. 741-749.

[71] Jehn, K.A., G.B. Northcraft, and M.A. Neale, *Why differences make a difference: A field study of diversity, conflict and performance in workgroups.* Administrative Science Quarterly, 1999. **44**(4): p. 741-763.

[72] De Dreu, C.K., *When too little or too much hurts: Evidence for a curvilinear relationship between task conflict and innovation in teams.* Journal of Management, 2006. **32**(1): p. 83-107.

[73] Olson, B.J., S. Parayitam, and Y. Bao, *Strategic decision making: The effects of cognitive diversity, conflict, and trust on decision outcomes.* Journal of Management, 2007. **33**(2): p. 196-222.

[74] O'Neill, T.A., N.J. Allen, and S.E. Hastings, *Examining the "pros" and "cons" of team conflict: A team-level meta-analysis of task, relationship, and process conflict.* Human Performance, 2013. **26**(3): p. 236-260.

[75] DeChurch, L.A., J.R. Mesmer-Magnus, and D. Doty, *Moving beyond relationship and task conflict: Toward a process-state perspective.* Journal of Applied Psychology, 2013. **98**(4): p. 559-578.

[76] Posthuma, R.A., M.L. Loughry, and A.C. Amason, *Why won't task conflict cooperate? Deciphering stubborn results.* International Journal of Conflict Management, 2014.

[77] Hu, N., et al., *Conflict and creativity in inter-organizational teams.* International Journal of Conflict Management, 2017.

[78] Lee, E.K., et al., *The dual effects of task conflict on team creativity.* International Journal of Conflict Management, 2019.

[79] Amason, A.C., *Distinguishing the effects of functional and dysfunctional conflict on strategic decision making: Resolving a paradox for top management teams.* Academy of Management Journal, 1996. **39**(1): p. 123-148.

[80] Tjosvold, D., *The conflict-positive organization: It depends upon us.* Journal of Organizational Behavior, 2008. **29**(1): p. 19-28.

[81] Martins, L.L., et al., *A contingency view of the effects of cognitive diversity on team performance: The moderating roles of team psychological safety and relationship conflict.* Small Group Research, 2012. **44**(2): p. 96-126.

[82] Van den Bossche, P., et al., *Team learning: building shared mental models.* Instructional Science, 2011. **39**(3): p. 283-301.

[83] DeChurch, L.A., K.L. Hamilton, and C. Haas, *Effects of conflict management strategies on perceptions of intragroup conflict.* Group Dynamics: Theory, Research, and Practice, 2007. **11**(1): p. 66-78.

[84] Alper, S., D. Tjosvold, and K.S. Law, *Conflict management, efficacy, and performance in organizational teams.* Personnel Psychology, 2000. **53**(3): p. 625-642.

[85] Dillenbourg, P., *What do you mean by collaborative learning?*, in *Collaborative-learning: Cognitive and Computational Approaches*, P. Dillenbourg, Editor. 1999, Elsevier: Oxford. p. 1-19.

[86] Deken, F., et al., *Tapping into past design experiences: knowledge sharing and creation during novice–expert design consultations.* Research in Engineering Design, 2012. **23**(3): p. 203-218.

[87] McDonnell, J., *Accommodating disagreement: A study of effective design collaboration.* Design Studies, 2012. **33**(1): p. 44-63.

[88] Bublitz, W., *Supportive fellow speakers and cooperative conversations*. 1988, Cambridge: University Press.

[89] Hsieh, H.-F. and S.E. Shannon, *Three approaches to qualitative content analysis.* Qualitative health research, 2005. **15**(9): p. 1277-1288.

[90] Gergen, K.J., *Social Construction: From "What is" to "What Could Be".* An Invitation to Social Construction (3rd ed., pp. 1-33). doi, 2015. **10**: p. 9781473921276.

[91] Kiernan, L., A. Ledwith, and R. Lynch, *Design teams management of conflict in reaching consensus.* International Journal of Conflict Management, 2019.

[92] Paulus, P.B., T. Nakui, and V.L. Putman, *Group Brainstorming and Teamwork: Some Rules for the Road to Innovation*, in *Creativity and Innovation in Organizational Teams*, T.H. Choi, Editor. 2006, Lawrence Erlbaum Associates: Mahwah, NJ. p. 69-86.

Section 2

Conflict and Company Performance

Chapter 3

Intergroup Conflict and Organizational Performance: A Case of Kiboga Hospital, Uganda

Antony Tebitendwa

Abstract

The study aimed at finding out whether there is a relationship between intergroup conflicts and organizational Performance, using the case of Kiboga hospital. The study contributes to the body of existing literature by laying down strategies for managing and reducing intergroup conflicts. The study employed a cross-sectional research design along with a quantitative approach. The study population was 95 of which a sample size of 76 respondents was selected using Krejcie and Morgan table. Data was collected by the use of a questionnaire which was self-administered. Data were analyzed by the use of Statistical Package for Social Science (SPSS) through descriptive statistics and correlation analysis. Results revealed that respondents consented that intergroup conflicts affect performance with an average mean of 4.154 and a standard deviation of 1.092. A correlation coefficient of 0.903 which is significant at 0.01, revealed that there is a significant relationship between intergroup conflicts and performance which lead to the rejection of a null hypothesis. The study concluded that moderate levels of conflicts improve performance since they stimulate thinking and creativity in decision making towards goal achievement. However, extreme levels of conflict reduce performance in terms of patient care for our case of investigation. The study recommended strategies management can employ to manage extreme levels of conflicts to improve patient care.

Keywords: conflict, intergroup conflicts, organizational performance, patient care, conflict management

1. Introduction

Conflicts are an inevitable part of organizational life since the goals of different participants such as managers and staff are often incompatible [1]. This results in a situation whereby they disturb each other in an attempt to achieve their objectives. Indeed, conflict is part of organizational life and may occur between individuals, and groups [1]. While conflict is generally apparently known as dysfunctional, it can also be functional because it may cause an issue to be presented in different perspectives. Therefore, conflict has both positive and negative effects [2]. It can be positive when it encourages creativity, new looks at old conditions, the clarification of points of view, improve quality of decisions by stimulating personality thinking and challenges individual to become better, and hence the growth of human capabilities to handle interpersonal differences.

Conflicts arise at different levels within the hospital as a social organization and this is identified as a global problem which is determined by internal reasons of organizational management, socio-psychology, personal and other external factors like; economic, social, and cultural factors that occurs over time. A study by [3] identified inter-professional conflicts which is between Nurses and Doctors as one of the major and frequent hospital conflict which affects the quality of patient care. This is mainly caused by income differences, prestige, and authority of doctors over other health care professionals. The physicians' power appears to arise from the knowledge and social class [4]. This situation shows that the potential for conflict to arise in a hospital setting is considerably high [5]. Just like Nigeria, in Uganda, the working relationships between doctors and nurses have been affected by withdrawal of services by both doctors and nurses which cripples hospital activities.

According to [6], conflict arises when people take on incompatible position, changes their perception and ideas, as these are inevitable and necessary for community life. He further states that conflicts can arise between co-workers, supervisors, team members, and subordinates, or between employees and external stakeholders. This statement supports the fact that the potential for conflict to arise in a hospital setting is considerably higher due to the complex and frequent interactions among the nurses, doctors, and other employees as well as the variety of roles they play. Specialization and organizational hierarchy often add to the intergroup conflicts in hospitals [7]. In health institutions where work-related conflict exists can interfere with nurses' roles performance if not well managed. Unresolved conflicts may be linked to poor communication resulting from refusal to cooperate, poor team collaboration and problem-solving, decreased clients' satisfaction, distrust, split camps, gossips, and disruption of work-flow in the hospital setting [8].

The World Health Report [9], estimates that there are 57 countries with critical shortages that have come as a result of either poor conflict management strategies or the absence of which is equivalent to a global deficit of 2.4 million doctors, nurses, and midwives. These may draw health care professional's attention away from patient care and drain their personal resources posing a threat to team safety climate and ultimately the quality of patient care. However, [10] states that well managed intergroup conflict in an enabling environment allows for issues to be tabled and discussed with objective language. Each party is empowered to state his or her position with confidence that the other party is genuinely listening, wanting to understand. Possible solutions are discovered with open minds therefore improving organizational performance.

Kiboga hospital is a government-owned hospital with a status of a general hospital. It is a hospital located in the central region of Uganda. The hospital is faced with intergroup conflicts among its different medical and support departments, and its performance has been declining over time. Given the functional and dysfunctional nature of conflicts, this study, therefore, seeks to establish whether there is a relationship between intergroup conflict and organizational performance.

2. Literature review

2.1 Intergroup conflicts

Organizational conflict is regarded as the discord that occurs when the goals, interests, or values of different individuals or groups are incompatible with those of individuals or groups block or frustrate each other in an attempt to achieve their objectives [1]. According to [11], organizational intergroup conflict is a condition between or among workers whose jobs are interdependent, who feel angry, who perceive the others as being at fault, and who act in ways that cause business problems. This analysis defines workplace intergroup conflict as a situation in which interdependent workers, perceive positions or action as irreconcilable, with the consequence that at least one of the parties perceive that disagreement are emotionally upsetting, causing a problem at workplace [12].

Many scholars [13, 14] equate the aspect of team-based structures as a result of increasing complexity and environmental demands that force organizations to specialize and diversify their workforce, to focus efforts and efficiently handle their subtasks. However, utilizing these combined efforts as well as resources can be a challenge for team-based organizations, due to structural and psychological barriers between groups that hinder effective intergroup relations [15]. This is because groups pursue their own interests at the expense of the overall organizational goal [10]; they compete over scarce resources [16]; and fail to manage the disruptive dynamics of social categorization [17]. The imbalance of both differentiation of subsystems and the need for integrating these subsystems in pursue of superordinate organizational goals represents an inherent potential for interface or structural conflict between work units [18]. If not managed well, such interface conflict result into negative interdependence with the likely result that one group's goal achievement decreases the possibility of another group's goal achievement [19].

2.2 Organizational performance

Performance is defined as the evaluation of the constituents that try to assess the capability and ability of a company in achieving the constituents' aspiration levels using efficiency and effectiveness. Since organizations perform various activities to accomplish organizational objectives, performance can also be referred to as the frequent assessments of organizations carried out in relation to the achievement or non-achievement of set objectives and goals [20]. However, many factors affect organization performance. Conflicts within the organization are among the factors that can either positively or negatively affect performance. Traditionally, conflicts are viewed as bad. It is considered harmful for organizational functioning since it is related to hostility, antagonism, and unpleasantness. A study carried out by [21], about the effects of conflict on employees performance pointed out that, in spite of the grim picture painted about conflict as an organizational tremor, this social action can also foster posterity for business ventures. With constructive and a prudent approach, conflicts can revolutionize new ideas which can take organizations to unprecedented heights in their endeavors. It was concluded that the effect of conflicts on the organization can either be positive or negative, but when managed properly, the positive effects can be used to encourage organizational innovativeness and build cooperation among the employees which enhances performance [21]. A recent research by [22] on the impact of conflicts on the Organizational Development, highlights the above point by stating that conflicts are not automatically destructive, but this aspect depends to a large extent on how they are perceived by those who observe them, but equally on how they are managed by the manager who has to take into consideration the constructive, positive aspects of a conflict and diminish the destructive peculiarities.

Indeed, conflicts are not all bad, it is just the level of conflicts that makes them functional or dysfunctional. According to [23], Organizational performance is low when conflict is at two extremes: high levels or low levels. Organizational performance is high at moderate levels of conflict. At a low level of conflict, that is, there is usually mutuality of opinion, people agree with each other and there is no stimulation to change. People are not adaptive to environmental challenges and, therefore, do not search for new ideas. The organizational performance, thus, tends to be low. At a high level of conflict, people do not agree with each other. There is lack of cooperation amongst their activities and behavior. This leads to lack of discipline in the organization resulting in low organizational performance. At optimum level of conflict, that is, people disagree with each other resulting in new ideas. People think differently in a constructive way. New solutions are developed to deal with problems and achieve the goals through optimum utilization of resources. Therefore, moderate levels of conflict are beneficial to organizational performance. A study by [24], elaborated this further by specifying the type of team conflict that benefit from moderate levels of conflict. The occurrence of moderate level of task conflict is more helpful during planning and strategizing phases of the work, when decision making is most needed, rather than during task execution phases. In fact, task conflict during task execution was found to interfere with effective integration of work activities and team creativity.

A study by [22], emphasized that conflicts are inevitable and often lead to the efficiency of the organization's activity, to its development. He adds that all organizations regardless of their size, the conflict is an integral part of the process of development and capitalization of human resources within the organization, which requires a permanent analysis in the direction of strategic development of those entities. This is because conflict is inherent in human interaction, appearing as a result of different systems of social values, differences in principles, culture, interests.

2.3 The effect of intergroup conflict on organization performance

One scholar [15] asserts that intergroup conflict is a common occurrence in workplace scenarios where one group of workers might find themselves at a face to face junction with another group. According to [25], goal differentiation between the organizational departments makes the environment competitive as each department has its own goals to achieve, for the magistrate's concern is primarily with quality and that of service staff primarily with speed. For each department to achieve its own goals and at the same time cooperate with other departments in achieving the overall goal of the organization while competing for scarce resources shared with other departments, results into both interdepartmental and intergroup conflict.

The above notion is supported by the Realistic Group Conflict Theory (RGCT), which states that perceived competition for limited resources can lead to hostility between groups. This is when valuable resources are perceived to be abundant, then groups cooperate and exist in harmony. However, if valuable resources are perceived as scarce, then these groups enter into a competition which leads to intergroup conflicts. The resources in question can be physical (such as land, food, or water) or psychological (such as status, prestige, or power). One group need only believe that competition exists for hostile feelings and discriminatory behavior to follow. How long and how severe the conflict becomes is determined by the perceived value and scarcity of the resource in question [26]. RGCT states that Interdepartmental or intergroup conflicts can be resolved when there is a performance situation that requires each group to depend on each other to achieve important goals equally valued by both groups where everyone's help and cooperation is needed. Therefore, management can solve intergroup conflicts by setting up organizational goals that require interdependence of different departments to maintain intergroup relations to improve performance.

Though the claim that well managed intergroup conflict automatically results in efficiency gains is challenged by some, it is generally accepted that the right kind of friction and constructive confrontation and arguments over ideas in an atmosphere of mutual respect can help an organization to have the potential to drive greater performance and creativity. Conflicts are also beneficial where intergroup conflict improves team dynamic within the group, by team increasing their cohesiveness and task-oriented when they face an external threat. Moderate intergroup conflict motivates members to work more efficiently toward their goals, thereby increasing the team productivity [27]. According to [28], there can be no intergroup conflict without a degree of information as to performance information in the basis period and, ideally, a targeted performance in a future time period. Intergroup conflicts can either be constructive or destructive in nature. However, it is important to note that intergroup conflict is a reality of our daily lives and intergroup conflict is thus inevitable in a human workplace.

A study by [29], states badly managed intergroup conflict, personal attacks are common, people can get visibly angry and feelings get hurt. When co-workers do not respect the fact that approaches in addressing issues at work can differ, everyone suffers due to unresolved intergroup conflicts risk with great potential to worsen the situation. Emotionally, the work environment grows more toxic and financially expensive, the toll can be a problem consequently affecting the performance of the organization from all angles. A big number of organizations are losing valuable resources including talent, time, and revenue from work conflicts arising from within and outside. So far, this matter has not been accorded much attention from a risk management perspective but, as a result of the emphasis on performance, researchers in human resource management have stressed the need for effective human resource strategy in conflict management with reducing conflict. Although conflicts differ in terms of sources and causes, they all have destructive consequences if handled poorly [30].

The Meta-Analysis research carried out on the three types of Team Conflict: Task, Relationship, and Process conflicts, highlights another perspective on how conflicts can be beneficial or unbeneficial. The research concluded that although relationship conflict which involves interpersonal tensions, frictions, and resentment can harm team performance, task conflicts which is concerned with different ideas, perspectives, and viewpoints regarding the work itself has the potential to improve team performance and team innovation [31]. In addition, the Pearson correlation findings by [21] indicated that whereas relationship conflict is negatively linked to performance, there is a positive correlation between task and process conflict and employee's performance. A recent study carried out by [32] regarding Conflicts on Team Trust and Team performance also concluded that task and relationship conflict, process conflict, team trust, have noteworthy effect on team performance. The study emphasized the importance of task conflicts on performance when members within a team engage in highly complex tasks. With highly complex tasks, task conflict fosters intensive information exchange as well as detailed information processing. Problems can be considered from different perspectives, different opinions or alternatives can be discussed, which may produce high quality solutions and enhance performance. Based on the literature the following null hypothesis was stated:

There is no significant relationship between Inter-group conflicts and Organization Performance.

3. Methodology

The researcher used a cross-sectional research design, this is where the data on the study variables are collected at the same point in time. There were 95 Health Care Providers at Kiboga Hospital in Uganda including Administration, Medical

Doctors, and Nurses. Krejcie and Morgan Table [33] was used to determine a sample size of 76 respondents. A quantitative approach was used and data was collected by the use of a questionnaire using a five-point Likert scale ranging from 1 for strongly disagree, 2 = disagree, 3 = not sure, 4 = agree to 5 for strongly agree. Interpretations were based on 4.21–5.00 – Very High, 3.41–4.20 – High level, 2.61–3.40 – Moderate, 1.81–2.60 – Low, and 1.00–1.80 – Very low. Data were analyzed using the Statistical Package for Social Science (SPSS). Descriptive statistics were used to measure the central tendency and correlations were used to test the null hypothesis. The reliability of the research tool was tested and the Cronbach alpha value was 0.821 which is above 0.5. This suggests that the questionnaire was highly reliable as suggested by [34]. Before data collection, permission was granted by Kiboga hospital administration.

4. Discussion of findings

4.1 Response rate

The researcher had a total population of 95 and from which a sample of 76 respondents was selected for the study. Of those sampled respondents, a total of 74 returned their questionnaire, it is most likely that the two questionnaires were misplaced. This represented a response rate of 97.4% which was considered appropriate for the study. This correlates with [35] recommendation that a response rate of 50% is adequate for analysis and reporting; Therefore, 97.4% was an excellent response rate for the study.

4.2 Demographics

Most respondents (60.7%) were Nurses, medical doctors (18.0%), administrative staff (16.4%) and support staff (4.9%). The majority (56.8%) were females while 43.2% of respondents were males. The majority of the respondents (74.3%) worked for the Hospital between 5 and 8 years, between 2 and 5 years (14.9%), and above 9 years (10.8%). The majority (49.2%) of the workers were Bachelor's Degree holder and Diploma holders (55.4% and 33.8%) Few respondents had Master's Degree and certificates (5.4% and 5.4%) respectively. The majority of the respondents were aged between 26–35 years (55.4%), between 36–45 years (23%) 46 years and above (12.2%), and between 18–25 years (9.5%).

4.3 Descriptive statistics of intergroup and organizational performance

In order to assess the level of agreement and disagreement on the different items used to measure intergroup conflict in the questionnaire, the mean and standard deviation were used to determine the central tendency. A low standard deviation implies that responses were closely related to the mean value while a high standard deviation implies that responses were highly deviating from the mean value. The results are shown in the table below:

According to **Table 1**, there is a high agreement on all the measures of intergroup conflicts and their effect on performance. The average mean of 4.154 and the standard deviation of 1.092 implies that the majority were in agreement although the responses were varying a lot.

From **Table 2** below the level of mean responses together with the average mean of 4.4831 regarding organizational performance indicate that functional intergroup conflicts positively affect organizational performance whereas dysfunctional conflicts if not managed well can have a negative impact on Organizational performance. Based on the average Standard deviation of 0.8858, the variance of responses was minimal.

	N	Minimum	Maximum	Mean	Std. Deviation
Intergroup conflict is a common occurrence at workplace in health institutions	76	1.00	5.00	4.1351	1.10198
Intergroup conflicts in health institutions have a positive effect on organizational performance	76	1.00	5.00	4.323	1.03511
Intergroup conflict has a negative effect on the performance of the health institution.	76	1.00	5.00	4.0676	1.22005
Intergroup conflict is avoidable at the workplace especially in health institutions	76	1.00	5.00	4.1892	1.11865
Goal differentiation in the health institution makes the environment competitive due to intergroup conflicts	76	1.00	5.00	4.4189	.89146
Competition over resources causes intergroup conflicts and consequently affect organizational performance	76	1.00	5.00	3.8649	1.20869
Lack of coordination is the common source of intergroup conflict among different department	76	1.00	5.00	4.0811	1.06959
Average Mean				**4.154257**	**1.092219**

Source: Primary data (2020).

Table 1.
Descriptive statistics on intergroup conflict and Organizational Performance.

	N	Minimum	Maximum	Mean	Std. deviation
Intergroup conflict results in poor organizational performance in your organization	76	1.00	5.00	4.4730	.90996
Conflict management lead to improved quality of organization performance in health institutions	76	1.00	5.00	4.6081	.77314
Employee performance is improved due to functional Intergroup conflict in health institutions	76	1.00	5.00	4.5270	.87934
Organizational conflict has a negative effect on the performance of the health institution	76	1.00	5.00	4.3243	.98075
Average Mean				**4.4831**	**0.8858**

Source: Primary data (2020).

Table 2.
Descriptive statistics on Organizational Performance.

4.4 Correlation analysis

The main aim of the study was to establish a relationship between intergroup conflicts and organizational performance. Pearson's correlation coefficient has been computed so as to establish this relationship. A high correlation coefficient would suggest a strong relationship between the intergroup conflicts and organizational performance and vice versa for a low correlation coefficient. The results are presented in the table below.

Research findings in **Table 3** below that there is a significant positive relationship between Intergroup conflicts and Organizational performance, generating a correlation coefficient of r = 0.903**, and significant at 0.01. This, therefore, implies that the null hypothesis that states: *There is no significant relationship between Intergroup Conflict and Organization performance,* is rejected and the alternative is accepted. The positive correlation indicated that as employees engage in intergroup conflicts it is likely to affect their performance positively or negatively. Intergroup conflicts can affect performance by causing changes to occur, both within the group and individuals, members will usually overlook individual differences in an effort to unite against the other side. According to [36], intergroup conflicts brings positive effects for the better, by removing barriers caused by different assumptions or misunderstandings about a team's tasks, or goals. Conflict can be constructive when it creates broader awareness about how team members are experiencing their work and thus leads to changes that improve members' productivity and they ought to work together toward achieving common goals. Conflict can also lead to process improvements, such as when it reveals a deficiency in how the team communicates, which can then be corrected. Clashes of ideas can lead to more creative solutions or otherwise provide perspectives that persuade the team to take a different approach that is more likely to lead to success [1]. The Pearson correlation findings by [21], indicated that whereas relationship conflict is negatively linked to performance, there is a positive correlation between task and process conflict and employee's performance. Therefore, it was concluded that the effect of conflicts on the organization can either be positive or negative, but when managed properly, the positive effects can be used to encourage organizational innovativeness and build cooperation among the employees which enhances performance. This is because organizational conflicts improves team dynamics by increasing cohesiveness among members.

A recent study carried out by [32] emphasized the importance of task conflicts on performance when members within a team engage in highly complex tasks. With highly complex tasks, task conflict fosters intensive information exchange as well

		Intergroup conflicts	Organizational Performance
Intergroup conflicts	Pearson Correlation	1	.903**
	Sig. (2-tailed)		.000
	N	74	74
Organizational Performance	Pearson Correlation	.903**	1
	Sig. (2-tailed)	.000	
	N	74	74

*******Correlation is significant at the 0.01 level (2-tailed).*

Table 3.
Correlation analysis between intergroup conflicts and organizational performance.

as detailed information processing since problems can be considered from different perspectives, different opinions or alternatives can be discussed, which may produce high quality solutions that enhance performance. Another recent research by [22], emphasized that conflicts are inevitable and if properly managed often lead to the efficiency of the organization's activity, which leads to its development.

On the negative side, a study by [3] found out that conflicts between nurses and doctors consumes much of the time and attention that should be committed to patients. Therefore, the consequences here range from poor coordination of patient care, less patient satisfaction, poor perception and utilization of health care services, medication error, failure to rescue patients, and even deaths. The results further revealed that patients suffered neglect and abandonment as they are caught in-between the conflicts of these two groups. Therefore, it is important for hospital management to identify and properly manage intergroup conflicts to avoid performance distractions.

5. Conclusions and recommendations

The study findings revealed that there is a strong positive significant relationship between intergroup conflict and organizational performance. This implies that intergroup conflicts that occur in an organization either result in a negative or a positive effect on performance in the organization depending on the level it occurs. It is important to note that organization performance increase when conflicts are at moderate levels. However, conflicts can negatively affect performance especially at a low level where mutuality of ideas exists between members and if not managed well to escalate to high levels where members lack cooperation regarding activities and behavior. Therefore, in order to offer quality patient care, it is crucial for management to identify functional and dysfunctional conflicts and effectively manage them so as to enhance hospital performance.

Management of health organizations should always address and manage the issues related to intergroup conflicts, by building trust, promote leadership, address cultural differences, establish ground rules, and finally promote good communication and listening skills among the group members and members of other groups so as to improve on patient care.

Where groups have differing goals, it is prudent for management to establish a superordinate goal that can only be reached when the conflicting groups work together. A superordinate goal not only helps alleviate conflict, it focuses more on performance, which is what the organization needs to survive. If this is done in the right way it will eliminate or reduce intergroup conflicts.

Misperception of the abilities, goals, and motivations of others often leads to conflict, so efforts to increase the dialogue among groups and to share information should help eliminate conflict. As groups come to know more about one another, suspicions often diminish, and greater intergroup teamwork becomes possible, which improves performance.

Management should identify and make significant changes in the structural variables involving the conflicting groups such as changing jobs or rearranging reporting responsibilities among health care teams. For effectiveness, groups involved should participate in structural change decisions. If done well, this can lead to permanent resolution of intergroup conflicts within health care institutions.

Given the relevance of task conflicts in decision-making teams, there is a need for better selection and training of team members, as well as a culture that enables team members to leverage task conflicts appropriately, as opposed to minimizing and avoiding them completely. By doing so, it enhances performance among health services teams.

Conflict of interest

There is no conflict of interest in this present study. This research work is not a part of any other studies and it is my original work.

Author details

Antony Tebitendwa
Uganda Martyrs University, Kampala, Uganda

*Address all correspondence to: tebitendj35@gmail.com

References

[1] Ongori, H., (2008). Organizational Conflict and its Effects on Organizational Performance. Research Journal of Business Management. Vol. 2(1), 16-24. Academic Journals Inc.

[2] Kankanhalli, A., Tan, B.C.Y. and Wei, K.K. (2007). Managing Conflict in Global Virtual Teams. Journal of Management Information Systems, 24(3), pp.237-274.

[3] Ifeanyi, E.E. & Babangid, B.B. (2020). Inter-Professional Relations and Conflicts between Nurses and Doctors in Tertiary Health Institutions. International Journal of Scientific Research in Humanities Legal Studies and International Relations. Vol. 5 (1)

[4] Zelek, B., & Phillips, S. P. (2003). Gender and Power: Nurses and Doctors in Canada, *International Journal for Equity in Health*, 2 (1). Retrieved from: https://equityhealthj.biomedcentral.com/articles/10.1186/1475-9276-2-1

[5] Akpabio, I. I., John, M. E., Akpan, M. I., Akpabio, F. F., & Uyanah, D. A. (2016). Work Related Conflict and Nurses' Role Performance in a Tertiary Hospital in South-south Nigeria. Journal of Nursing Education and Practice, Vol. 6 (2), 106-114. Retrieved from: http://www.sciedupress.com/journal/index.php/jnep/article/view/7774

[6] Rahim, M.A. (2002). Toward a Theory of Managing Organizational Conflict. The International Journal of Conflict.

[7] Lee, D., Huh, Y. and Reigeluth, C.M. (2015). Collaboration, Intragroup Conflict, and Social Skills in Project-based Learning. Instructional Science, 43(5), pp.561-590.

[8] Greer, L.L. and Jehn, K.A, (2007). Chapter 2: The Pivotal Role of Negative Affect in Understanding the Effects of Process Conflict on Group Performance.

[9] The World Health Report (2006). Working together for Health

[10] Tjosvold, D. (1991). Forging Synergy. In D. Tjosvold (Ed.), Team Organization: An Enduring Competitive Advantage (pp. 219-233). Chichester, UK: Wiley.

[11] Dana, D., (2001). Conflict Resolution: Mediation Tools for Everyday Work Life. McGraw-Hill Professional.

[12] Sääksvuori, L., Mappes, T. & Puurtinen, M. (2011). Costly Punishment Prevails in Intergroup Conflict. Proceedings of the Royal Society B: Journal of Biological Science

[13] Lawrence, P. R., & Lorsch, J. W. (1967b). Organization and Environment: Managing Differentiation and Integration. Boston: Harvard Graduate School of Business Administration.

[14] McCann, J., & Galbraith, J. R. (1981). Interdepartmental Relations. In P. C. Nystrom & W.H.

[15] Van Knippenberg, D. (2003). Intergroup Relations in Organizations. In M. A. West, D. Tjosvold, & K. G. Smith (Eds.), International handbook of organizational teamwork and Cooperative working (pp. 381-400). Chichester, UK: Wiley.

[16] Mohrman, S. A., Cohen, S. G., & Mohrman, A. M. (1995). Designing Team-based Organizations: New Forms for Knowledge Work. San Francisco: Jossey-Bass.

[17] Terry, D. J., & Callan, V. J. (1998). In-group Bias in Response to an Organizational Merger. Group Dynamics: Theory, Research, and Practice, 2(2), 67-81.

[18] Richter W.A, Scully J., &West, A.W (2005). Intergroup Conflict and Intergroup Effectiveness in Organizations: Theory and Scale Development. European Journal of Work and Organizational Psychology. Vol. 14 (2), 177-203.

[19] Thomas, K. W. (1992). Conflict and Negotiation Processes in Organizations. In M. D. Dunette & L. M. Hough (Eds.), Handbook of industrial and organizational psychology (2nd ed., Vol. 3, pp. 651-717). Chicago: Rand-McNally.

[20] Jenatabadi, S.H., (2015). An Overview of Organizational Performance Index: Definitions and Measurements. Accessed through Researchgate.

[21] Donkor, P., Afriyie, S., AdjeiDanquah, B., KwakuNimsah, W., (2015). Effect of Conflict on Employees Performance: Evidence from Coca Cola Company Limited, Kumasi Branch. American Scientific Research Journal for Engineering, Technology, and Sciences. Volume 14, No 3, pp. 44-53.

[22] Ene, A.M. (2020). The Impact of Conflicts in the Organizational Development. The 15th Edition of the International Conference: European Integration, Realities and Perspectives.

[23] Tanuja A. (n.d). Relationship between Conflict and Organisational Performance. https://www.businessmanagementideas.com/notes/managementnotes/conflictmanagement/relationship-between-conflict-and-organisational performance/5013. Online Access: 20/12/2020.

[24] Farh, J., Lee, C., & Farh, C. I. C. (2010). Task Conflict and Team Creativity: A question of how much and when. Journal of Applied Psychology Vol. 95, pg1173-1180.

[25] Curşea S. (2010), Revisiting the Relationship between Team Diversity, Conflict and Trust. Group Dynamics: Theory, Research Practice, Volume 14.

[26] Encyclopedia of Social Psychology. Realistic Group Conflict Theory of 1960. Retrieved from: http://psychology.iresearchnet.com/social-psychology/social-psychology-theories/realistic-group-conflict-theory/ Online Access: 22/12/2020.

[27] O'Neill, T.A. (2018). Conflict Management, Efficacy, and Performance in Organizational. Journal of Management.

[28] Rahim, M. A. (2011). Managing Conflict in Organizations. Transaction Publishers.

[29] Kiglai J. (2006) Training Manual on Conflict Management: The National Unity and Reconciliation Commission, Republic of Rumania.

[30] Spaho, K. (2013). Organizational Communication and Conflict Management. Management. Journal of Contemporary Management Issues.

[31] O'Neill, A. T., Allen, J.N. & Hastings, E. S., (2013) Examining the "Pros" and "Cons" of Team Conflict: A Team-Level Meta-Analysis of Task, Relationship, and Process Conflict. Human Performance. Vol. 26:3, pg. 236-260.

[32] Yuni, Y., Tham, J., Azam, S.M.F. (2020). Conflicts on Team Trust and Team Performance at the University Scientific Research Teams in Jiangsu Province, China: Structural Equation Modelling Approach. European Journal of Management and Marketing studies. Vol.6:1.

[33] Krejcie, R.V. and Morgan, D.W. (1970), 'Determining Sample Size for Research Activities', Educational and Psychological Measurement. Vol. 30, 607-61.

[34] Sekaran, U. (2003). Research Methods for Business: A Skill Building Approach (4 ed). New York: John Wiley & Sons Inc.

[35] Mugenda, O. & Mugenda A. (2003). Research Methods Laban Graphics Services, Nairobi Rutgers University. Psychology, 85(1), 102-111.

[36] Cox, K.B., (2003). The Effects of Intrapersonal, Intragroup, and Intergroup Conflict on Team Performance Effectiveness and Work Satisfaction. Nursing Administration Quarterly.

Chapter 4

Conflicts in Environmental and Agricultural Organizations in the Far North Region of Cameroon

Nanche Billa Robert

Abstract

The population of the Far North Region of Cameroon suffers the most from poverty and huge environmental challenges. As a result, they have the highest concentration of environmental organizations in Cameroon. Data was collected by interviewing key informants who work in environmental and agricultural companies. It was discovered that conflicts in such organizations are caused by the differences people have in terms of opinions, interests and needs as they work together with each other. Their strictness with one another also causes conflict especially when doing dirty or difficult work tasks. Conflict also comes about when the religious values of each other is not respected especially that of the Muslims in Christians dominated companies. There is also generational conflict which is characterized by the confrontation between the older and less educated generation who have some experience and young graduates who would like to implement new practices. Other causes are discrimination where workers are not promoted basing on merit but on their ethnic relation to one another. There is equally an economic cause which is due to the non-distribution of part of the substantial profits that some companies make to their employees as well as too low salary and poor work tasks distribution.

Keywords: environment, agriculture, organization, discrimination, Cameroon, religion, work task, relation, conflict, generational, economic

1. Introduction

Conflict has different meanings and is used differently depending on people's subjective experiences. The main problem is not the many different definitions but rather the ways scholars have conceptualized the term. As a result, scientists have defined conflict in broad terms: Jehn and Bendersky (2003) [1] defined conflict as "perceived incompatibilities or discrepant views among the parties involved". De Dreu et al. (1999) [2] state that conflict involves "the tension an individual or group experiences because of perceived differences between him or herself and another individual or group". The term conflict reflects the assumption of involving not only differences but incompatible goals and is a win-lose affair. In order to better understand conflict, Elisabeth N. and Stewart C. (2019) [3] ask the following questions which equally interest us: What does conflict look like? How should it be identified in the workplace? And how can we capture its dynamics in our theorization?

Louis R. (1967) [4] state that the term "conflict" can be used to describe various conditions and states such as the scarcity of resources, policy differences of a conflicting behavior, or an affective states such as stress, tension, hostility, anxiety, etc. of the individuals involved, or a cognitive states of individuals, which can be their perception or awareness of conflicting situations, and even still behavior, ranging from passive resistance to overt aggression. An industrial dispute means any dispute or difference between employers and employers or employers and workers or between workmen and workmen, which is connected with employment or non-employment or terms of employment or conditions of labour of any person. According to Priyakshi M (–) [5] *Conflict can be considered as a breakdown in the standard of decision making and it occurs when an individual or group experience difficulty in selecting an alternative. Conflict arises when individual or group encounters goal that both parties cannot obtain satisfactorily.*

Organizational Conflict or otherwise known as workplace conflict is described as the state of disagreement or misunderstanding, resulting from the actual or perceived dissent of needs, beliefs, resources and relationship between the members of the organization. At the workplace, whenever, two or more persons interact, conflict occurs when opinions with respect to any task or decision are in contradiction (Business Jargon, –) [6].

Task conflict is disagreement about the content of the work that workers perform; relationship conflict exists when employees have interpersonal incompatibilities arising from differences in personality or opposing values (De Dreu & Beersma, 2005) [7]. Process conflict is closely related to task conflict: Whereas task conflict has to do with the actual task, process conflict concerns how the task is done (Jehn, 1997) [8]. While the concepts of task and relationship conflict are widely used in conflict research, the application of process conflict is still limited. More recently, the concept of status conflict (Bendersky and Hays, 2012) [9] has emerged, and it concerns disputes over members' status positions in social hierarchy.

Despite disagreements, task conflict is commonly considered constructive and relationship conflict dysfunctional. Relationship conflict interferes with performance by lowering effectiveness, creativity, and the quality of decision making (de Wit, Jehn, and Scheepers, 2013) [10]. By contrast, task conflict is healthy and necessary because it stimulates discussions and prevents premature consensus, leading to enhanced decision-making quality, work-team effectiveness, and performance. Since the 1980s, major strand in organizational conflict research has concentrated on refining the conflict-type framework to distinguish between negative and productive conflict, by showing out how "these two types of conflict differentially affect work group outcomes" (O'Neill et al., 2013) [11].

Therefore conflict is an instrumental means to achieve authoritatively sanctioned ends. "It is through conflict that teams can be productive and enhancing and leaders effective" Tjos-vold's (2006) [12]. Depending on the situation and the kind of outcome desired by management, there is a widespread interest on how to attain the "right" kind of conflict for the achievement of goals.

Conflict equally occurs in the routines of work and the norms embedded in everyday social interaction as organizational members go about their daily activities which constitutes the cultural context of conflict (Mikkelsen, 2013) [13]. Therefore, conflict is an inherently dynamic process of communicating which pays particular interest to the role of language and symbols in shaping and co-developing it (Mikkelsen and Gray, 2016.) [14].

Specifically, there are three distinct and competing ways on conceptualizing conflict: as a distinct behavioral phenomenon, as an instrumental means, and as a social construction.

It is a process in which one party suggests that its interests are being opposed by another party. As a role, people see only the observable part of conflict –angry words and actions of opposition. But this is only a small part of the conflict process (Mcshane, S. and Glinow, M, 2008) [15] because the conflict process consists of five stages: firstly, a.potential opposition or incompatibility; secondly a cognition and personalization, thirdly, an intentions; fourthly a behavior; and finally an outcome.

Internal Sources of conflict refer to factors which are inherent within the framework of an organization. The major prime factor of internal sources of conflict is the "Opposing interests" of industrial actors. Differing interests bring about conflict because the two parties in organizations try to share the "industrial cake". Equally, there is usually "power relationship" between the two actors in an industry which make conflict production inevitable (Bernard O. Ashimi R. 2014) [16].

According to Gatlin, J. et al. (2019) [17], there are eight potential reasons which cause conflict in an organization: conflicting needs, styles, perceptions, goals, pressures, roles, differing personal values and unpredictable policies. An organization is a system of position roles with each member belonging to a role set. Conflict role occurs when an association of individuals sharing interdependent tasks and performing formally defined roles are influenced both by the expectations of others in the role set and by their own personalities and expectations. A person's role joins with that of other members' as well as their set of organizational roles to produce opportunities for a role conflict. This type of conflict increases individual's anxiety and frustration and reduced efficiency as it can as well motivate him to do better work (Henry P., Börje O. (1971) [18].

Unmanaged conflict in the workplace can lead to miscommunication which bring about confusion or non-cooperation, non-respect of deadlines or delays, increased stress among employees, weak creative collaboration and team problem solving, disruption to work flow, knowledge sabotage Serenko, A. (2020), Serenko, A. (2019) [19–20], reduced customer satisfaction, distrust, split camps, and gossip (De Angelis, Paula 2008) [21]. The win-lose conflict in groups may have some of the following negative effects: Divert time and energy from the main issues, delay decision, create dead locks, drive unaggressive committee members to the sidelines, interfere with listening, Obstruct exploration of more alternatives, reduce or destroy sensitivity, cause members to drop out or resign from committees, Arouse anger that disrupts a meeting, provoke personal abuse, cause defensiveness. It causes strains such anxiety, depression, physical symptoms, and low levels of job. Equally, interdependence recognizes that differences will exist and that they can be helpful, so members learn to accept ideas from dissenters (which does not imply agreeing with them).

An environment organization is one which is part of the conservation[1] or environmental movements[2] that seeks to protect, analyze or monitor the environment against misuse or degradation from human forces. In this sense, the environment may refer to the biophysical environment or the natural environment (Wikipedia the free encyclopedia List of environmental Organization) [22]. The organization may be a charity, a trust, a non-governmental organization, a governmental organization or an intergovernmental organization. Environmental organizations can be global, national, regional, or local. Some environmental issues that environmental

[1] seeks to protect natural resources, including animal and plant species as well as their habitat for the future

[2] Also known as the ecology movement, it includes conservation and green politics, and is a diverse philosophical, social, and political movement for addressing environmental issues. The movement is centered on ecology, health, and human rights.

organizations focus on include pollution, plastic pollution, waste, resource depletion, human overpopulation and climate change.

Agriculture places a serious burden on the environment in the process of providing humanity with food and fibers. It is the largest consumer of water and the main source of nitrate pollution of groundwater and surface water, as well as the principal source of ammonia pollution. It is a major contributor to the phosphate pollution of waterways OECD (2020) [23] and to the release of the powerful greenhouse gases (GHGs) methane and nitrous oxide into the atmosphere (IPCC.. Climate change 2001) [24]. Increasingly, however, it is recognized that agriculture and forestry can also have positive externalities such as the provision of environmental services and amenities, for example through water storage and purification, carbon sequestration and the maintenance of rural landscapes (Murgai, R., Ali, M. and Byerlee, D. 2001) [25].

In the Far North Region of Cameroon, there are seven organizations, that deals with issues related to the environment and agriculture: GIZ, PNDP, HYSACAM, ACEFA, SOLKAMTECH, COPPRESSA, SAHEL AGRO. We noticed that most environmental organizations intervene as much as possible to ameliorate the precarious environmental problems of the region while those dealing with agriculture are mostly transformative: transforming raw materials into finished goods.

We examine the causes of conflict in the above agricultural and environmental organization in the Far North Region of Cameroon whose population suffers the most from poverty and huge environmental challenges and which has the highest concentration of environmental organizations. Therefore our objective is to find out the causes of conflicts in environmental and agricultural organizations in the Far North region of Cameroon.

2. Theories of organization conflicts

Functionalists state that a conflict serves a social function and they ask the following questions: "Why is there conflict? What purpose does it serve?" George Simmel views conflict as designed to resolve divergent dualisms; as a way of achieving some kind of unity, even if it will be through the annihilation of one of the conflicting parties". Conflict serves as a social purpose even if reconciliation comes with the total destruction of one party. Conflict socializes members into a group and reduces the tension between group members. Furthermore, a conflict may end with a victory of one party over another or it can be resolved through compromise; or through conciliation.

Functionalists define conflict as "the clash of values and interests, the tension between what is and what some groups feel ought to be." Conflict serves the function of pushing society to new institutions, technology and economic systems. It is a "situation which generates incorruptible goals or values among different parties".

Functional, constructive forms of conflict is the conflict that supports the goals of a group and improves its performance (Robbins, S., et al., 2003) [26]. Conflict leads to competition among groups and they work harder to produce more, it is advantageous to the group and the institution. It is viewed as a confrontation between two ideas, goals and parties that improves employees and organizational performance. One of the main benefits of constructive conflict is that it gives its members a chance to identify the problems and see the opportunities. It also inspires new ideas, learning, and growth among individuals (Robbins, S., et al., 2003).

Conflict is "an expressed struggle between at least two interdependent parties who perceive incompatible goals, scarce rewards and interference from the other party in achieving their goals" Floger, J. P (1993) [27]. This approach introduces two important concepts: Interdependence and perception. Interdependence is connected to such situations where one party's future actions depend on another party's actions. The differences are created by conflict, for example, values, goals, motives, resources and ideas. In the business world, differences in such characteristics as work experience, personality, peer group, environment and situation, all lead to difference in personal attitudes, beliefs, values or needs".

3. Methodology

We first of identified all the environmental and agricultural organizations in the Far North Region of Cameroon. Then we prepared a semi-structured interview guard which consisted mainly of questions that helped us to know the causes of conflict in the various organizations. We obtained a research permit from the director of the Higher Institute of Polytechnique Maroua in which the department of Environmental Studies is found. We then selected fifteen students Master students and trained them on how to conduct the interview and sent them to the field. They dropped the research permit at the head-office of each company and they were granted permission to conduct the interview with key-workers. They purposely selected experienced workers, that is, those who have been working in the companies for long and who had an in-depth knowledge of the functioning of the companies. They met them at convenient areas where the interview was conducted: some in their offices during break time or when their colleagues had gone out for break and others in the quarters and some in a quiet environment in the companies. Follow-up information were given in a created Whatsapp group. The experienced workers shared their views on the organizational culture and sources of conflict.

4. The results

4.1 Areas of expertise of the environmental and agricultural enterprises

The environmental and agricultural organizations in the Far North Region of Cameroon are either cooperation (GIZ), private structures (SOLKAMTECH, COPPRESSA, SAHEL AGRO) or parastatal structures (HYSACAM, PNDP, ACEFA). They have very diverse fields of activity: sanitation and waste management, reforestation, the fight against climate change, environmental protection, and the processing of agricultural products.

These organizations have varied domains of expertise: the PNDP operates on small scale micro-projects. It carries out: reforestation, waste management, small-scale disaster management, sanitation and pollution reduction. In the domain of reforestation, it fights against the advancement of the desert and it works in collaboration with the GIZ cooperation. In disaster management, it reconstructs schools that have been destroyed by floods. In the area of sanitation, it builds latrines for needy populations. In the area of biodiversity, it builds artificial ponds for animals and shelter.

SOLKAMTECH[3] SARL was founded in 2010 by a renewable energy and the environment engineer and its activities extend to other regions of Cameroon: the East, Adamawa, North regions where it has already implemented numerous projects. It aims at providing renewable energy as a solution to people who do not

[3] Solar Kamerun Technology

have access to electricity and those who cannot afford to pay huge electricity bills as well as those who have unstable electricity supply. This company is multifunctional because it is also involved in the business sectors: buildings and doing other public works, providing solar photovoltaic, thermal as well as wind and biomass.

Sahel Agro, also called Sahel Agro Wilfec Holdings was created in 2013 and it launched production in January 2015. It aims at improving the overall food conditions of the Sahelian zones and to set up a new method of consuming industrial product. It's main activity (area of expertise) is Agribusiness. It works in the processing and marketing of high quality corn flour and provides customers with product ranges of 500 g, 1 kg, 5 kg, 10 kg, 25 kg and 50 kg which are available anytime and anywhere.

The ACEFA[4] program was created in 2013 in Diamaré and it contributes to the sustainable improvement of producers' incomes in order to reduce poverty in rural areas and also helps to improve Family Farms and Producers' Organizations (POs).

GIZ has been working in Cameroon since the early 1960s. Its regional office is in Yaoundé where the company's activities are coordinated. The main sponsor of GIZ is the German Federal Minister for Economic Cooperation and Development. It operates in 12 different programs but we are interested in its PROFE[5]. This program operates in four regions of Cameroon: the Center, the East, the North and the Far North. In the far north region, it is aim at restoring landscape, responsible for wood and energy (improved stoves) and the management of non-timber forest products (NTFPs).

GIZ is a cooperation while SOLKAMTECH, COPPRESSA, SAHEL AGRO are private structures and HYSACAM, PNDP, ACEFA are .parastatal structures.

4.1.1 Sources of conflicts in environmental and agricultural organization

The conflicts in environmental and agricultural organizations in the Far North Region of Cameroon are: relational conflict of authority, generational conflict, discrimination, economic and work task conflicts. However, not all these conflicts are necessarily negative because for executives, the absence of conflict can even be a problem since it can mean the lack of collaborators or their inability to work with other workers to produce the best of them.

4.1.2 Relational conflict

Conflicts in organizations are regularly triggered by the differences people have in terms of opinions, interests and needs as they work together. These relations may be between employees or with senior colleagues, there are always misunderstandings between collaborators; that is, collaborators hardly understand each other when sharing opinions with each other. There are romantic relationships which create conflicts in enterprise or when employees are strict with one another especially when doing dirty or difficult work like keeping the environment clean. This exists when one person of the same hierarchical rank encroaches the competent domain of the other which produces conflict of authority and then leads to jealousy

In COPRESSA, there are conflicts between employees and in some cases with senior colleagues. For example in 2019, a colleague decided not to share the

[4] programme d'Amélioration de la Compétitivité des Exploitations Agropastorales (Programme to Ameliorate the competivity of Agropastoral Exploitation)

[5] forest, fauna and environment program.

company's vehicle with her colleague. This was because her colleague scolded her at the wrong time and place while they were in the field in front of people who were not members of their company. According to her, the population ought not to have been aware of it. As a result, they did not speak to each other for almost 4 months when they returned to the company until their hierarchy resolved their misunderstanding during a weekly meeting and resolutions were taken to restore peace and calm between them. It significantly affected the functioning of the organization and rendered workers less productive and there was a slowdown in the advancement of projects.

The sources of conflicts at COPRESSA are varied and diverse. When executing projects for example, there are always misunderstandings between collaborators; that is, collaborators hardly understand each other when sharing opinions with each other. Members are primarily focused on completing their tasks for projects to get through, although they hardly share ideas with other members. As a result, stress is generated through the rationalization of work. There is also a dysfunctional hierarchical relationship which does not only smoothly coordinate workers but also fail to communicate with them. As a result workers face personal difficulties and at times, they lack the motivation to work etc. It produces tensions which lead to social conflicts among workers.

There are romantic relationships which create conflicts in enterprises. One of the employees of the SOLKAMTECH was at logger head with his supervisor because they both fell in love with their colleague. In addition, two other employees also loved the same girl and it created bitterness and lack of collaboration between them.

Strictness is also a source of conflict in the sense that it causes tensions between employees, and brings about rivalry. For example in HYSACAM, when filling the dumpsters, workers hardly allow their fellow colleagues to leave even to satisfy their natural needs. Whenever it is done, the response is often a negative one even if the colleague concerned is a senior worker. Most often, the staff representative reports them to the hierarchy which summons them and sanctions them if necessary. The disciplinary council can punish them by either giving them a three-day warning or a permanent dismissal as it has been the case of several employees who were victims for leaving work for one reason or the other.

It also exists when one person of the same hierarchical rank encroaches the competent domain of the other which produces conflict of authority and then leads to jealousy. For example, in 2018, the technical head of the departmental cell was in a conflict of authority with the coordinator of PCP-ACEFA Maroua because he had established a good organizational culture in the establishment and it led to competition or rivalry: it is also present in the ACEFA program because employees are called upon to express their skills in order to produce an unbeatable final results and as a result, they are in constant competition with each other. As an illustration, last year's best employee was jealous of his co-workers and it caused huge conflicts which affected their relationship as well as their performance at work. There is an ACEFA employee of the same rank like his colleague who gave order to his fellow colleague and it created a tense atmosphere between them and he warned him to stop ordering him about. This type of conflict produces psychological problems: violence, anxiety, depression, aggression, frustration etc. which equally affects the personality of individuals).

Conflict also negatively affects the psychological well-being of employees. If it is severe, conflicting thoughts, ideas and beliefs can lead to resentment, tension and anxiety. It can also destroy collaboration and team spirit in the structure and structure will render the company less productive.

4.1.3 Religious conflict

Maroua is a Muslim dominated community and the Muslim do not joke with prayer and especially the hours they have to pray. Most often they close their businesses and stop their other activities in order to pray. However, some companies in the Far North Region where the Muslim do not hold dominant positions do not respect their prayer hours but the work tasks they have to complete thereby affecting the religiosity of its Muslims workers. At ACEFA for example, when it is prayer time for its Muslim employees, the coordinator will ask them to complete their work task before going for prayer. Therefore the Muslim employees are dissatisfied with this attitude and it generates conflicts. It must noted that the Muslims consider their prayer time seriously and they ensure to pray at affixed times of the day therefore, this generates a lot of conflicts between the Muslim workers and the company.

4.1.4 Generational conflict

Generational conflict is characterized by the confrontation between an older generation of workers who have some experience and young graduates who would like to implement new practices. Young graduates have more theoretical knowledge as compared to older workers who are less-educated or who are not graduates. When the young graduates try to put theories into practice or try to innovate the manufacturing process, they face opposition from the older generation. Young workers apply theory or try to maintain the standard in the laboratory to the letter to process products and respect the smallest details in the production process in order to avoid any possible risk. On the other hand, the older workers with practical experience are often careless and often do trial and error tests which often produce poor results.

A clear example is at Sahel Agro, during the grinding process of grains, young graduate will let the corn grains to naturally dry while older workers will put the grains in the oven (over 180 °C) in order for it to get dry faster which of course destroys the properties of the grains and render the flour produced less rich and of reduced quality. The older and experienced workers argue with the young graduates when they explain it to them and it leads to conflict between the two generations of workers. It was a serious problem between the two groups until an expert engineer in transformation intervened to clearly explain the young graduates' approach in transforming corn into flour to the older employees.

This confrontation between older people who have some experience and young graduates who would like to set up new practices is also visible at PCP-ACEFA and the most affected are the older generation because young people who have just graduated from the training schools have more improved knowledge of organizational culture, in other words an update of the corporate organizational culture.

This clash of opinion or ideology or technology that arose between the workers generally affected their morality and religion. Misunderstanding from a false interpretation of facts or actions affect the company and workers in various way: violence, anxiety, depression, aggression, frustration and the personality of individuals is hurt. It affects the organization work tasks, the psychology of the workers, the technological progress of production and retards the economic activities of the company and makes interdependence of tasks or heavy work methods difficult.

4.1.5 Ethnic discrimination

Workers are not promoted basing on merit but on their ethnic relation to one another. Position intended for one worker is most often given to a completely different person. This leads to a kind of jealousy, lack of respect, denigration between employees hence widening the conflict between them in the company. At SOLKAMTECH excellence premium and other bonuses are given to employees basing on their relationship with the hierarchy and not necessarily on merit. Some workers work more and receive fewer bonuses while those who work less receive more bonuses. Tribalism is due to the fact that Bamilekes are the most favored in the structure and are the only ones who occupy the major positions in the company and this creates tension and disagreement between the employees.

4.1.6 Economic cause

The scarcity of resources (spaces, equipment, training, etc.) creates conflict in environmental and agricultural enterprises. Conflicts are present due to the non-distribution of part of the substantial profits that ACEFA makes to its staff. Employees complain that the bonuses that suppliers pay do not reach employees not even half and there is also the problem of too low salary at especially the private companies.

The delay in payment of wages at HYSACAM forces the employees to borrow money from their colleagues or they borrowed cooked-food from the women who carries out restaurants business around the organization. When salary is retarded for long, they find it difficult to pay back the food vendors and even their colleagues and it creates conflict between them, their colleagues and the food vendors. The debt conflict tarnishes the image of the company in the outside world and the personnel do not command the respect of the surrounding population and it tarnishes their dignity.

4.1.7 Conflict of work tasks

In the Far north Region of Cameroon, environmental organizations such ACEFA suffer from frequent poor distribution of work tasks. Our respondents (the employees) of ACEFA confirmed that workers of the same rank in the organization have unequal distribution of tasks while some workers have more tasks, others have less. Work is mostly informal, unplanned and therefore unpredictable. There are cases where some employees leave work much earlier than others. That is to say, they work overtime while others do not. However, some aspects of the work tasks of employees are well organized in this organization, the respect of the arrival and departure time are well managed. Interdependence of tasks (This is when the work of one person depends on the work of another). There is poor adequacy between the objectives set and the means made available, low investment in production tools (hardware, software, etc.), cumbersome, unclear working methods and procedures.

Conflicts have a negative impact on ACEFA Maroua it diverts certain efforts from bearing fruits and the achievement of set-down goals become difficult. At a time when efforts should be made to converge the resources of ACEFA Maroua towards the goals set, a conflict can arise that wastes the structure's resources and it leads to wasted time and money that have been invested in the project. Conflicts equally have a positive impact on the performance of the structure too because the birth and/or resolution of a conflict often makes it possible to find a constructive solution to a problem help members to improve or get better at the tasks. It also improves interpersonal relationships and increases team cohesion and performance.

4.1.8 Organizational type and conflict resolution

In Maroua, organizational conflict depends on the type of organization whether it is a co-operation, private or Organizational conflict is as a result of lack of team work and organization of work. Where there is teamwork in organizations, there will hardly be conflict. In PNDP which is a cooperation where employees are better paid, there is harding conflict in its structure because there is solid teamwork and they work in harmony and all its departments are linked.

GIZ socializes its new recruits to respect its code of ethics and integrity which helps them to learn and understand how cooperation works. Communication is simple, fluid, without fear but the employee and the hierarchy must respect each other. The languages spoken are: French, English and the local language to facilitate the integration of new employees. The hierarchy supports employees facing a difficult task to enable them better advance in their tasks and for them to quickly integrate in the cooperation. At the GIZ cooperation, the concept of conflict is not a topical issue because it has a small and efficient staff with an exemplary behavior. The absence of conflict promotes an excellent working environment which always produces satisfactory result at the end of most projects.

At SOLKAMTECH the various conflicts are discreetly managed by the hierarchy without the intervention of other members which the conflict does not concerned. They always try to find a common ground for the conflicting party, at times the management board also takes particular cases to the court. The management does everything to prevent conflict from affecting the production and the returns of the company, and ensures that every worker gives the best of himself. However, personal problems are not managed by the company. They also manage conflict through negotiation which helps to reconcile opposing points of view, Mediation versus arbitration, in which case the mediator facilitates discussion, guides conservation or provokes it. At times too, the hierarchy may decide in an authoritarian manner (with or without the party concerned). This type of conflict resolution is necessary in emergency situations.

Equally through an amicable way, the hierarchy explains to the young people that despite their knowledge, it would be better to recognize the place of the elders and explain to them new ways of doing things in a humble and gentle way. In this case, the parties become involved in the resolution of the problem and the conflict is solved peacefully.

The circulation of information within the SOLKAMTECH company is provided by the company using an internal communication network, that is, an internal Internet, telephone and also through posting within the company. This is how the respondents are often informed about the organizational changes, set out objectives as well as the internal regulations, and any new development concerning work. Circulation of information at SOLKAMTECH between its employees is very important because it plays a role in letting everyone know the work tasks the company engages in. It also integrates interpersonal communication which facilitates the exchange of information between workers.

At COPRESSA Communication is facilitated through exchanges by organizing weekly meetings (every Monday) which allow the coordinator and employees to discuss the important activities of the previous week. This meeting helps staff to set goals for the current week and the coordinator use it to draw the attention of dishonest and misbehaved employees in the course of the week and congratulates all those who distinguished themselves throughout the week. It is a means intended to enable staff to present their suggestions and express their ideas on matters relating to the running of the business. There is also a platform in which employees communicate after working hours on good news concerning them like births and unfortunate events such as death.

The dialog or communication in this structure varies according to the post people occupy: executives communicate using a WhatsApp platform where they exchange on topics concerning the company. Information notes are pasted on bulletin board for other employees. There is a rally with all company staff every Monday which helps to keep cohesion and allows new employees to learn about the hierarchy.

5. Discussion of results

This research shows that economic reason is responsible for the conflict that affects a good number of environmental and agricultural companies in the Far North region of Cameroon. This is because in many work situations, workers have to share common resources; therefore, the scarcer the resources in an organization, the greater the chance for a conflict situation. Resource scarcity leads to a conflict because each person that needs the same resources necessarily undermines others who pursue their own goals. Limited resources may include money, supplies, people or information Mcshane, S. L and Glinow, M.A. (2008). [15] but in this case, it is money. Equally, concerning the environmental companies in Maroua those in the private sector particularly suffer from this scarcity the more. This is due to conflict of interest in which there is a disorientation between the personal goals of the individual and the goals of the organization. As *Daniel K.; Robert L. (1966)* [17] puts it, this conflict of interest arises when the individual fights for his personal goals which hinders the overall success of the project.

This scarcity of resources creates conflict between the hierarchy as well as the workers and the surrounding environment as it is the case in HYSACAM. More so, the benefits of the organization are not equally shared; most often, the hierarchy takes everything giving little or nothing to the employees as it is the case in ACEFA. This shows that, the major prime factor of internal sources of conflict is the "opposing interests" of industrial actors. Differing interests bring about conflict because the two parties in organizations try to share the "industrial cake". Therefore, members of a company competes with each other over scarcity of resources like time, money, materials etc. leading to conflict between them.

Equally, the research also shows a generational gap between the older generation who is less-educated with a long experience in the company and a younger and educated generation who are more qualitative in the production process than the older generation thereby producing a generational conflict between them which is later resolved most often in favor of the younger generation. This shows that, conflict serves a social purpose even if reconciliation comes with the total destruction of one party. Conflict socializes members into a group and reduces the tension between group members. Conflict may end with a victory of one party over another or it can be resolved through compromise; or through conciliation. One of the main benefits of constructive conflict is that it gives its members a chance to identify the problems and see the opportunities. It also inspires new ideas, learning, and growth among individuals (KInicki, A. and Kreithner, R., 2008) [28]. The generational conflict at Sahel Agro was resolved through an expert engineer of raw material transformation giving reason to the younger generation to the detriment of the older generation.

The win-lose conflict in groups may have some of the following negative effects: Divert time and energy from the main issues, delay decision, create dead locks, drive unaggressive committee members to the sidelines and interfere with listening. The older and experienced workers argue with the young graduates when they explain it to them and it led to conflict between them. It was a serious problem between the two parties until an expert engineer in transformation intervened to clearly explain the young graduates' approach in transforming corn into flour to the older employees. This confrontation between older people who have some experience and young graduates who would like to set up new practices is also visible at

PCP-ACEFA and the most affected are the older generation because young people who have just graduated from the training schools have more improved knowledge of organizational culture, in other words an update of corporate organizational culture. This affects the older generation and they either drop out or resign from committees, their anger is arouse that disrupts a meeting, provoke personal abuse and cause defensiveness. It causes strains such as anxiety, depression, physical symptoms, and low levels of job performance (Richard A 1976) [14].

At the workplace, there is conflict whenever, two or more persons interact, especially when opinions with respect to any task or decision are in contradiction (Business Jargon: -) [6]. Our research clearly shows this when people or workers have it difficult to cooperate because of the attitude of one another either through an impolite usage of language or disrespect for a colleague in front of the population as it was the case at COPRESSA.

6. Conclusions

In this chapter, we have examined the causes of conflict in the agricultural and environmental organizations in the Far North Region of Cameroon whose population suffers the most from poverty and huge environmental challenges and which has the highest concentration of environmental organizations. We discovered that:

There are disputes over how revenues should be divided, how the work should be done, and how long and hard people should work. There are jurisdictional disagreements among individuals, departments and between unions and management. These subtler forms of conflicts involve rivalries, jealousies, personality clashes, role definitions, and struggle for power and favor. There is also conflict within individuals- between competing needs and demands – to which individuals respond in different ways.

We discovered also that conflicts in organizations are regularly triggered by the differences people have in terms of opinions, interests and needs as they work together. These relations may be between employees or with senior colleagues, there are always misunderstandings between collaborators; that is, collaborators hardly understand each other when sharing opinions with each other. There are equally romantic relationships which create conflicts in organizations when two or more male employees fall in love with the same female employees it creates conflict. It also occurs when employees are strict with one another especially when doing dirty or difficult work tasks like cleaning the environment. Equally when one person of the same hierarchical rank encroaches the competent domain of the other, it produces conflict of authority and then leads to jealousy. It also comes about when the religious values of each other is not respected especially that of the Muslims where a majority of the workers are non- Muslims, it provokes conflict because the prayers hours of the Muslims are hardly respected.

There is also generational conflict which is characterized by the confrontation between those who have some experience and young graduates who would like to implement new practices. Young graduates have more theoretical knowledge as compared to older workers who are less-educated or who are not graduates. When the young graduates try to put theories into practice or try to innovate the manufacturing process, they face opposition from the older generation.

One of the causes of conflict in environmental and agricultural organizations is discrimination: workers are not promoted basing on merit but on their ethnic relation to one another. Position intended for one worker is most often given to a completely different person. This leads to a kind of jealousy, lack of respect, denigration between employees hence widening the conflict between them in the company.

Another source of conflict is economic which refers to the scarcity of resources in environmental and agricultural enterprises. Conflicts are present due to the non-distribution of part of the substantial profits that ACEFA makes to its staff. Employees complain that the bonuses that suppliers pay do not reach employees not even half and there is also the problem of too low salary at mostly private organization unlike cooperation like GIZ.

Finally, the poor distribution of work tasks is another source of conflict in these companies. Our respondents (the employees) of ACEFA confirmed that workers of the same rank in the organization have unequal distribution of tasks while some workers have more tasks, others have less. Work is mostly informal, unplanned and therefore unpredictable. There are cases where some employees leave work much earlier than others. That is to say, some employees work overtime while others do not.

Acknowledgements

I thank Dr. Obono Felicité the Head of Department of Environmental Sciences and Prof Mohamadou Alidou the Director of the National Advanced School of Engineering of Maroua for issuing a research permit for the Master 1 students of Environmental Sciences to carry out this research.

Author details

Nanche Billa Robert
Department of Sociology, Anthropology and Social Sciences for Development, Faculty of Arts, Letters and Social Sciences, University of Maroua, Cameroon

*Address all correspondence to: nanchefile@yahoo.co.uk

References

[1] Jehn, K.A. and Bendersky, C. "Intragroup conflict in organizations: a contingency perspective on the conflict-outcome relationship", Research in Organizational Behavior, 2003, Vol. 25, pp. 187-242.

[2] De Dreu, C.K.W., Harinck, F. and Van Vianen, A.E.M. 1999, "Conflict and performance ingroups and organizations", in Cooper, C.L. and Robertson, I. (Eds),International Review ofIndustrial and Organizational Psychology, 1999 No. 14, Wiley, Indianapolis, IN, pp. 369-414

[3] Elisabeth N. and Stewart C. Conception of Conflict in Organisational Conflict Research: Toward Critical Reflexivity Journal of Management Inquiry 2019 Vol 28(2) 166-179 (2019)

[4] Louis R. Pondy. Organizational Conflict: Concepts and Models Administrative Science Quarterly, 1967, Vol. 12, No. 2, pp. 296-320: Sage Publications, Inc. URL: https://www.jstor.org/stable/2391553

[5] Priyakshi M. Organisational Conflict available at https://www.yourarticlelibrary.com/organization/conflict- management/organizational-conflict/99695

[6] Business Jargon: Organisational Conflict available at https://businessjargons.com/organizational-conflict.html

[7] De Dreu, C., & Beersma, B. Conflict in organizations: Beyond effectiveness and performance. European Journal of Work and Organizational Psychology, 2005. 14, 105-117.

[8] Jehn, K. A qualitative analysis of conflict types and dimensions in organizational groups. Administrative Science Quarterly, 1997. 42, 530-557.

[9] Bendersky, C., & Hays, N. Status conflict in groups. Organization Science, 2012 23, 323-340

[10] de Wit, F., Jehn, K., & Scheepers, D.. Task conflict, infor-mation processing, and decision-making: The damaging effect of relationship conflict. Organizational Behavior and Human Decision Processes, 2013 122, 177-189.

[11] O'Neill, T., Allen, N., & Hastings, S. (2013). Examining the "pros" and "cons" of team conflict: A team-level meta-analysis of task, relationship, and process conflict. Human Performance, 26, 236-260.

[12] Tjosvold, D. The conflict-positive organization: It depends upon us. Journal of Organizational Behavior, 2008. 29, 19-28.

[13] Mikkelsen, E. An analysis of the social meanings of conflict in nonprofit organizations. Nonprofit and Voluntary Sector Quarterly, 2013. 42, 923-941.

[14] Mikkelsen, E., & Gray, B. Everyday conflict at work: An organizational sensemaking ethnography. In A. Pedersen & D. Humle (Eds.), Doing organizational ethnography 2016. (pp. 17-39). New York, NY: Routledge.

[15] Mcshane, S.L & Glinow, M.A. Organizational Behaviour. (2008). New York: McGraw –Hill Companies.

[16] Bernard O. Ashimi R. International Journal of Academic Research in Economics and Management Sciences, 2014, Vol. 3, No. 6I SSN:2226-3624126www.hrmars.com

[17] Gatlin, J. et al., Understanding Conflict in the Workplace, University of Florida IFAS Extension, 2019

[18] Henry P Knowles; Börje O. (1971). Personality and leadership behavior, 1971, Mass.: Addison-Wesley Pub. Co.

[19] Serenko, A. Knowledge Sabotage as an extreme Form of Counterproductive Knowledge Behaviour: The Perspective of the Target Journal of Knowledge Management, 2020. 24(4): 737-773.

[20] Serenko, A. Knowledge Sabotage as an Extreme Form of Counterproductive behaviour: Conceptualisation, Typology and Empirical Demonstration. 2019. Journal of Knowledge Management, 23(7): 1260-1288.

[21] De Angelis, Paula: Blindsided: Recognizing and Dealing with Passive-Aggressive Leadership in the Workplace, 2008.

[22] Wikipedia the free encyclopedia List of environmental Organisation available at https://en.wikipedia.org/wiki/List_of_environmental_organizations#:~:text=An%20environmental%20organization%20is%20an,environment%20or%20the%20natural%20environment

[23] OECD. OECD environmental outlook to 2020. Paris, OECD 2001.

[24] IPCC.. Climate change 2001: synthesis report, by R. Watson & the Core Writing Team, eds. 2001 Cambridge, UK, Cambridge University Press

[25] Murgai, R., Ali, M. & Byerlee, D. Productivity growth and sustainability in post-green revolution agriculture: the case of the Indian and Pakistan Punjabs. World Bank Research Observer, 2001, 16(2). Washington, DC.

[26] Robbins, S., et al, Management Forest NSW: 2003. Pearson Education, Pp 385-421.

[27] Floger, J.P. Working through Conflict 1993. New York: Harpes.

[28] KInicki, A. & Kreithner, R. Organizational Behaviour: Key Concepts,Skills and Best Practice 2008. New York: The McGraw-Hill Companies.

Section 3

Conflict and Communication

Chapter 5

Rhetoric Communication to Handle Interpersonal Conflicts at Workplaces

Mitashree Tripathy

Abstract

Organisations are large platforms amalgamating people from diverse backgrounds, mindsets, experiences, opinions and beliefs. It is likely that at times there may be a clash in personalities leading to conflicts. While conflicts resolved create productive workplaces, on the contrary unresolved conflicts generate dissatisfaction and discontent among the people further leading to inefficiency among the employees directly hampering the organisation as a whole. Communication is understood as the most indispensable factors that moulds and reflects in our everyday relationships. Because of its dynamism and complexity, communication forms the essence of interpersonal relationships in organisational contexts. Understanding the vitality of communication, the concept this paper explores is how rhetoric communication, an Aristotelian principle may help resolving interpersonal conflicts, creating a win-win situation and further extending healthy interpersonal relationships at workplaces.

Keywords: communication, rhetoric, organizational, conflict, philosophy, management

1. Introduction

The concept of communication plays a major role in building interpersonal connections. The concept, the scope and the essentials of communication is dynamic and at the same time complex. Dynamic, because it involves and depends on the perception that feeds human interaction and that evolves over time and complex because it includes several steps before finally receiving a feedback from a receiver. Interestingly, its complexity does not merely gets restricted to individuals, rather expands to groups, organisations and cultures all around the globe. This dynamism and complexity in communication together form the essence of interpersonal relationships. Studies claim "through communication individuals describe and propose their preferred relationship to objects or others" [1]. Communication helps individuals to question and reply and it is in this fashion that they develop objectives regarding their favoured relationships and the manners for progressing with them. This is how interpersonal relationships sustain or abstain.

Particularly in organisational contexts, communication is more intricate where people spend a significant quantity of their lives. Working with others, sharing interests and activities form a work environment where a great deal of connections takes place through correspondence. Transactions with superiors, subordinates, managers, peers, customers, clients and other members internally or externally linked at workplaces frame the day to day schedules making workplaces all the more collaborative and blended. This system is indispensable and inevitable as employees at workplaces need to understand what their organisations demand and how are they proceeding to meet the demands. While organisations demands may vary however, it is expected that the interpersonal relations at the workplaces remain constant, although may get stronger but should not feeble. This is because "achieving goals is possible only when employees form a strong bond between each other at workplaces" [2]. Stronger bonds create excellent interpersonal relationships thereby converting workplaces as a potential source of satisfaction and contentment. However, on the contrary, "relationships at work can be source of great distress and dissatisfaction when conflicts do occur" [3]. This is because while people spend a considerable proportion of time at workplace, they somehow tend to underrate this time and neglect the "the effect that their behaviour has on the way others behave and therefore on the achievement of personal and organisational goals" [4]. Communication becomes dysfunctional during conflicts. Ultimately, these intricacies may interfere in the business performances and smooth running of the organisation. Interestingly, it is communication again that resolves conflicts.

2. Literature review

Communication is an activity of relaying information from one source to another. Communication helps to create the world we live in. The way we interact, make relationships both personally and professionally, understand, develop, manage, lead, experience is all dependent on communication. In fact it is communication that offers strength and vitality to our existence. The concept of communication is very vast and means different to different people. For example, communication scholars will understand communication as a theory. Similarly, people from the business world understand communication as crucial information to be executed. In personal relationships communication would mean to share opinion, emotions and beliefs. For a vendor, communication may mean to present or persuade someone to buy their products. In short, communication is any such activity that includes exchange of views, information, messages, and opinions between two parties that are expected to promote a healthy relationship. However, there is no fixed definition of communication. Literature is replete with several definitions like "communication is a process of passing information and understanding from one person to another" [5]. Further studies claim "communication is essentially the ability of one person to make contact with another and make himself or herself understood" [6]. Still more definitions claim "communication is a process by which information is transmitted between individuals and/or organizations so that an understanding response results" [7]. Although, there can be indistinct definitions based on various studies on the theory and definitions of communication, it seems reasonable to summarize and assert that communication is an activity that is commenced by a source and gets executed to another to provide some meaning with a purpose to build a bridge between the two.

While communication is inevitable and its value can never be disparaged, its expertise in organisational contexts holds of greater significance. The reason is the purpose of the organisations is focussed for long-term goals that are executed meticulously through equally efficient structures. The implementation of communication in such strategies certifies the result of the efforts given. One study claims "communication is perceived as a magical elixir, one that can ensure a happy long term relationship and can guarantee organisational success". But at times, there arise discrepancies or misinterpretation of communication when people work for common goals that result in conflicts. Authors mention "a disagreement often begins when two people or parties have different interest and work against each other in pursuit of their own objectives" [8]. This can also be between subordinate and superior or between c0workers where superiors may coerce forced strategies using their power and co-workers may even become ugly so much that at times they "become destructive, leading to anger, burnout and stress directly affecting mental, physical and emotional wellbeing" [9].

Studies mention that "conflict management refers to the systematic prevention of unproductive conflict and proactively addressing those conflicts that cannot be prevented" [10].

Conflicts can take place at various levels in an organisation. For example, there can be conflicts between departments, teams and individuals as internal communication structure is concerned and between customers, clients and third parties when external communication is concerned. Interpersonal conflicts although inevitable can be hazardous. Its seriousness emerges when the consequences of conflicts are taken lightly and easy and for granted in similar ways just like conflicts are taken. Hence, a constructive conflict handling system in organisation is a must. Many studies argue that both conflict resolution and conflict management are same and that if an organisation lacks conflict this symbolizes that the conflict has already been solved but, for a temporary moment. However, "if the removal of the symptoms of conflict does not remove the causes of conflict, then the solution reached is an illusory one" [11]. Thus, it may be fruitful if a conflict is managed rather than simply solved for better results.

Blake and Mouton (1964) were first to develop a scheme for managing "interpersonal conflicts into five types like forcing, withdrawing, smoothing, compromising and problem solving" [12]. Further these five modes were reinterpreted by Thomas (1976) where "he considered the intentions of a party through cooperativeness and assertiveness in classifying the modes of handling conflict into five types" [13]. Cooperativeness is an act that originates from within an individual in need to suit and agree to other's concerns while assertiveness to satisfy one's own concerns through respect for other people.

Many studies have also attempted to find if there could be an intervention of emotional intelligence in conflicts management. Or more possibly does there sustain any relationship between emotional intelligence and conflict management. Results indicated that "individuals' conflict management preferences predicted actual conflict management behaviours and EI was found to moderate this relationship" [14]. More recent studies on emotional intelligence depict it is always advisable to know a person in person in order to anticipate challenges and avoid objectionable surprises. In such aspects emotional intelligence plays a major role as "knowing the confronter, one will need to understand and work through one's own feelings about the subject matter of the confrontation as well as one's feelings about those who hold opposing views" [15]. Comprehending how one feels and counters when confronted is a key element in emotional intelligence.

In the above studies one common link and a key factor in all findings is communication. Most of the times and most during conflict management if the sender before giving any message to the receiver gives a thought to the intended message and attempt to stimulate the receiver in a way that is intended to achieve a specific result, probably then not only the conflict is managed but also it would have long term effects in organisational growth as well. Such communication is known as rhetoric communication, a strong principle prescribed by Aristotle. This paper attempts to explore the relevance of rhetoric communication in interpersonal conflict management in the organisation. This paper declares rhetorical communication is not simply a prudent approach to solve interpersonal conflicts but it's an instant win-win over an audience. The upcoming section will study interpersonal conflicts in organisational contexts in details and rhetorical communication as an intervention in the same.

3. Organisational conflicts

Conflict is as inevitable as breathing. It is a natural process. It takes place during when two or more individuals, groups, organisations or even nations interact with each other while attaining their objectives. Often during the process there might arise unavoidable inconsistencies or incompatibilities "when two or more of them desire a similar resource that is in short supply when they have partially exclusive behavioural preferences regarding their joint action; or when they have different attitudes values, beliefs, and skills" [16]. This suggests that during conflicts one of the parties have a differing perception of beliefs, opinions, interests, and aspirations from that of another thus causing an incongruity between the two. Although the concept of the conflict is not a novel one and has influenced out thinking process since quite a long time, its dealing and acceptance has been largely underrated. Efficient dealing with conflict is highly indispensable if it is realized that the changes associated with it will have immense benefits.

The success of every organisation either large or small largely depends on the profit it makes. Many business organisations mostly centre on daily functions and operations and extend strategies and standards to proceed in order to achieve the desired results. However, these objectives and plans disappear when there occur conflicts between one or more parties that impact everyone associated with the organisation so much that at times, when conflicts are unchecked they can bring down an organisation's moral and image in the market. Hence organisational conflict can be described as "a phenomenon that depicts disagreement within or among individuals or group working together in an organisation over means or ends; or in an attempt to establish their views in preference to others" [17]. And when the conflict takes place between two or more individual, it is termed as interpersonal conflict. It's true that sometimes perception of interference from others can act as a reason of conflict; however, perceptions are not always true. Studies reveal that organisational conflict commonly originates because of "power, relationships, substantive and task issues, emotion, information, structure, values, and styles" [18]. Power struggles, perceptual differences in relationships due to roles and responsibilities, conflicts arising from tangible items, disagreement on the accuracy of or withholding a data or information, hurt feelings associated with various relationships, are some of the common reasons behind the instigation of organisational conflict. Interestingly, each of the reasons is unique in itself and demand different management application and strategies.

There may be various reasons behind organisational conflicts however, the impact that conflicts create are at times hazardous as sometimes they can be life threatening. Employees may have commitment issues resulting to reduced turn over and complete absenteeism. Put differently, workplaces seem like war spaces as employees continue to be on stress gradually, that impacts their problem-solving, decision making and thinking abilities. Studies indicate that "enduring stress further increases irritability and tendencies to distance oneself from social environment" [19].

Many organisations have already learned how unproductive conflicts can hamper their success and adapted fruitful methods to develop a structural framework to conflict management there are still many organisations that are struggling to find out suitable ways out. While destructive conflicts act as a barrier in workplace performance and many employees at their workplaces in fact are inclined more towards destructive conflicts sometimes voluntarily or involuntarily, with absolutely no approach towards developing constructive manners to resolute the issues between them, organisational theorists and researchers are still struggling to probe deep into what can be the only, if not, probably be more appropriate solution to manage conflicts apart from what the literature provides. The following section will explore if rhetoric communication as an Aristotelian principle be considered as a constructive and practical approach to handle interpersonal conflict. The following section studies in details about the same.

4. Rhetoric communication

The word rhetoric means "the art of persuasion" [20]. As an art rhetoric is of utmost importance to every part of a society. And that's why perhaps, rhetoric as a subject has been written in every age and realm wherever and whenever the study of arts and sciences have been encouraged. Ancient studies believe that "the power of pleasing and persuading those whom we address has excited every faculty in the mind of man, to detect, if possible the secret springs of that pleasure and persuasion, which give us such dominion over the feelings of our fellow creatures" [21]. It in fact speaks about the production of belief that one creates in the mind of an individual while persuading in considerations with fact and its possibility that also provide pleasure.

Good contributions to the rhetoric emerged with the intervention of Aristotle views and his contributions in the subject where he explored the unexplored realm of the art. In fact it was his treatise on the art of rhetoric that acts a structural and a systematic treatment of the subject so much that it remains as the quickest and the most direct form of any works related to any subject. Aristotle in his book Rhetoric focuses on the use of language in persuasive argument. He detects that if there is an appropriate blend of both practical and aesthetic elements this will lead to an effective presentation. On the same grounds Aristotle writes "proofs that depend on the spoken word fall into three categories that are the speaker's character or ethos, putting listener in a certain frame of mind through emotion or pathos and through demonstrating or seeming to demonstrate something through argument or logos" [22]. Many studies understand this concept as "the triadic classification of arguments that persuade by virtue of an appeal" [23]. The mode of communication through ethos, pathos and logos is a crucial discovery reflecting a standard classification of a practical discourse contributing to conflict management. The following sections will traverse through all the three modes of communication to unravel the contribution of the same in conflict management.

5. Ethos

Ethos "is a Greek word meaning character that is used to describe the guiding beliefs or ideals that characterize a community, nation, or ideology" [24]. And as Aristotle elucidates ethos is related to the character of the sender or the speaker in the process of communication. A character is a key trait that frames the personality of an individual. Aristotle defines character as "what shows a man's disposition the kind of things he chooses or rejects when his choice is not obvious" [25]. Hence character can be understood as any such act by an individual in terms of goodness and badness of the morals and values. Studies mention "the core characters are respect, responsibility, honesty, trust, caring fairness, perseverance, self discipline, courage, citizenship and life skills" [26]. And in fact these moral and values build a character of an individual and put a claim on the conscience of an individual to act in a certain manner.

During an interpersonal conflict at least one party or one source lack character or in simpler words when at least one party fails to exhibit morals and values interpersonal conflict happens and sometimes fails to get managed. While managing conflicts it's very essential to understand and evaluate the ethics of the source because ethics inspires credibility and credibility promotes belief. An individual with moral character would always gain trust and belief from others. Hence, the credibility of the individual would provide a quick help in assessing the wrongness or rightness of situations thereby offering solutions to conflict management.

6. Pathos

Pathos in Greek is associated with emotional appeal. However, many studies consider that "a better equivalent might be appeal to the audience's sympathies and imagination" [27]. This is because through emotional appeal, an audience doesn't merely respond emotionally but also attempts to identify and understand about what the points the speaker intends to convey. This emotional appeal instigates a feeling of pain and misery in the mind of audience creating an impact on the audience. It would not be counterfeit to express that emotions do an important work while negotiating particularly during interpersonal conflicts. Many observational studies reveal that "negotiators rely on emotions to overcome obstacles such as initial mistrust and interpersonal friction" [28].

During interpersonal conflict management, pathos acts as a powerful principle as it connects its sources through emotions. Although the emotional appeal depends on how it is conveyed, however, its impact necessarily overcomes much of suffering. One must have a concrete grip over one's passions. One of the studies refers that "passions matter in real- life deal making and dispute resolution" [29]. One ought to have clarity on the medium of communication and discover what the emotions are conveying in order to adapt to the situation thereby engaging others successfully. This indicates one must be prepared to negotiate or manage conflicts through emotions. Although it is obvious that anxieties and resentments may skulk under the surface, however, once festered the communication can go out of control and may not be acceptable. Hence, emotions have to be used judiciously while conflict management, to arouse empathy and not tense up.

7. Logos

Logos in Greek "means reasoning or argument" [30]. It is associated with logical appeal and is used to persuade an audience by the use of rational claim in order to support an argument. Studies suggest that "*logos* refers to the internal consistency of the message, the clarity of the thesis, the logic of its reasons and the effectiveness of its supporting evidence" [31]. The main motive of the use of logical reasoning during an argument is to create an impact on the audience through validation of proof in order to support the argument by substantiating it.

During an interpersonal conflict management, although the speaker is able to provide an apparent proof in order to convince the audience. Most of the time during an interpersonal conflict lack of proof or essential evidence may either give rise to conflicts or deepen the existing conflict. However, through the valid appeal of logic, the speaker tends to prove his/her point and bring truth to the surface. Evidently, a speaker may be able to provide facts, statistics, figures and analogies as proof in order to showcase his/her views before the audience.

However, the point is focusing only on one mode of communication and rejecting the other two would make the purpose of conflict resolution dilute and the outcome may largely seem vague. For example, if one only focuses on the credibility part, even if the morality of the individual appears right, but if he/she lacks the emotional approach or fails to provide sufficient proofs to keep the views, the speaker may not be able to manage the conflict. Similarly, if one focuses only on the emotional part and disregards the integrity and the logical reasoning appeal of the individual still the conflict won't be managed. Likewise, if the emphasis is given to the scope through logical argument excluding the emotional and the ethical aspect of the communication the conflict may not still be managed. Hence, during an interpersonal conflict management one must be able to blend all the three modes of persuasive communication in order to make it more effective.

Discussing all the three modes of communication in order to handle interpersonal conflicts it must be understood that at the core, the conflicts need to be handled also considering the fact that how during conflicts the needs of the people get affected by the conflicts. Hence, "for a solution to be lasting, it must meet the needs of all those involved in the conflict" [32].

8. Conclusion

The most important element in interpersonal conflict management at workplaces is communication and the usage of persuasive approach in the communication process. Beyond the ethos versus pathos versus logos according to the Aristotelian principle of communication, the key factor that helps in interpersonal conflict management is identifying the aspects of the managing the conflict sensibly. The element of ethical, emotional and logical standards cue must be well picked during interpersonal conflict management so that one knows exactly how to strike the bull's eye. Interpersonal conflicts can be well managed when all the three modes of persuasion are appropriately influencing each mode of communication over the other. Focusing on only one of the modes and implementing only one agenda creates more incoherency and incoherency during the conflict management. Communication without ethics or character can be manipulative. Communication without emotions can lead to coercion and inflexibility and communication without facts, logic, reasoning and argument can be misguiding during interpersonal conflicts. After analyzing the derivatives of ethos, pathos and logos, in the paper, we now have the residue of reinforcing a richer appreciation of how all the three modes of persuasion must work in consistency during an interpersonal conflict management. Hence, ethos pathos and logos, can provide a braided thread that is not only strong but also sustainable in interpersonal conflict management.

Author details

Mitashree Tripathy
Faculty of Management Studies, Sri Sri University, Odisha, India

*Address all correspondence to: mitashreetripathy84@gmail.com

References

[1] Cushman DP, Cahn DD. Communication in interpersonal relationships. Albany: State University of New York Press; 1985.

[2] Tripathy M. Interpersonal act at Workplace Through Discreet use of Humor. Israeli Journal for Humor Research. 2018;7(2):64-78.

[3] Edelmann RJ. Interpersonal conflicts at work. Leicester: BPS Books; 1993.

[4] Hayes J. Interpersonal skills goal-directed behaviour at work. London: Routledge; 2013.

[5] Davis K. Organizational behavior- a book of readings. 4th ed. Montreal: Mcgraw-Hill; 1974.

[6] Adair JE. Effective communication. London: Pan Books; 2009.

[7] Little P. Communication in business. Second edition. London: Longman; 1970.

[8] Proksch S. Conflict management. , Switzerland: Springer; 2018.

[9] Tripathy M. Practicing the Strategies of Interpersonal Conflicts Management in Business Organisations to Accede Development and Effectiveness in Personal Health. 1st ed. Vol. 10. Noida: Institute of Medico-Legal Publications; 2019.

[10] Raines S. Conflict management for managers: resolving workplace, client, and policy disputes. Lanham; Boulder; New York; London: Rowman et Littlefield Publishers; 2020.

[11] Eunson, B. Conflict Management. John Wiley & Sons; 2012.

[12] Samaras JT. Management applications: exercises, cases, and readings. Englewood Cliffs, NJ: Prentice Hall; 1989.

[13] Fenn P. Construction Conflict Management And Resolution. S.L.: Taylor & Francis; 2020.

[14] Moeller C, Kwantes CT. Too Much of a Good Thing? Emotional Intelligence and Interpersonal Conflict Behaviors. The Journal of Social Psychology. 2015;155(4):314-324.

[15] Blank S. Managing organizational conflict. Jefferson, NC: McFarland & Company, Inc., Publishers; 2020.

[16] Rahim MA. Managing Conflict in Organizations. New Brunswick (U.S.A.): Transaction Publishers; 2011.

[17] Alice VBA. Organizational Conflict. London: IntechOpen; 2018.

[18] McCorkle S, Witt SL. People Skills for Public Managers. Oxfordshire, England: Routledge; 2015.

[19] Dreu CKWD, Beersma B. Conflict in organizations: Beyond effectiveness and performance. European Journal of Work and Organizational Psychology. 14(2):105-17.

[20] The British Controversialist, and Literary Magazine. United Kingdom; 1865.

[21] Walker J. A Rhetorical Grammar: In Which the Common Improprieties in Reading and Speaking Are Detected. London: Printed for T. Cadell; 1823.

[22] Aristotle, Waterfield R. The Art of Rhetoric. United Kingdom: OUP Oxford; 2018.

[23] Hall DL, Ames RT. Thinking from the Han: Self, Truth, and Transcendence in Chinese and Western Culture.

Albany, NY: State University of New York Press; 1998.

[24] Gathing DT. Ethos: A Look inside Ourselves. United States: Xlibris Corp; 2012.

[25] Aristoteles, Potts LJ. Aristotle on the art of fiction. Cambridge: Cambridge Univ. Press; 1968.

[26] Thompson TL. Fulfilling Special Needs in Scouting Guide to Finding Resources to Help the Special Needs Scout. Tawny Lee Thompson; 2014.

[27] Penny M. Political Pathos. United States: Xlibris US; 2010.

[28] Bolton GE, Croson RTA. The Oxford Handbook of Economic Conflict Resolution. New York, NY: Oxford University Press; 2012.

[29] Kimberlyn Leary JPand MW. Negotiating with Emotion [Internet]. Harvard Business Review. 2014 [cited 2020Nov21]. Available from: https://hbr.org/2013/01/negotiating-with-emotion

[30] Thompson P. Persuading Aristotle the Timeless Art of Persuasion in Business Negotiation and the Media. Sydney: Allen & Unwin; 2014.

[31] Abdul-Raof H. Text Linguistics of Qur'anic Discourse An Analysis. United Kingdom: Taylor & FrancisU; 2018.

[32] Omisore BO, Abiodun AR. Organizational Conflicts: Causes, Effects and Remedies. International Journal of Academic Research in Economics and Management Sciences. 2014;3(6):118-136.

Chapter 6

Managing Conflict in Faith-Based Organizations in Zimbabwe

Norman Chivasa

Abstract

One of the basic theories commonly believed in the secular world today is that conflict is inevitable which means that individuals and groups have needs, interests, dislikes, likes, partnerships, values and preferences which are often not compatible. This is also true of faith-based organizations. Using the Apostolic Faith Mission in Zimbabwe church as a point of reference, this article argues that in Christian circles there is need to deliberately develop a perspective of conflict that reflects conflict as a positive force that generates both co-existence and growth in the church to counter the conventional view in the majority of churches that consider conflict as a destructive force. In the Apostolic Faith Mission church, intra-church disputes have a negative effect on the wellbeing of individuals and groups (the church) as conflict creates rivalry, hostility, divisions, hate, breakaways, among others. This is because a strongly adversarial attitude to conflict of all sorts is reflected in the approach of the church to conflict and in particular, some pastors have responded with legal action against the disciplinary activities of the church. Consequently, this article suggests that faith-based organizations should appreciate the importance of conflict for positive growth and development as a good number of Christians today are still pessimistic about conflict.

Keywords: Apostolic Faith Mission church, conflict, faith-based organization, Zimbabwe

1. Introduction

The phenomena of conflict, world over, is experienced at different levels and in varying degrees of human interaction. This is so because "Every relationship... no matter how close, how understanding, how compatible there will be times when ideas, actions, needs or goals won't match those of others around" [1]. In a real world such situations do occur and usually there are negative feelings that go along with them. For this reason, in some circles conflict is feared because it is viewed as a social ill that always negates development and a source of all distressed relationships that militates against harmony sustenance. While in other circles it is perceived as a necessary ingredient for human survival which potentially helps individual people to understand each other better whenever it occurs.

Within this framework, the contemporary world now looks at conflict as unavoidable and a beneficial phenomenon that exists wherever people live. This perspective demonstrates a shift from the unschooled and myopic view that regarded conflict as a vice to human survival yet when better managed it provides the opportunity to learn more about other people's needs, values or rights.

As such, instead of working hard to avoid conflict societies must be ready through experience and training to meet and manage conflict constructively. Thus, well-managed conflict can yield up positive relationships.

This Chapter explores conflict management strategies employed by faith-based organizations taking the Apostolic Faith Mission in Zimbabwe (AFM) church as a point of reference. The AFM in Zimbabwe church has set procedures to curb conflicts that potentially threaten the life of the church. By coming up with conflict managing strategies, the AFM in Zimbabwe church has acknowledged that conflict in itself is not necessarily a vice, but a challenge, which when carefully handled may benefit the church and society at large. Accordingly, the AFM in Zimbabwe church has also demonstrated a shift in its view of conflict by championing for the non-violent resolution of conflicts following a realization that human diversity does not threaten harmony but enhances meaningful relationships when the parties to a conflict keep engaged to dialogue following disagreements.

2. Research approach

The aim of this article was to assess how conflict involving pastors in the AFM in Zimbabwe church is being managed. To systematically achieve this aim, qualitative research approach was followed through the descriptive, explorative and normative tasks [2]. The descriptive task led the researcher to establish the current state of affairs relating to the nature of conflict and how they are being managed in the faith-based organization under review. The explorative task led the researcher to evaluate structures responsible for handling conflict in the AFM in Zimbabwe church. The normative task led the researcher to recommend strategies ought to be employed by the AFM in Zimbabwe church when addressing conflicts involving pastors.

Sources of data came through document analysis, in particular the church's two primary documents: Constitution and the Policy Document, which represent data for public consumption. Other sources of data include literature on dispute handling procedures of the AFM in Zimbabwe by Chivasa [3] and intra-church or group conflicts from Blackburn and Brubaker [4]; Schrock-Shenk et al. [5] among others. To keep an updated record on conflicts involving pastors in the AFM in Zimbabwe local Zimbabwean newspaper articles from Herald, Sunday Mail, Chronicles, Newsday, and H-Metro among other newspapers were instrumental. The major reason for consulting local newspapers was due to that conflicts involving pastors receive media coverage in local newspapers in Zimbabwe.

3. Statement of the problem

Conflicts in the AFM in Zimbabwe involve everyone from church members, laypersons and high profile leadership such as pastors. In the AFM church pastors are responsible for resolving conflicts, administering church doctrines, enforcing Christian values and constitutional regulations. The issue facing the article is if, for example, the pastor is engaged in misappropriation of church funds, extramarital affairs or some other misdemeanor, the church would not expand both numerically and spiritually. Such circumstances, if anything, generate discontent, break apart the church and blackmail the whole Christian culture.

Such activities religiously and morally stain the church's purity. For the broader community, now that the leaders (pastors) of whom they seek divine support are involved in such vices, people who may wish to convert to Christianity may be discouraged. The key research question is who will help pastors to resolve their conflicts without causing the church to degenerate into a spiritually paralyzed religious body bearing the mere label of Christianity?

4. The rationale for studying the AFM in Zimbabwe church

Of the major Pentecostal denominations in Zimbabwe, the AFM in Zimbabwe church boasts the singular honor of having been in existent for more than a century. In 2015, the AFM in Zimbabwe celebrated 100 years of active ministry across Zimbabwe. She claims to have an estimated membership of about 2, 3 million. In 2006, the denomination claimed that its membership was estimated at 2, 5 million [6]. Due to lack of updates on denominational records, membership figures are liable to amplification [7]. However, commanding a large membership following was not the impetus behind the choice of AFM in the present article, but numerical age of the denomination was the major drive. The AFM in Zimbabwe is the oldest Pentecostal of them all in Zimbabwe. As a matter of fact, the numerical age of the AFM in Zimbabwe cannot be overlooked considering that the rise of other popular Pentecostal denominations in Zimbabwe (for example, Johane Masowe) which trace their origins from the AFM in Zimbabwe [8]. Other popular denominations that broke away from AFM in Zimbabwe which have been in existent for more than 50 years or so include Apostolic Faith Mission of Mugodhi which broke away in the 1940s and Zimbabwe Assemblies of God Africa which broke away between the 1950s and 60s. As if that was not enough, in 2010 the AFM in Zimbabwe gave birth to other popular denominations such as: United Family International Church, Heartfelt International Ministries, Apostolic Flame Ministries [7, 8] and the list is still on-going. Thus, numerical age was an important factor in the selection of the denomination under review, as well as the nature of conflict experienced up to this day.

5. Overview of conflict involving pastors in the AFM in Zimbabwe church

The AFM in Zimbabwe church is one of the oldest Pentecostal denominations in Zimbabwe, hereinafter referred to as a faith-based organization, tracing its origins as far back as 1915. Ever since its establishment, the AFM in Zimbabwe, formerly Rhodesian African Church in 1915, was largely run under the supervision of the Apostolic Faith Mission of South Africa but even then conflicts involving pastors have been an integral part of this church's life.

In 1989, the AFM's self-autonomy in Zimbabwe ushered in a new period in which the church encountered a multitude of head-on conflict situations involving pastors and the majority of cases arising from sexual immorality, violent tendencies, drunkenness, forced transfers, misappropriation of church funds, confiscation of church property, disputes over leadership roles and personality clashes [3]. To exemplify practical instances of conflict among pastors, the researcher identified cases that occurred between 1990 and 2018. The researcher, therefore, made a conscious choice of the period 1990 to 2018, which covered an upsurge of conflict situations resulting from the behavior of AFM in Zimbabwe pastors which resulted in the split of the church under review in 2018. Most of these conflict situations were both glossed over and degenerated into various levels of intractability, which have troubled this faith-based organization for 28 years.

For instance, in 1990, Masvingo Province experienced a conflict situation involving allegations of sexual immorality, leveled against a pastor by the church elders. After investigations by the Provincial Committee the matter was discussed in the Provincial Council meeting and a resolution was passed to suspend the pastor indefinitely. Another example of conflict situation of similar nature, an extra-marital affair, was also witnessed in 1994. The case was unearthed following reports by the church elders to the Provincial Overseer. The Provincial Committee made investigations and a resolution to place the pastor under censure for one-year pending reinstatements was passed.

In 1995, two cases were unearthed. The first involved a Provincial Overseer, who faced allegations of promiscuity. Following investigations a resolution was passed by the Apostolic Council to depose him from serving as Overseer with subsequent indefinite period of censure. The second case involved allegations of extra-marital affair, which the probing committee found no substantial evidence.

Also, in 1996, four gruesome conflict situations haunted and shook the church in the same year. A surge of tension occurred within one congregation following allegations of extra-marital affair leveled against a pastor. A report was forwarded to the Provincial Committee and the pastor denied the allegations. Following this, a resolution was made by the Provincial Committee to transfer the pastor to another congregation and the case came to a standstill.

During that same period three more cases heralded. The first one involved allegations of confiscating church property by a pastor and before investigations were made, it appears the pastor unceremoniously left for another province and the case was left insoluble. The second case involved allegations of polygamy. Following reports to the Provincial Overseer, the Provincial Committee made investigations and the matter was deliberated at a Provincial Council meeting and a resolution to suspend the pastor indefinitely was agreed upon. The third mishap involved a wrangle over the control of an assembly between a deputy Overseer and a junior pastor. Tension occurred following a decision by the Provincial Committee to place the deputy Overseer at the congregation which was already under a junior pastor. As pressure from the Provincial Committee was mounted on the junior pastor to create space for the deputy Overseer, the matter was left insoluble following the junior pastor's decision to unceremoniously leave the church to join another denomination.

In 1997, a resident pastor was alleged of attempted rape. The Provincial Committee made investigations following the pastor's arrest amidst allegations by family members of the victim. Subsequently, the matter was brought to court which some Provincial Committee delegates did attend and the pastor pleaded not guilty. And findings from the court proceedings were presented to the Provincial Council by the Provincial Committee delegates. The Provincial Council resolved that the pastor was to be suspended pending placement under censure by the Apostolic Council.

Apart from that, 1999 saw the province under review recording another conflict situation which spilled over to 2005 resulting in factions in the same church. Tension occurred following allegations of embezzling church finances being leveled against a Provincial Overseer by some members of the Provincial Committee. The case subsequently translated into violence between 2001 and 2003 and police had to be called in to restore order at the church premises where the alleged Overseer was stationed. The Provincial Committee and the Provincial Council discussed over the matter and recommendations were made to the Apostolic Council, which did not resolve the matter promptly. The Daily News newspaper of Tuesday 28, January 2003, confirms that police arrested the alleged Provincial Overseer on allegations of misappropriating church funds, common assault and malicious injury to property. According to the newspaper, the arrest followed disturbances in which the

Provincial Overseer was alleged to have teamed up with other members and turned the church premises into a boxing ring. After a week, the newspaper of February 4, 2003 reported that the alleged Provincial Overseer appeared in court for a similar case in which he was charged with embezzlement of church funds but was not asked to plead against the charges. According to the newspaper report, the pastor had loaned church funds to a church member who returned it within a week and instead of depositing the money into the church's bank account the pastor allegedly converted it into his own use [8].

Furthermore, after the alleged pastor's acquittal the Apostolic Council cleared the charges and the pastor's suspension was lifted pending expiry in April 2003, a resolution contested against by the Masvingo Provincial Council, which demanded ostracization of the alleged pastor from pastoral duties. Accordingly, the Provincial Committee refused to abide by the decision of the Apostolic Council and this resulted in the alleged pastor's congregation splitting into two camps. And the two factions waged bitter war to gain control over the affairs of the congregation in which some youths resorted to physical force to ensure their favored pastor retains control. As the story goes, about four youths were arrested in connection with fighting, demolition of church property, the use of force to take over the church premises and driving the church vehicle with flattened tyres [8]. According to the newspaper report, despite the alleged pastor's acquittal by the Masvingo Magistrate who declared that "There was no evidence for the clergyman to warrant prosecution" [8], tension was still raging between Apostolic Council and Provincial Council over the status of the alleged pastor in the church until 2007.

As if that is not enough, to give an update information on some of the conflicts involving pastors that received wide media coverage. The following newspaper titles demonstrate the size of the problem;

1. Just who is Emmanuel Makandiwa? Herald, 11 February 2011.

2. AFM should go back to the drawing board, Newsday, 21 April 2012.

3. AFM Church members in demo against overseer, H-Metro, 18 January 2013.

4. AFM Church Overseer accused of being used by the devil, H-Metro, 16 January 2013.

5. AFM Church pastors bribe overseers to be transferred to 'profitable' assemblies, H-Metro, 15 January 2013.

6. Nemukuyu B, Lawsuits lead to AFM Pastor's suspension, Herald, 13 August 2013.

7. Apostolic Faith Mission in Zimbabwe and other vs. Murefu.

8. Nemukuyu B, AFM top brass sued over 'looting spree', Herald, 31 December 2015.

9. Zimbabwe riot police beat up Waterfalls members in Church.

10. Jachi F, AFM pastor fined for ungodly behavior, Herald, 18 February 2015.

11. Laiton C, AFM Pastor screams at the High Court, Newsday, 28 February 2015.

12. Mbanje P, Fierce leadership row rocks AFM, Newsday, 14 April 2015.

13. AM Pastor, congregants clash, Manica post, 17 March 2016.

14. Kadirire H, AFM members want defrocked pastor reinstated, Daily News, 06 January 2016.

15. Mhlanga B, AFM fires senior pastor, closes Assembly, The Standard, 03 January 2016.

16. Chaos As AFM Finally Breaks Up, Zimeye, 14 October 2018.

In the first case, for example, the headline was a response following Makandiwa's decision to leave the church unceremoniously against the background of allegations of conflict of interests with the AFM in Zimbabwe church. Case of concern is number six, which records the pastor taking a complaint after misunderstandings against the church's decision. His decision resulted in him being indefinitely suspended. Another case of concern is number 15, which documented the ostracization of a pastor arising from misunderstandings between the parties to the dispute. Case number 16, represents a watershed conflict that changed the membership the AFM in Zimbabwe church. According to reports, the 2018 break-up was due to power struggle and other factors between top leadership involving the long-time and out-going church president, former deputy and the general secretary. At the time of writing this article, the once united AFM in Zimbabwe church has two rival church presidents one group has identified itself as the 'Original AFM and its rival identifies itself as 'Reformist AFM' with each camp claiming legitimacy and ownership of church property. These issues are still being decided by the courts of the land. From these cases, one can conclude that the church under review is more inclined toward adversarial position in which case the majority of pastors respond by going through the courts of law as they fight for what they consider as a violation of their rights (we discussed in detail on the principles focused on powers and privileges below). Against this background, this article assess the extent to which the faith-based organization is dealing with conflicts involving pastors with a view to recommend effective strategies. Whether the current strategies produced sustainable outcomes or just alleviated the impact or not resolved at all, are questions to be considered?

6. Conceptualizing conflict

Conflict is part and parcel of human life, and neither is the church spared [9]. As such, if the church wants to make the most of circumstances of conflict, conflict dynamics must be known. Although it is difficult to define conflict because of a variety of meanings in circulation, this article is closely associated with Adler & Towne's concept of conflict, who understand conflict as' an expressed struggle between at least two interdependent parties who perceive conflicting goals, scarce rewards, and the other party's intervention in achieving their goals' [1]. There are two major points to remember about conflict here. Conflict, in the first place, is an expressed struggle that implies that it is an open confrontation. In that sense, when all the parties concerned become aware of their differences, that is, in one way or the other, conflict may be said to exist; each party involved must realize that there is discord, tension or clash between them.

Second, disputes are made up of interdependent groups. This is so because "Any relationship... no matter how close, how detailed, how compatible there will be times when feelings, acts, needs or priorities will not match those of those around" [1]. The tension inside an interaction is crystal clear. Thus, as family, colleagues, workmates, church mates or neighbors, the parties experiencing a conflict engage in different spheres of social interaction. Since this article is interested in a church organization's conflict situations, it is important to remember that faith-based organizations are like family structures. Faith-based organizations are made up of people who affect each other, such as the teacher of the Sunday school, usher, deacon, deaconess, elder, priest, overseer, church president, to name a few. The actions of one participant impacts others as these individuals interact, thereby necessitating conflict, misunderstandings or disagreements. Conflict thus exists during an interaction [4].

There are three levels of social interaction from which conflict frequently arises: interpersonal, intra-community or intercommunity interactions [10, 11]. Conflict at an interpersonal level includes tension between people. Conflicts typically arise from variations in personality, attitudinal issues, communication failure, different expectations, limited resources and incompatible behaviors at this stage. Such factors may also fuel tensions between individuals.

An Intra-community tension includes tension within a community between individuals or groups that can also erupt due to, among other factors, personality differences, attitudes or limited resources. A conflict between a pastor and an over scarce resources is a good example. A common example of an intragroup conflict includes tension between cultures or community members, a clash of ideologies between Christians and Muslims [10].

The majority of researchers believe that conflict is a dynamic phenomenon that can be positive or negative [10, 12, 13]. When contained, handled and resolved, conflict becomes constructive in a way that prevents it from escalating into abuse (harm by intention). In contrast, it is considered destructive and thus harmful when a dispute transforms into hate, resentment, hatred, animosity and hostility between the parties [13]. Conflict only becomes negative if conflicts or misunderstandings are not adequately resolved, then conflict will turn into a crisis that will probably have a negative impact on human life [14]. The possible negativity or positivity of conflict is reflected below:

Conflict is not always a mechanism that is negative. Conflict, therefore, is one of the most important positive forces for social change. It tells us that something is wrong; conflict is a growth and development driver. There will be stagnation without conflict [15].

The above sentiments imply that conflict is not inherently a bad experience, but it helps to reveal other people's goals, priorities and roles, which can in turn foster development and positive social interactions between individuals and groups. This article is more concerned with the management of intra-church conflict.

7. An evaluative discussion on models of managing conflict in faith-based organizations

7.1 Frameworks for managing conflict in the AFM in Zimbabwe

The fact of conflict has contributed enormously to the establishment of an internal conflict management system called the Code of Conduct and Grievance Handling Procedure (CCGHP) in the AFM church in Zimbabwe [16]. Simply put, the AFM recognized that conflict in itself is not inherently a vice, but a challenge, which can improve the church and society at large when carefully handled.

The AFM in the CCGHP was established to act as a "guideline for rules and standards of conduct and procedures within the church to foster unity and discipline"

[17]. It is important to focus on the priorities of their CCGHP in order to assess the grievance management structure within AFM in Zimbabwe. There are institutionalized ways of coping with conflict in groups and societies [10]. The CCGHP is an institutionalized structure for conflict management at the AFM church in Zimbabwe. It includes policies, corrective steps, and actions to be made and recognizes leaders with dispute resolution responsibilities. A reflection of the aims of the CCGHP offers us the aspirations of the church under scrutiny in relation to issues of dispute. The code's goals are:

- To create consistent principles of code of conduct and maintain discipline within the church;
- To allow fulltime church leadership, lay employees and general staff to resolve conflicts among themselves;
- To outline actions that constitute disciplinary action-responsible misconduct;
- To state the disciplinary action that can be taken when the code is not complied with;
- To take corrective action in the event of inappropriate conduct or behavior; to develop clear, equitable and timely disciplinary processes that aim to remedy rather than punish unacceptable behavior; to include a vehicle or process within the church to address grievances [17].

The goal of the CCGHP was to resolve disputes in order to promote peace and harmony as desired results within the church. Another element of a happy church is unity. The mechanisms used by the AFM's CCGHP in Zimbabwe are built to create unity in the church. What is odd about AFM in Zimbabwe, however, is that the church mainly uses church discipline as its key conflict response mechanism in which the perpetrator is granted a period of censure ranging from three months to 12 months, depending on the nature of the offense as described in the Constitution of the church [18], Chapter 13.

7.2 Conflict-handling systems at the AFM in Zimbabwe

Despite attempts to demonize and minimize conflict by some individual Christians, there have been positive efforts by church leadership to deal constructively with conflict. The formation of the Local Council of Elders, the Regional Committee and the Apostolic Council to mediate disputes at the various levels of the Church can also be viewed as a positive step for the resolution of conflicts. It is important to stress that these structures are elected by a ballot system that uses the winner to take over all democratic processes and majorityitarianism. It is only the office of a pastor that is not voted into office, but appointed to be a member of the local council of elders [18].

A three-year theological training at a denominational college and the completion of a probationary period (internship) of at least one year are the requirements for one to qualify for the office of a pastor in the AFM in Zimbabwe. When employed to serve in an assembly, the pastor immediately becomes the chairman of the elderly council, which consists of seven adults. The members of the board are chosen on merit. One of the key merits is that such a person must pay tithes faithfully after which he/she can be elevated from deaconship to eldership, which is the highest rank before one becomes a pastor.

There are six lay staff on the local board of elders (mostly elders and, in some cases, deacons) and a local pastor as chairman. The local elders' board is responsible for the local congregation's affairs and this means resolving disputes at that level. The elders' local board is accountable to the provincial committee [17, 18].

Seven people are part of the provincial committee. The provincial overseer is the chairperson. An overseer is an administrative position assumed only by a pastor who, every three years, wins an election. The key qualification for being an overseer is that he or she must have reached the age of 40 years and worked in ministry in the church for more than ten years. Therefore, the provincial committee consists of pastor, elders and deacons who, on merit, assume these positions [18]. The provincial committee supervises a province's affairs and reports to the Apostolic Council. With political and administrative provincial demarcations in Zimbabwe, a province in the AFM in Zimbabwe does not drop squarely. There are three times more provinces in the AFM than in Zimbabwe's political and administrative provinces. The Apostolic Council, containing ten office bearers, is the supreme structure. The chairperson is the church president, who is chosen triennially from within the provincial overseers' ranks. The Apostolic Council is the protector of the Church and responsible, among other duties, for handling conflict [17, 18].

As evidence suggests, structures in Zimbabwe's AFM are built on the basis of experience, not necessarily on conflict resolution skills. Experience is supposed to indicate the number of years one has served in the church's leadership system. Some of the attributes taken from some biblical scriptures, such as 1 Timothy 3:13 and Titus 1:19, include qualities such as faithfulness, ability to lead, charismatic skills and good standing among peers. In terms of ability, a person who is chosen should be a dynamic preacher or teacher in either of these roles. Conflict resolution skills are also not taken into account when choosing individuals for leadership in the AFM church in Zimbabwe.

A more in-depth study of the state of affairs at the AFM in Zimbabwe shows that the development of the CCGHP can be seen as an effort to achieve sustainable conflict outcomes. However, these mechanisms (local elders' board, provincial and apostolic council) were challenged for not being able to deal constructively with conflict because most conflict situations appeared to have adversarial results where some pastors called 'black shepherds' or dangerous wolves in the skin of sheep are perceived as a threat. In most cases, it would be very difficult for so-called black shepherds to rise to higher positions in the church, such as overseers and president of the AFM. The boards have appeared in some cases to be used by some senior pastors in the church hierarchy to settle scores and create personal vendetta. These mechanisms are notorious in the AFM church in Zimbabwe for putting offending pastors under censorship, suspension and, in some cases, ostracizing them for good [3, 19].

Typically, after charges of sexual immorality were brought against them, three former senior pastors were indefinitely silenced in the 1990s. About the same time, more than 10 pastors quit the church unceremoniously in the Midlands province following accusations of insubordination. AFM witnessed a number of new Pentecostal Churches in Zimbabwe from 2008 to 2015, founded by their former pastors, who have left AFM in Zimbabwe with two influential pastors from Harare Province and another from Chitungwiza East Province.

These and other cases that followed are classic examples that have been tendered by provincial committees and the Apostolic Council to facilitate adversarial dispute approaches rather than to pursue reconciliatory approaches. One example of an adversarial approach is driving a minister out of the church. Adversarial tactics are listed as unilateral decisions [4]. In the case of AFM in unilateral decisions typically take place at the provincial level where the overseer may be a dominant figure in the decision-making processes and procedures. Normally, the national executive endorses disciplinary actions. Dissatisfaction with dispute resolution has resulted in many court cases being brought in Zimbabwe against the Church and the AFM executive. Unilateral decisions do not always settle a conflict, but tend to reinforce factionalism, which can be more serious since certain parties with decision-making powers can attempt to force another party to bend to their will, which can often be resisted to create more bitter feelings between leadership and ordinary church members [16].

7.3 How should conflict be managed in faith-based organizations?

Due to conflict situations such as dismissal of pastors, insubordination, pastors accused of sexual immorality, misappropriation of funds, fabrications focused on personal vendettas, extramarital affairs or divorce cases, among others, the existing internal conflict managing strategies in the AFM in Zimbabwe church tend to be under serious strain. Drastic steps taken against some pastors due to the alleged conflicts of interests between pastors engaged in activities of independent ministries from 2010 onwards caused the offended pastors to leave the church unceremoniously. These acts are disruptive patterns of conflict that usually do not settle the conflict, but help to blow it out of proportion [5].

The move led to the accused pastors attracting a number of members of the former AFM in Zimbabwe. As for the pastors who want to stay within the AFM in Zimbabwe, they turn to secular courts for remedies. In 1 Corinthians 6:18, critics then accuse them of going against Paul's biblical stance that states that Christians do not pursue resources from secular courts, but resolve their issues through local church systems. Paul recognized that, because of Christ in them, Christians would never be driven by self-interest when resolving disputes in the Church.

If Paul had lived longer, He would have known that, Christians might be so greedy and biased against brothers who turn to secular or conventional courts. Incidences of case overload in coping with disputes in the church of the AFM in Zimbabwe also indicate that a large percentage of workers, especially pastors, have no or little training in conflict resolution.

Furthermore, the fact that the CCGHP was designed to deal with disputes without actually going through the courts, but there are still some conflicts going through the courts brings to mind a multitude of concerns as to whether or not the CCGHP is really achieving its goals. In view of this, it can be assumed that the CCGHP's capacity is not as efficient as desired, given that certain disputes, particularly those that continue for a prolonged period of time, end up in the courts of law, causing uncertainty in the church.

As mentioned in local newspapers cited above, there are many cases of disputes involving pastors, including, among others, two supervisors from Masvingo Province, one from Harare Province, one provincial youth leader from Harare Province, one pastor from Midlands North Province, and one from Masvingo Province and Harare east province to not provide an exhaustive list.

Conflicts in the AFM in Zimbabwe are handled, according to the CCGHP, by the Local Council of Elders, the Provincial Committee or the Apostolic Council [17]. Therefore, since protocols and methods are already set down, resolving disputes in the court of law implies that internal mechanisms have either been exhausted or that specific dispute may be beyond the ability of the internal conflict handling committee. In the same way, it can be concluded that it is a sign that the internal mechanisms of the AFM in Zimbabwe are either not sufficiently used or not completely understood that they go through the direction of the courts of law. It should be remembered that disputes that go through the court are expensive and that route is not a fair investment for the AFM to pursue in the church of Zimbabwe [12, 13].

7.4 Principles focused on powers and privileges

The CCGHP is focused on values based on authority and freedom. As is often the case in AFM, a senior person such as the pastor, overseer or church president is responsible for coping with conflict in the power-based relationships. The attribution of seniority to dispute resolution is characteristic of the African approach to conflict.

As mentioned above, it is believed in traditional cultures that a senior individual has developed the capacity to deal with disputes over time. In addition, seniority is linked to wisdom to deal with any emerging dispute [19]. This seems to be the case with the AFM in Zimbabwe, in which the responsibility for presiding over certain disputes, especially those involving pastors, is provided to senior pastors or supervisors.

The distinction is that the relationship oriented African approach to conflict is driven by the desire to strengthen relationships or reconcile the contending groups as opposed to an approach that seeks to decide who is right or wrong, as is the case with the rights-based approach. There are several commonalities, but the rights based approach varies greatly from the conventional dispute resolution process. In the rights-based system, decision making authority is vested in the hands of a senior person, which suggests that the power to determine the outcome of the dispute is based on rank or position. Usually, in this situation, the most powerful party wins while the less powerful loses. This kind of conflict solution typically produces winners and losers in a real world, which ensures that the conflict will reappear because it remains unresolved [12].

A dispute resolution is assured only by a mutually satisfying outcome of a conflict. The management (in this case, the Provincial Committee or the Apostolic Council) relies heavily on laws, rules and regulations to decide the outcome of a dispute in the rights-based approach. Under this model, management ensures that laws are respected and that sanctions are imposed if not adhered to. The perpetrator is also not consulted in the process of imposing punishments, and the ultimate objective in most situations is to win over the perceived opponent or offender at this stage, thereby producing a winner-loser outcome. The dispute may seem to have vanished in some way, but since there is a winner and loser, it may come again, but at a higher cost [12]. The solution focused on rights does not really allow reconciliation between the perpetrator and the offended.

It should be understood that the settlement of disputes is focused on mediation between the parties to the conflict. It allows the parties to work together cooperatively (offender and victim, in this case the pastor and the aggrieved assembly or vice versa) by listening to each other, not with the intention of winning a debate, but to consider the situation, desires and needs of each other. Dialogue includes skills such as empathy, which is "to listen with your opponent's ears, see with your opponent's eyes, and feel with your opponent's heart. Lack of empathy allows the parties to the dispute to get swept up and confused in the competition for "dog-eat-dog... [20].

Open communication is another important skill that sustains dialogue, as someone said: "People don't get along because they fear each other. Since they don't know each other, people dislike each other. They do not know each other and they have not interacted with each other properly" [20]. As a central element of dispute resolution, mediation between the parties (offender and victim) can also theoretically produce win-win results.

To this end, both leadership and follow-up in the church of the AFM in Zimbabwe will need to accept that the existing internal conflict management processes do not always yield win/win results, and possible reasons for this are that they are neither derived from the model of criminal law nor the model of African Ubuntu Restoration.

8. Conclusion and recommendation

The question that this article sought to address was how best can the AFM in Zimbabwe manage conflict effectively to help to promote unity and growth instead of fanning divisions, animosities and factionaries among the conflicted pastors? As results indicate, the church under scrutiny uses adversarial tactics that ostracize those with which the leadership of the church disagrees. The propensity of the stronger party to ostracize the other party to a dispute does not help to foster cooperation and progress, but rather fans factionalism as it produces win/lose results, generating animosities particularly for those pastors against whom loss is incurred.

Conventional wisdom does not advocate ostracization of the person or party with whom church leadership is in dispute, but rather encourages mediation between the parties to a conflict, the idea being that there is a greater possibility of better relationships if the parties engage in influencing the results of the conflict. This article argues that the church should accept the view that tension is natural and good for the life and development of the church in order to move toward a relationship-oriented outcome.

The whole church must take it seriously to deal with conflict involving groups and establish basic assumptions that there is nothing satanic about conflict. Based on selected biblical texts, which encourage dialogue rather than ostracization, pastors, local elders' councils, the provincial committee and the Apostolic Council must establish optimistic conclusions about conflict. In view of this, the article suggests that, in order to deepen their understanding of conflict as a positive force, the church under review may conduct conflict resolution training courses, seminars or Bible study sessions. AFM in Zimbabwe and its affiliate institutions that train pastors should continue to advance subjects or courses in Conflict or Peace Studies in their curricula to empower student pastors on conflict-related issues. It has been argued in other quarters that instruction in dispute resolution is not the essence of Christianity. This article argues that conflict resolution training is a valuable investment for the church and must be supported if the church is to help create harmony and growth.

Author details

Norman Chivasa
International Centre of Nonviolence, Department of Peacebuilding, Durban University of Technology , Durban, South Africa

*Address all correspondence to: normanchivasa@gmail.com

References

[1] Adler, R. B. & Towne, N. Resolving interpersonal conflicts, in Looking out, Looking in, USA: Holt, Rinehart and Winston Inc, 1990: 355, 357.

[2] Osmer, R. Practical theology: an introduction. Grand Rapids: Eerdmans, 2008.

[3] Chivasa, N. Handling of pastoral misconduct and discipline: evidence from the Apostolic Faith Mission in Zimbabwe. HTS Teologiese Studies/ Theological Studies, 73(3), 2017, a4518. https://doi.org/ 10.4102/hts. v73i3.4518, 1-8.

[4] Blackburn, R. and Brubaker, D. Conflict in congregations, in C. Schrock-Shenk, and L. Ressler, Making peace with conflict: practical skills for conflict transformation, Pennsylvania, Herald Press, 1999:167-175.

[5] Schrock-Shenk, C., et al. Making peace with conflict, Pennsylvania: Herald Press, 1999.

[6] IRIN, People Flock to Church as Inflation Tops 1000 Percent. Harare, 2006, 16 May, Available from: http:// www.irinnews.org/news/2006/05/16/ people-flock-churchinflation-tops-1000-percent. (Accessed on 2017/02/17.)

[7] Machingura, F. The Significance of Glossolalia in the Apostolic Faith Mission, Zimbabwe. Studies in World Christianity, 2011: 17, 1: 12-28.

[8] Togarasei, L. Historicising Pentecostal Christianity in Zimbabwe. Studia Historiae Ecclesiasticae, 2016, 1-13.

[9] Mckay, A. How does the church handle conflict in its midst and what challenges doex it face in handling conflict constructively? Bridge Builders, 2016. Available from: https://www. bbministries.org.uk/wp-content/ uploads/2016/04/ (Accessed 2017/09/17).

[10] Tillett, G. The conflict resolution process, Resolving conflict: a practical approach. Oxford University Press, 1999, 96-112.

[11] Kent, G. Analyzing conflict and violence, in Peace and Change, 1993, 18(4), 373-398.

[12] Harris, G. Conflict resolution and mediation services in South African Universities: A cost benefit analysis, Durban: UKZN, 2007.

[13] Bendman, H. An Analysis of the problems of the labour dispute resolution system of SA, ACCORD, 2006.

[14] Cornelius, H. & Faire, S. Everyone can win: how to resolve conflict. Roseville: Griffin Press, 1989.

[15] Bloomfield, D., Ghai, Y. & Reilly, B. Analyzing deep-rooted conflict, in P.Harris and B.Reilly (eds.), Democracy and deep-rooted conflict: options for negotiators, Stockholm, Institute for Democracy and Electoral Assistance, 1998, 31-48.

[16] Chivasa, N. The nature, extent causes and consequences of conflicts involving pastors. GMHB Publishing House, 2012.

[17] The Apostolic Faith Mission in Zimbabwe Policy Document

[18] The Apostolic Faith Mission in Zimbabwe Constitution & Regulations

[19] Gombe, J. M. (2006). Tsika dzavaShona. Harare: College Press.

[20] Snyman, G. (2002). The Ethics of reading the Bible. Pretoria: UNISA.

Chapter 7

Conflict of Power and Leadership among Afro-Pentecostal Churches: Resurrecting the Traditional Model of Transferring Power and Managing Appreciations in Faith-Based Organisations in Zimbabwe

Ngoni Chikwanha

Abstract

It is commonly believed that democratic elections lead to the election of good leaders and help to mitigate conflict of power within organisations. However, power struggles that are associated with leadership succession at the top level and the appreciation of leaders who occupy top positions seem to engender strife in faith-based organisations. Using the Apostolic Faith Mission in Zimbabwe church (AFM) as a point of reference, this article sets out on the premise that the change of the traditional model of transferring power that occurred from 2000 up to the time of this study and the appreciation of leaders at the top level trigger strife in the AFM. Up to the time of this study, in the Apostolic Faith Mission in Zimbabwe Church (AFM), there are some innuendos that suggest that during the time that the AFM followed the traditional model of transferring power the older, senior, and mature leaders who assumed top positions of leadership did not put much emphasis on appreciations. Consequently, this article suggests that faith-based organisations should not change their traditional models of transferring power at the top level as well as manage the appreciation of top leaders as a way of mitigating organisational conflict.

Keywords: Apostolic Faith Mission Church, organisational conflict, power, appreciations, faith-based organisation, Zimbabwe

1. Introduction

The transferring of leadership and handling of appreciations (hefty financial gifts and benefits associated with top positions of leadership) in faith-based organisations generally trigger a conflict of power. This chapter examines the model of transferring power and the handling of appreciations employed by faith-based organisations, taking the Apostolic Faith Mission Church (AFM) as a point of reference. One of the most critical problems facing the AFM is the conflict of power that is associated with leadership succession and handling of financial benefits called appreciations which manifest in diverse forms such as delay in the holding of tri-annual elections, perceived or real reluctance to relinquish power, handpicking of successors, implementation of contested constitutional reforms and schisms among other issues. Such conflict of power has yielded undesirable consequences both for the image of the AFM in general and the general spiritual well-being of the majority of the ordinary church members in particular. Therefore, there is a need to examine the model of transferring power in the AFM as well as to revisit the handling of appreciations as a way of addressing organisational conflict. This essay explores the need to revisit the traditional model of transferring power and handling of the appreciations as a way of resolving organisational conflict in the Apostolic Faith Mission in Zimbabwe.

2. Research approach

This research aimed to assess leadership is transferred at the top level in the Apostolic Faith Mission in Zimbabwe. To systematically achieve this aim, a qualitative research approach was followed through descriptive, explorative, and normative tasks. The descriptive approach led the researcher to find out the status quo about how power is being transferred in the faith-based organisation under review. The explorative task led the researcher to make a comparative analysis of the traditional models of transferring power practised by both the Apostolic Faith Mission of South Africa (AFMSA) and the Apostolic Faith Mission in Zimbabwe (AFM). The normative task led the researcher to recommend the traditional model of transferring power and management of appreciations as peace-building models that ought to be employed by the Apostolic Faith Mission in Zimbabwe (AFM). Sources of data include document analysis and in-depth interviews. The in-depth interviews and focus group discussions were employed and they yielded data that were analysed to inform this study. To identify informants for in-depth interviews and focus group discussions purposive and snowballing convenient sampling techniques were instrumental. I used purposive and snowballing sampling to target pastors, elders, deacons, deaconesses (who include pastors' wives) and the leaders of the Young People's Union (YPU). In-depth interviews were held with pastors and lay workers of the AFM in Manicaland North and Manicaland Central Provinces. These sampling techniques proved useful to elicit data from pastors and lay leaders. I considered this group of informants as experts in the ongoing dynamics of power in the church under review. According to Duve and Maitireyi [1], 'data are the facts, figures and other materials, past and present, that serve as the basis for study and analysis'. Literature on the AFM in Zimbabwe and grey literature on power struggles in the AFM were reviewed, based on their advantage of appraising this study with current and existing dynamics relating to the power contestation being experienced in the AFM. The inclusion criteria for selecting literature on Google involved key concepts such as AFM power struggles. Also, as an active member of the church under review for a period amounting to 24 years, I used my experience as well as my research findings to reach the conclusion that disrespect of seniority which is symbolised by the relegation of the traditional institutionalised leadership succession planning trend, the appreciations, among other issues precipitated widespread power contestation and unrest in the AFM.

3. Statement of the problem

Conflict of power is becoming evident within the AFM's top leadership ranks. It also seems the conflict of power that is affecting the leadership succession process of the Apostolic Faith Mission in Zimbabwe (AFM) is further complicated by appreciations. If the legitimacy of the top leader is contested and the appreciations are not managed well it engenders strife in the church. It also triggers appellate court appeals, break-ups, tarnishes the image of the church, and generates civil unrest in the body of Christ. Some church members backslide and those who want to join the church will not be able to do so. The key research question is, how can power be transferred amicably and appreciations managed well in a way that does not degenerate into hostility, appellate courts appeals, and schisms?

4. The rationale for studying the AFM in Zimbabwe Church

According to Ndlovu ([2], pp. 1-4) is presently one of the fastest-growing Pentecostal churches in Zimbabwe. It is also considered to be the mother of Pentecostalism in Zimbabwe [2, 3]. AFM is an offshoot of the Apostolic Faith Mission of South Africa (AFMSA) (Hwata, 2015; [2–6]). Ndlovu ([2], p. 119) further argues that;

> *Langton Kupara became the first A.F.M.Z.'s black Superintendent in 1983. According to Madziyire and Risinamhodzi (2016, p. 73) Pastor Gashwend officially handed over A.F.M. to local leadership in 1983. During the occasion Gashwend gave Langton Kupara a golden watch, making the complete transformation of A.F.M.S.A. into A.F.M.Z.*

Several studies that have been undertaken from within the context of the AFM have both directly and indirectly alluded to the leadership crisis that is becoming evident in the AFM [2, 3, 5–10]. It is also worth noting that right at the beginning of this work to this present day, AFM has been characterised by innuendos that suggest that the gigantic Pentecostal movement is embroiled in its worst power contestation ever since it became an indigenous church ([2], pp. 1-4; [3, 5, 8]). According to The AFM New Life Assembly Church of Chitungwiza, Harare, website: 'The work of the AFM in Zimbabwe is said to have begun in 1915 in Gwanda through the preaching of Zacharias Manamela, a convert of the AFM of South Africa.'[1] Similarly, Chivasa [7] observes that, "It has long been recognised that the Apostolic Faith Mission (AFM) in Zimbabwe church is the mother of Pentecostalism in Zimbabwe (Hwata 2005, p. 27; [4], p. 18; [3], p. 31; [6], p. 2). In 2015, the AFM in Zimbabwe celebrated 100 years of active ministry across Zimbabwe (Madziyire & Risinamhodzi 2015, p. 105; Murefu 2015, p. 1) and the denomination claims to have more than two million members (http://www.pindula.co.zw) in a population of 13 million people ([4], p. 17)."

Additionally, several young churches look up to AFMZ as a role model of Pentecostalism that is not only pastoring its members only but it is pastoring other churches too. Machingura [4] further posits that, "The interest on AFM cannot be overlooked considering the number of followers that the church commands, yet surprisingly not much has been done by scholars in terms of research save to mention in passing its existence as one of the biggest Pentecostal churches" [4]. The motivation to conduct this analysis was sparked by two factors. The first was the prevalence of leadership succession-related power contestation in the AFM. The second was that no efforts to date have been made to examine the change of the traditional model of transferring power as the main contributing factor to the widespread power contestation that has engendered incessant schisms in the church under review. As such the current study attempts to fill this gap and it makes a case for the need to resurrect the traditional institutionalised

[1] See, for example, [11].

leadership succession planning trend as well as advocates for the responsible management of appreciations as the panacea to the conflict of power that is currently rocking the AFM in Zimbabwe. To interrogate the conflict of power, this research was guided by the following three questions: What evidence is there that there is a conflict of power associated with leadership succession in the AFM? Which factor(s) mainly contributed to the widespread conflict of power in the AFM? How significant is the traditional model of transferring power and appreciations at the top level in the AFM?

5. Overview of organisational conflict and leadership succession in the Apostolic Faith Mission in Zimbabwe (AFM)

The findings of this study show that there is a nexus between organisational conflict and leadership succession in the AFM. Of late there has been considerable interest in leadership succession issues in the Apostolic Faith Mission in Zimbabwe (AFM) ([3], Nhumburudzi and Kurebwa 2018). To give up-to-date examples of the most typical leadership-related conflict of power experienced in the AFM from 2015 to 2019, I refer to seven articles elicited by the Google search mentioned in the previous paragraph. These eight articles were carried in local newspapers in Zimbabwe:

- AFM Factions Come Close To Blows In Milton Park [12]
- AFM Top Brass Suspended [13]
- AFM leadership wrangle persists [14]
- WATCH: 'Jambanja MuChurch!'—DRAMA As FIST FIGHT Breaks Out In 'AFM Church' Over Power Struggle [15].
- AFM power wrangle rages [16].
- AFM church saga deepens [17]
- AFM remains in limbo [18]
- AFM remains in limbo [19]
- Overstaying AFM leader splits church [20]
- AFM church hires NIKUV to rig pastors' election [21]
- AFM church in dirty election rigging: Court papers [22]

At the time of this study, the ongoing leadership succession-related conflict of power in the AFM have since spilled into the court of law that is yet to decide on who is the legitimate leader of the AFM as reported by the following contribution on Good Morning Zimbabwe of 17 February 2019 which thus elaborates, "This (leadership succession contestation)... resulted in the two factions electing parallel leaderships with one led by Rev. Madawo and the other siding with Rev. Chiangwa. The legitimacy battle has since spilled into the courts and is yet to be decided" [23].

The above-mentioned conflict of power has also yielded undesirable consequences both for the image of church organisation in general and the well-being of the ordinary church members in particular. The study further stresses that resurrecting the traditional model of transferring power and managing the appreciations will help the church to address the leadership succession power contestation that has arguably led to the AFM's first wholesale schism since it became an indigenous church in 1983. This schism occurred on the 22nd of September 2018. The AFM split is confirmed by the following report which thus elaborates;

> *AFM's total split was yesterday confirmed with the holding of elections by the faction led by Reverend Cossum Chiangwa held at the church's Rufaro Conference Centre in Chatsworth. The faction aligned to Rev. Chiangwa participated in the elections that were held on Saturday putting a stamp to the split with the Reverend Aspher Madziyire grouping [24].*

The history of the traditional model of transferring power in the AFM cannot be fully comprehended without linking it to the history of transferring power in the AFMSA. AFM is an off shoot of AFMSA (Hwata, 2015; [2–6, 10]). Since this research is based on insights that were gained from the field research conducted in pursuance of a doctoral programme [25] part of my PhD, both the AFM gatekeepers and the University of KwaZulu-Natal provided ethical clearance. Ethical approval to conduct the study was obtained from the University of KwaZulu-Natal, Humanities and Social Sciences Research Committee (reference no. HSS/1768/017D).

There is a need to examine the model of transferring power and the management of appreciations in the AFM to know how best to address the current standoff. To do this, examining the history of the leadership succession trend in both the AFMSA and the AFM is critical as it provides the bedrock for addressing the conflict of power rocking the AFM. It seems right from their inception both the AFM and AFMSA followed the model of transferring power at the top level that valued seniority. Nhumburudzi [3] posits that the AFM of South Africa was founded in 1908 by two American Missionaries, who are John Graham Lake and Thomas Hezmalhalch. Nhumburudzi [3] further postulates that, "When the Mission was formalised, Thomas Hezmalhalch was elected the first President of the Apostolic Faith Mission Church on 27th May 1909 while John G. Lake was the Vice President, probably because Hezmalhalch was older than Lake." In support of the traditional model of transferring power alluded to above, Nhumburudzi [3] categorically states that it was the AFM of South Africa deputy president, Lake who succeeded Hezmalhalch as president as narrated below; "By the end of 1910, Thomas Hezmalhalch had returned to the U.S.A after serving a one year term and John G. Lake became the President for three years until 1913 when he also went back to U.S.A."

Coming to the AFM, Nhumburudzi [3] notes that, "The history of the AFM presidential succession has mostly seen the Deputy President succeeding the President. Reverend J. Mvenge was Deputy to the first black AFM in Zimbabwe leader, Reverend Langton Kupara and succeeded him after his death. Reverend Mvenge was also succeeded by his deputy Reverend Stephen Mutemererwa." Rev. Mutemererwa was also succeeded by his deputy Manyika and up to the time of this study it is only Rev. Manyika and Rev. Madziyire who have not been succeeded by their deputies and somehow the above shows a violation of the institutionalised leadership succession trend. Similarly, Ndlovu ([2], p. 120) reinforces that;

> *After his departure, his then Deputy Superintendent, Rev. Jeffries Mvenge was appointed the next A.F.M.Z. According to Madziyire and Risinamhodzi (2016, p. 93) Mvenge retired in 1996 and his Deputy President Rev. Stephen Mutemererwa was elected the President." Ndlovu ([2], p. 121) adds that, Reverend Enos Manyika was Stephen Mutemererwa's Deputy President and was elected his successor in the year 2000 after Mutemererwa's retirement.*

Related to the foregoing, Murefu [26] posits that, "The correct position is that the previous presidents were actually elected from among the then executive council members by the executive council itself and mandated by the workers' council. We then went for an electoral college with equal representatives from the provinces to elect Rev. Enos Manyika then Rev. Madziyire respectively." Murefu further clarifies that, "the term executive was used before it became apostolic council. There were only 6 provinces then, then the bible college principal and other heads of departments" [26]. So from the time, the AFM in Zimbabwe became an indigenous church in 1983 ([3], p. 34) and during the successive years up to the time of the immediate past president, the church followed a traditional model of transferring power at the top level which saw the outgoing presidents always being succeeded by his deputy president up to the time of Manyika. This model of transferring power enabled older, senior, experienced and mature leaders to assume leadership at the top level. In support of the traditional model of transferring power, C. Reus-Smit [27] reinforces that, "In a nutshell, the concept of binding institutions suggests a constitutional order that helps to lock-in a set of rules that will outlast change in the distribution of power. In the same vein, E. Frantz and E.A. Stein [28] posit that, "institutionalised succession rules hamper coordination efforts among coup plotters... by assuaging the ambition of some elites who have more to gain with patience than with plotting."

My analysis revealed that it is mainly the changing of the traditional model of transferring power which valued seniority which has triggered a widespread conflict of power in the AFM. This is an analysis of the fourth chapter of my doctoral thesis on the dynamics of power and its implications on leadership succession, governance and peacebuilding in the Apostolic Faith Mission in Zimbabwe (AFM).

Both the print and electronic media are rife with stories relating to conflict of power that is becoming evident in the AFM. Consequently, for the past couple of years, AFM has been characterised by innuendos that suggest the prevalence of conflict of power which have since spilled into the secular courts [2, 3, 8]. In support of the above standpoint, Nhumburudzi [3] echoes identical sentiments when he contends that, the immediate past president's "Administration has suffered the most break-aways ever experienced in the history of the AFM church."

Although, conflict of power is common within organisations including Christian organisations, it is a cause for great concern that the conflict of power that the church has been experiencing over the past couple of years has finally resulted in the church's worst split ever since it became an indigenous church. The conflict of power that is becoming evident in the AFM is linked to appreciations. Historically, from the time that AFM started in Zimbabwe until 2003, leadership succession in the AFM followed a trend that saw the deputy president succeeding the outgoing president. This ensured smooth transfer of power as leadership easily changed hands from one senior pastor onto another senior pastor. However, both in 2003 and 2018, relatively young presidents took over the leadership of the gigantic Pentecostal movement and this has sparked conflict of power in the church. The church has since split into two major factions, the Madawo and the Chiangwa factions. Chiangwa is a relatively old senior pastor who is also a former long-time provincial overseer and deputy president of the AFM while Madawo is a relatively young pastor who is a former long-time provincial overseer and general-secretary of the AFM. During the in-depth interviews, the informants reported that the traditional model of transferring power valued seniority. Even though the Constitution and Regulations outline how the president is elected from among the overseers who have served for at least two terms [3], all the respondents who were interviewed in this study strongly believed that revisiting the traditional model of transferring power that valued seniority leadership appointment at the top level and managing appreciations are the panacea to the leadership difficulties being experienced in the church.

6. Conceptualising conflict of power and resurrection

6.1 Conflict of power

To a greater extent, this study concurs with Mapuranga [29] who conceives conflict of power as a struggle for power that occurs between individuals and among groups. She further argues that the general conception that power struggles are associated with secular politics only is erroneous. She adds that wherever we find a contest for power between individuals and groups, dynamism of power is present. She further contends that there is nothing amiss in problematizing power struggles occurring in the church or analysing it using a political lens, hence this study [29].

6.2 Resurrection

To avoid the ambiguity associated with the use of terms in everyday usage, this study relied on the following dictionary definition of resurrection which is proffered by the Cambridge Dictionary to mean, "*the act or fact of bringing someone back to life, or bringing something back into use or existence*" [30]. Similarly, the Merriam Webster Dictionary defines the concept resurrection to mean, "to bring to view, attention, or use again" [31].

7. An evaluative discussion of traditional models of transferring power in faith-based organisations

Chivasa [32, 33] laments that; it is adversarial conflict resolution that has engendered unrest in the AFM. However, this study proposes the need to revisit the traditional model of transferring power as the panacea to the leadership difficulties that are being experienced in AFM for a plethora of reasons. First, the ballot system is believed to have led to the appointment of novices. Resonating with the findings of this study, in his study Nhumburudzi [3] notes that the election system has led to the election of ungroomed leaders. Similarly, Ndlovu ([2], p. 140) observes that;

> *It was found that the leadership wrangles, church politicking and association of leadership positions with financial benefits have led to great complications in the patterns of successions within A.F.M.Z.*

Commenting on the advent of elections in the AFMZ, Ndlovu ([2], p. 68) reinforces that from its inception the AFMZ used an institutionalised leadership succession trend which used the appointing system before it transitioned to the ballot system. He thus elaborates that;

> *The A.F.M. Church from its inception used to appoint its leaders in positions of authority. The system of appointing leaders in positions later proved to be problematic and the church opted for elections through secret ballots (Madziyire and Rinamodzi, 2016, p. 91).*

Nhumburudzi [3] further observes that the;

> *The history of the AFM reveals that schism within the AFM started in the early years of the Church in South Africa under the leadership of Reverend Le Roux, John G. Lake's successor,* **who was elected President in 1913***, a role he filled until 1943. According to Horn (2006), in 1919, under Le Roux's leadership, the*

> *black African Zionist Church withdrew accusing the AFM leadership of practicing racism in the church.*

Although by and large his study decries the shortcomings of the ballot system due to its manipulability by the incumbency, and the unprecedented strife that it has caused and so on, Nhumburudzi [3] surprisingly seems to proceed to endorse the same ballot model by claiming when he claims that:

> *The responses indicated that the election succession system ensured stability to the church during leadership changes when Pentecostal leadership power was transferred from one leader to another. The AFM Church in Zimbabwe had continued to survive through four successive leadership power transfers in the past by using the ballot. ([3], p. 8)*

Chivasa concurs that the ballot has caused discord in the AFMZ but he does not argue well how this leadership succession power contestation that has spilled into the court of law can be addressed serve for the institution of dispute resolution mechanisms which he proposes. However, to me Chivasa's Dispute Resolution Framework is an attempt to address the fruits and not the root causes of the power contestation in the AFMZ [8]. Similarly, Machingura [9] laments the prevalence of win-lose conflict resolution that is practiced in the AFMZ and has seen some pastors being pushed out of the church but he again does not seem to offer any feasible solution about how the prevalent power contestation can be addressed.

However, it is on record that, by and large Ndlovu ([2], p. 68) categorically castigates the ballot system when he posits that;

> *This study made an enquiry to assess the reliability of the use of elections within the A.F.M.Z. today. Responding to the question of how they observe the use of elections as a system of appointing leaders into positions of authority, the respondents revealed that this has created untold problems.*

Ndlovu ([2], p. 68) elaborates that the;

> *The idea of holding elections was never there in the A.F.M.Z. Initially, we were told that the man in charge would order people to pray, after prayer the Spirit of God will lead the church to the right leader. This was possible because the church was still growing and there were less complications. Since then the church opted for the conduction of elections. However, it has turned to be a problem again. Respondent E.M48 observes that elections have created a lot of challenges within the church. In the run-up to elections, many people are deliberately doing ungodly things in order to get into power or remain in power. As a result, a lot of dirty dealings, unimaginable, are happening in the church to the extent of some being victimized and tainted so that they do not contest the elections (Respondent E.M48). In support of this observation Respondent M.G52 points out that there is are a great number of campaigns and pulling down each other during election years. Hence this puts the unity of the church in a compromised position.*

However, after immaculately observing the shortcomings of the ballot, Ndlovu [2] proceeds to make insinuations that suggest that the leadership-succession-related power contestation that is being experienced in the AFMZ can only be sufficiently addressed if the existing constitution is amended with the active participation of all the key stakeholders. It is however noteworthy that Ndlovu ([2], p. 197) recommends that, "*More research is recommended in coming up with an effective, transparent and accountable system of appointing leaders into positions within the Pentecostal churches in Zimbabwe*" and this is a gap that this study has attempted to fill.

The majority of the participants who took part in this study expressed the view that the changing of the traditional model of transferring power gave rise to the handpicking of a successor by the outgoing president.

> *The former president (Rev. Manyika) influenced the election of the incumbent president Bishop (Rev. Madziyire) and now Bishop Madziyire now wants to facilitate the appointment of his successor (Rev. Madawo) who would protect his interests and also the interests of his predecessor. At the time that the incumbent Bishop was elected to be the president he was not the best leader. There were other more deserving more experienced, more senior and more mature leaders who included, Rev. T.I. Murefu who was the then General Secretary of AFMZ and the renowned late Evangelist Phanuel Chiweshe who were expected to take over the reins of power. Chiweshe was appointed in America [34]*

The data collected in this study suggested that in 2003 Manyika used the ballot to facilitate the handpicking of his preferred successor. The above-mentioned handpicking of a preferred successor is also alleged to have been done by Madziyire in 2018. Madziyire is alleged to have delayed the elections to allow his preferred successor Madawo to attain the minimum age of 50 years. Chivasa [8] argues that the minimum age required for one to become the president in the AFMZ is 50 years. It is also possible that the relegation of the ILST was facilitated by the fact that according to Nhumburudzi [3] "*Both president and his deputy, were retired in 2003 when their ages hit the 65 line.*" Nhumburudzi ([3], p. 35) further claims that consequently, "*a young president was voted in 2003.*" According to Murefu [35], the president (2003–2018) "*served his probation under his predecessor (Rev. Manyika) in Bulawayo.*" The findings of this research demonstrate that the election of the president (2003–2018) was received with mixed feelings in the church. A focus group discussion with elders suggested the above handpicking of the successor. One elder said;

> *It's Rev. Manyika who cooked the whole controversial top leadership succession which led to the election of the immediate past president (Rev. Madziyire). At the time he was elected the immediate past president (2003–2018) was little known and when he was elected everyone expressed dismay. There were other more senior and experienced leaders who were better qualified to become president the likes of Rev. T.I. Murefu and the late renowned Evangelist Rev. Chiweshe [36].*

Another elder who participated in the focus group discussion was of the view that, "*The president (2003–2018) is the project of the immediate past president. It is the immediate past president who facilitated the election of the incumbent president*" [37]. It is therefore possible that one of the most senior pastors Rev. T.I. Murefu who was the then general secretary of the AFM and was highly expected to succeed Rev. Manyika was possibly side-lined from the leadership succession race consequent to the allegation of sexual misconduct that was levelled against him. According to Chivasa [7] alleged acts of misconducts such as sexual misconducts of pastors are not taken lightly in the AFM. He however does not unpack how the handling of pastoral misconducts could be linked to leadership succession power contestation in the AFM. In addition to his seniority, it also seems Rev. Titus Murefu qualified to succeed Manyika by virtue of his being the then general secretary of the AFMZ. The fitness of the general secretary in the leadership succession equation is observed by Nhumburudzi [3] notes that some of the participants he interviewed in his study on leadership succession on ZAOGA categorically stated that, the Secretary-General appeared to be the second favourite to the succession of the ZAOGA leadership post after Mai Guti. The fitness of the Secretary-General in the top leadership succession equation is also reinforced by Magaracha and Masengwe [38] in their study on the leadership succession in the Johane Marange Apostolic Church where they argue that the church's secretary Mushati was also expected to succeed Johane Marange. The other favourable candidate who was heir apparent was Evangelist Chiweshe. According to the former Secretary-General of AFM in Zimbabwe who is the incumbent president (Rev. Madawo), "*Evangelist Chiweshe had been an evangelist since 1985 and he also worked as a pastor in the United States between 2001 and 2003*" [39]. So it seems when the elections were held in May 2003, Evangelist Chiweshe had been away for nearly 2 years which made it very difficult for him to make it even if he participated in the elections. However, upon returning from America an informal discussion that was held between the late Evangelist and the researcher, the late renowned Evangelist Chiweshe [40] claimed that in America he had been appointed at a non-existent congregation by the then president Rev. Manyika and the above suggests relegation of some sort. However, it is no secret that late Evangelist Chiweshe is highly regarded in the history of the AFMZ as reported below, "*We last heard of AFM crusades during the days of the late Rev Masiyambiri and the late great general of God Rev. Chiweshe*" [41]. It, therefore, seems it was through the side-lining of both Murefu and Chiweshe that Manyika managed to create room for his preferred handpicked successor.

The foregoing discussion sought to illustrate how the research participants in this study think that the AFM president (2003–2018) was handpicked to become the president against the ILST of the AFMZ which valued seniority. Related to the foregoing, commenting on the premature election of the president (2003–2018), Ndlovu ([2], p. 123) posits that, "In 2003, he (immediate past president 2003–2018) was elected Overseer of Bulawayo Province and the same year he was elected the A.F.M.Z. President, a post he never expected to hold at that time (Madziyire & Risinamhodzi, 2016, p. 101)." In support of the above, Madziyire and Risinamhodzi (2016) echo that the long-time serving president (2003–2018) was elected to become president at a very young age in 2003.The importance assigned to the institutionalised leadership succession trend in the AFMZ is further emphasised by an Elder [42] who was one of the research participants who pointed out that the immediate past bishop (2003–2018) was not the rightful candidate for the post of president. He thus elaborated; "The president is too junior. The leadership succession trend was such that the more senior would lead. While in the secular world it is acceptable for a junior to lead a senior in church it is not acceptable for a junior to lead a senior."

The supremacy of the traditional model of transferring power is authenticated by the below-mentioned findings that came from the research participants who participated in this study.

- When the AFMZ became an indigenous church it did not follow the constitution in electing its top leaders. Consequently, the late Reverend Kupara who is the first black superintendent was not elected using the ballot but he was simply appointed based on age, leadership experience, seniority and maturity [43].

- Rev. Kupara was appointed based on seniority. In the past the one who was appointed first would be the leader. It had become the tradition of the church that the president is succeeded by his deputy president [44].

- It had become our tradition in A.F.M.Z that the deputy will always succeed his senior. Reverend Kupara was appointed based on seniority. The failure to respect seniors started in Harare when the late Rev. Mazadza was removed from leadership by Rev. T.I. Murefu. It then spread to other provinces [45].

- In the past people used to have a lot of respect for their leader in the church because leadership was earned through seniority. People would look forward to lean more from them. It seems people do not have much to learn from the current president (2003–2018). The precedent that has been set is enabling novices to assume key leadership positions and this is creating problems [46].

- Moreover, the current president is too junior. He did not do anything to qualify for that top position. In the secular world some junior people are qualified to lead adults by virtue of their education, training and skills [47].

- The president (2003–2018) is too junior. The leadership succession trend was such that the more senior would lead. In the past people used to have a lot of respect for their leaders in the church because leadership was earned through seniority [46].

- The leadership succession was such that the more senior would lead. But after president Manyika a more junior president took over and this caused leadership problems in the AFMZ [47].

- The church was supposed to use its traditional way of appointing leaders [48].

- In the past it was easy to predict that so and so was going to become the next leader [49].

A closer examination of the above-mentioned key research findings that came from the research participants who participated in this study show that they unanimously concur that the traditional model of transferring power was the best as it valued seniority and also made it possible for the deputy to succeed the president. It may be possible that one weakness of the ILST was that it made no provision for the situations where the president retired together with his deputy. Nhumburudzi [3] claims Manyika retired together with his deputy. Madziyire also cites similar allegations that his deputy Chiangwa who was also supposed to retire together with him in 2018, altered his birth certificate to reduce his age. The above sentiment of self-qualification is echoed by the remarks that were made by a Bishop who was interviewed in this study who categorically stated that, "*The system of electing leaders has been hijacked and those who do not qualify want to qualify themselves*" [50].

In the foregoing discussion, it was argued that the ILST was practiced in both the AFMSA and the AFMZ. According to Leavy and D. Wilson [51], institutionalised leadership succession patterns dominate unless crisis (real or manufactured) force the hand of change. While an elder who participated in this study alluded that the changing of the traditional model of transferring power was caused by the generation gap that was mainly necessitated by the absence of pastors who were in their 60's who would replace Manyika [44], this view was refuted by a Bishop who was interviewed in a separate interview in this study, who instead argued, "The sitting leaders kill others who have potential and thereby create an artificial leadership vacuum so that there is no one who qualify to take over from them" [52].

In the same line of thought, Ndlovu ([2], p. 68) posits that "The A.F.M. Church from its inception used to appoint its leaders in positions of authority. The system of appointing leaders in positions later proved to be problematic and the church opted for elections through secret ballots (Madziyire and Risinamhodzi, 2016, p. 91)."

It however seems both Murefu, and Ndlovu [2] do not elaborate on what went wrong with the traditional model of transferring power in the AFM. However, somehow, discarding the traditional model of transferring power, Ndlovu ([2], p.

142) alludes that, "there was always a tendency to centralise authority in a few figures or councils." Similarly, Musariri [5] argues that the ILST was dropped because it ended up being manipulated by a few but still he does not elaborate on how the manipulation occurred.

In support of the traditional model of transferring power that ensured the election of mature senior leaders, Musariri ([5], p. 36) argues that, "It has been discussed in various AFM WhatsApp chart groups such as AFM national pastors' forum and AFM in Zimbabwe Gotekwa where AFM is accused by some for failing to play a fatherly role to avoid splits." In support of the traditional model of transferring power, where leadership changed hands from the president to the deputy president, Musariri ([5], p. 17) notes that:

> *In 1983 Rev. Gashwend officially handed over AFM to Langton Kupara to mark the complete transformation of AFM South Africa into AFM in Zimbabwe. The church continued to rapidly grow all over the country until now. Rev. Jeffries Mvenge became the next AFM president taking over from Langton Kupara and was succeeded by Steven Mutemererwa. Mutemererwa was succeeded by Enos Manyika and Aspher Madziyire tookover.*

Related to the foregoing, Ndlovu ([2], p. 119) reinforces that;

> *Langton Kupara became the first A.F.M.Z.'s black Superintendent in 1983. According to Madziyire and Risinamhodzi (2016, p. 73), Pastor Gashwend officially handed over A.F.M. to local leadership in 1983. During the occasion Gashwend gave Langton Kupara a golden watch, making the complete transformation of A.F.M.S.A. into A.F.M.Z.*

Furthermore, Ndlovu [2] categorically states that;

> *After his departure (Rev. Kupara), his then Deputy Superintendent, Rev. Jeffries Mvenge was appointed the next A.F.M.ZAccording to Madziyire and Risinamhodzi (2016, p. 93) Mvenge retired in 1996 and his Deputy President Rev. Stephen Mutemererwa was elected the President. Reverend Enos Manyika was Stephen Mutemererwa's Deputy President and was elected his successor in the year 2000 after Mutemererwa's retirement." ([2], pp. 120-121).*

In the same vein, Nhumburudzi [3] posits that;

> *When the Mission (AFMSA) was formalized, Thomas Hezmalhalch was elected the first President of the Apostolic Faith Mission Church on 27th May 1909 while John G. Lake was the Vice President, probably because Hezmalhalch was older than Lake [3]. The history of the AFM presidential succession has mostly seen the Deputy President succeeding the President. //Reverend J. Mvenge was Deputy to the first black AFM in Zimbabwe leader, Reverend Langton Kupara and succeeded him after his death. Reverend Mvenge was also succeeded by his deputy Reverend Stephen Mutemererwa [3]*

The foregoing supports the research findings which stated that the traditional model of transferring power saw the outgoing president being succeeded by his deputy president. The traditional model of transferring power suffered a major blow when it was replaced by the ballot system which led to the election of juniors' key positions of influence which is believed to have engendered leadership difficulties in the AFMZ. Resonating with the above standpoint, Ndlovu ([2], pp. 2-7) states that currently AFMZ is facing leadership challenges which are "fast destroying the great work done by those who shouldered it first."

Ndlovu ([2], p. 140) further argues that, It was found that the leadership wrangles, church politicking and association of leadership positions with financial benefits have led to great complications in the patterns of successions within A.F.M.Z.

Ndlovu ([2], p. 140) further reveals the secret behind the traditional model of transferring power as follows, "succession tended to be bestowed on those who most imbibed the ethos of the Pentecostal movement." Similarly, scholars also confirm the pattern through which leadership changed hands in both the AFMSA and the AFM. According to Nhumburudzi [3] it was the AFMSA deputy president, Lake who succeeded Hezmalhalch as president as follows; "*By the end of 1910, Thomas Hezmalhalch had returned to the U.S.A after serving a one year term and John G. Lake became the President for three years until 1913 when he also went back to U.S.A*." ([3], p. 32) So it can be safely argued that the top leadership succession trends of both AFMSA and AFM followed a pattern that saw the deputy president succeeding the president.

In support of the institutionalised leadership succession trend, Govea & Holm ([53], p. 130) posit that, "the leadership succession system conforms to a set of predetermined and widely acceptable rules. Legitimacy is claimed by the process of selection to the extent that it honours those rules." Similarly, Habisso concludes by recommending that to eradicate the leadership succession woes there is a need to ensure:

> *In conclusion I wish to emphasize that any country, organization or institution worth its name and reputation should have a well-defined, regulated and transparent system for determining leadership succession. Such an institutionalized system is a key requirement for good governance.*

In the same vein, C. Reus-Smit [27] reinforces that, of some elites who have more to gain with patience than with plotting." "In a nutshell, the concept of binding institutions suggests a constitutional order that helps to lock-in a set of rules that will outlast change in the distribution of power." In the same line of thought, Frantz and Stein [28] assert that, "institutionalised succession rules hamper coordination efforts among coup plotters... by assuaging the ambition".

Related to the foregoing, Nhariswa [54] castigates the ballot system as a viable means of effecting leadership succession. He further claims that elections can be manipulated and consequently engender strife in the Church and he recommends the need to have institutionalised leadership succession planning systems.

It also goes without mentioning that although Nhumburudzi [3] immaculately observes that; "It was established that in previous elections, only 3 candidates out of over 1000 pastors would be eligible to contest for the Presidency. Voters were thus forced to come out with a president from the few presented qualifying candidates," it seems he failed to appreciate how the traditional model of transferring power made it possible for only one person that is the deputy president to qualify to succeed the outgoing president. Consequently, there was virtually no need to have many qualifying candidates. However, one elder [44] who was interviewed in this study argued that the violation of seniority did not first occur at the national level but it first occurred at the provincial level as explained below, "the violation of the seniority-based top leadership succession started in Harare when Rev. T.I. Murefu removed Rev. M. Mazadza as overseer and it then spread to other provinces" [45].

The above resonates with Ndlovu ([2], p. 62) who categorically states that his study, "...also noted the leadership succession patterns as a concern today." In light of the foregoing discussion, it is the position of this study that it is mainly the change of the traditional model of traengendered strife in the AFMZ. The above explains why, Ndlovu ([2], pp. 2-7) is of the conviction that currently A.F.M.Z is facing acute leadership challenges which are "*fast destroying the great work done by those who shouldered it first.*" Ndlovu ([2], p. 3) further laments that;

The A.F.M.Z conducted and celebrated its centennial existence in style in August 2015 at Rufaro National Conference Centre2 in Chatsworth, Masvingo. The event was meaningful but the researcher observed many areas of concern in the church's managerial and leadership preparedness to face the future and remain spiritually effective. However, the imminent danger is the collapse of the unique spiritual culture and ethos within the Pentecostal churches if they do not keep themselves focused and aligned with the apostolic vision.

Ndlovu ([2], p. 5) adds that, "It was found that the leadership wrangles, church politicking and association of leadership positions with financial benefits have led to great complications **in** the patterns of successions within A.F.M.Z." It, therefore, seems it is the above scenario that led Ndlovu ([2], p. 197) to conclude his study by recommending that, "More research is recommended in coming up with an effective, transparent and accountable system of appointing leaders into positions within the Pentecostal churches in Zimbabwe" and this study attempted to fill that gap.

To this end, it can be firmly stated that from its inception until 2003, AFM followed a traditional model of transferring power that valued seniority and ensured that the outgoing president was succeeded by his deputy president. As shown above, the traditional model of transferring power made it possible for senior and mature leaders to assume leadership at the top level of the church. These leaders who were appointed using the traditional model of transferring power did not emphasis appreciations. Consequently, there was little or no widespread conflict of power which was triggered by the love for appreciations by the top-level leaders in the AFM and the church experienced relative peace.

8. An evaluative discussion of management of appreciations in faith-based organisations

A close analysis of the findings of this study shows that in addition to the changing of the traditional model of transferring power, conflict of power in the AFM was also triggered by appreciations. Up to the time of this study, some pastors, all the overseers, and the president in the AFM have access to hefty monetary benefits called 'appreciations'. It is argued that the leadership succession patterns in the AFM are being complicated by appreciations ([3]; Nhumburudzi and Kurebwa, 2018). The appreciation is also cited as having triggered the dynamics of power in the AFM [2, 5]. Similarly, Ndlovu [2] reinforces those appreciations are causing strife and hatred in the AFM. He proceeds to lament that the concentration of monetary benefits is creating divisions and economic disparities among pastors and engendering unethical practices in managing resources. This is harming followers in the AFM ([2], p.138). Chivasa [33] defines conflict as an expressed struggle for scarce rewards among other contributing factors. According to Baser and Ozerdem [55] many scholars agree that for any peace process to be successful, it must address the underlying causes of the conflict in question [55]. This section will explore the conflict of power in the AFM. A closer examination of the above-mentioned research findings clearly shows that there is power conflict in the AFM. The prevalence of conflict of power in the AFM is also alluded to by scholars who include, but are not limited to, Nhumburudzi (2017), Nhumburudzi and Kurebwa (2018), Chivasa and Mupangwa and Chirongoma (2020), Musariri [5], and Chivasa [33] who are cited above among other writers. The conflict of power in the AFM is triggered by the financial benefits that are associated with the positions of overseer and president [2, 5]. All the respondents who were interviewed in this study alluded to the conflict of power that is becoming evident in the AFM. It is also highlighted that the conflict of power is a result of financial benefits that are popularly known as "Appreciations" in the AFM. Resonating with the findings of this study, Ndlovu ([2], p. 140) argues that appreciation-related power struggles are "complicating the leadership succession patterns in the AFM." According to one Pastor B (not his real name, interviewed, 31 May 2018), "The love for appreciations has engendered conflict of power. Right now we have overseers and president whose term of office has expired and they are clinging to power" [56].

In the same vein, Elder E who was also interviewed in this study had the following to say "There is power contestation as to whether we should start with elections or reforms" [57]. Resonating with the findings of this research, Chivasa [8] notes that "The increasing number of disputes involving leadership in the AFM in Zimbabwe has been so dramatic." Resonating with the findings of this study on the prevalence of the conflict of power in the AFM, Musariri [5] advances that conflict of power is prevalent in the AFM. He, however, seems to blame the young pastors who broke away from the AFM as power-hungry. He, therefore, does not argue well how the senior pastors also exuded power-hungry tendencies to remain in positions of authority for extended periods. "It was announced during AFM (National Workers Council) in 2016 that the church leadership has been taken to secular courts by people who were challenging the legibility of 2015 national elections. Hunger for power may result in splits in the AFM because of its system" ([7], p. 42).

Additionally, indirectly alluding to the conflict of power existing between the clergy and the lay workers in the AFM, Musariri [5] argues that:

> *Overseer Nhira in an interview says that in AFM after the missionaries left, the congregations were led by elders because the pastors were very few. These elders were not hungry for title and even for money because they served without receiving any payment from the church. However, they were willing to work for free because they did it on a part-time basis. The current AFM constitution does not allow any pastor to be employed in a secular job except after being given written permission from the Apostolic Council (AFM constitution Chapter 15.30.1). This can also be a reason for pastors to end up manipulating the Scriptures for personal gain especially during the time of scarcity of resources like in the current Zimbabwean economic instability. An attempt to control them may end in a split.*

However, it is noteworthy that the majority of the male participants who were interviewed in this study considered the above conflict of power as having been engendered by the competition for financial resources. It is argued that the leadership succession patterns in the AFM are being complicated by appreciations ([3]; Nhumburudzi and Kurebwa, 2018). The appreciation is also cited as having triggered the dynamics of power in the AFMZ [2, 5]. It is therefore suggested that there is a need to revisit the appreciation in the AFMZ.

Gathogo [58] belabours to convince his readers that Afro-Pentecostal churches need money to acquire new technology and advises that people should not be quick to condemn the churches on monetary grounds [58]. However, while he advocates for the need for a balance in handling of church and personal finances he does not seem to offer practical solutions about how that balance can be attained. All the respondents across the subgroup divide alluded to the hefty appreciations associated with the position of the president as triggering conflict of power in the AFM. It is, therefore, important for the AFM to find a way of managing the finances that are raised towards the president's office. The church ought to encourage people to mobilise resources towards the presidential office and not towards the individual who is occupying the office. Resonating with the findings of this study, and writing from within the context of the AFM, Ndlovu ([2], p. 140) argues that appreciation-related power struggles are "complicating the leadership succession patterns in the AFM." Again, similar to the findings of this research, (Kurtz 1982), argues that the reasons why there are tension and struggle in churches are because of money, power, values and beliefs, and factions among other issues. He adds that ensuring an equitable distribution of resources in the church will go a long way in resolving conflicts. The above sentiment is supported by the remarks that were made by the Pastors wife during an interview that was held on the 31st of May 2018. She had the following to say, "Power is sweet and there are benefits attached. The AFM church system has a lot of money especially for the top leaders and this brings problems. The issue of money is causing a lot of problems" [59]. Similar sentiments were echoed by Elder F who argued that "The appreciation is the major source and reason why people fight for positions. Overseer's appreciation is at both the local assembly level and provincial level. The president is appreciated at the assembly, provincial and a very large scale at the national level" [44].

The observation that was made in this study about appreciations is in line with the findings of Musariri [5]. Writing from within the context of AFM, Musariri [5] argues that, "The Overseer, who is the leader of the province, is now being appreciated at provincial conferences and the same also happens to the president." Musariri [5] also posits that while in the past AFMZ experienced doctrinal difference-related schisms the current schisms are mainly engendered by "power and money issues."

Similarly, Ndlovu [2] reinforces those appreciations are causing strife and hatred in the AFM. He proceeds to lament that the concentration of monetary benefits is creating divisions and economic disparities among pastors and engendering unethical practices in managing resources. This is harming followers in the AFM ([2], p. 138). Taking the debate further, Ndlovu ([2], p. 197) further notes that the fight for appreciations has bred the preaching of false and heretic gospel which is now rife in Zimbabwe.

On the origin of appreciation in the AFM, Elder E who was interviewed in this study had the following to say;

> *The issue of financial benefit came during the period of president Manyika and from there, people took leadership as an opportunity to make money. The mobilisation of resources towards the individual(s) is believed to have started during the time of Rev. Manyika as the president and it was implemented at a grand scale during the time of Madziyire" [60].*

Alluding to the origin of appreciation, Rev. Madziyire claimed that when the AFMZ started there was no appreciation. The triple appreciation of pastors per annum was then introduced in the AFMZ (The Daily News Live, 13 January 2019). However, contrary to the remarks that were made by an Elder G, who participated in this study, Elder F has the following to say "When the president (2003–2018) came into power it is him who started mobilising and channelling funds towards an individual" [61]. Ndlovu ([2], p. 121) further argued that Rev. Mutemererwa's administration introduced the appreciation of pastors at the local assembly level in the AFM. In the same vein, Chitando [62] argues that as a result of the emphasis placed on money by preachers, they end up valuing and worshipping "those members who have money and class" [62].

While the majority of the participants spoke against appreciations, the deputy overseers hoped to assume these lucrative positions for them to be appreciated as well. This is shown below, "I am tired of raising money for someone else, I also need that opportunity to become an overseer. At the moment, we are saying God stop heaven, so that we also have our opportunity to enjoy here on earth" [63].

Similar sentiments were echoed by an Elder who argued that "The deputy president is the one who organises the president's appreciation in the hope that he is going to be the next president. The enthusiasm is driven by the fact that he hopes to be the next leader" [47]. It, therefore, follows that if those hopes of the deputy chairman becoming the chairman are shattered through the handpicking of successors by the outgoing leaders, dynamics of power are created. This seems to be what occurred in the AFM where Rev. Manyika president is believed to have handpicked his preferred successor, hence altering the traditional model of transferring power.

In resonance with the claim made above about the appreciations, Obiakor [64] argues, "African leaders misinterpreted the concept of western leadership, equating it to amassing of wealth by the leader" [64]. It seems it is because of the laity's great distaste for appreciations that Elder D suggested that "The incoming president need to find a compromising ground. He has to leave the issue of appreciations" [65].

In the same vein, Masengwe and Machingura (2010) concur that;

> *In the Apostolic Faith Mission Church in Zimbabwe, most gospreneurs engage in questionable ministerial practices. Related to the foregoing, Shoko & Chiwara (2013, pp. 226-227) reinforce that the church minister, expects his adherents to come back to him with some appreciation packages to acknowledge that they would be blessed with the miracle of prosperity. They expect their clients to come back and offer some token of appreciation for services rendered to them.*

Similarly, A. Chitando [62] notes "one of the most contentious characteristics of newer Zimbabwean Pentecostalism is the emphasis on wealth. Members and visitors are encouraged to give generously to the "man of God" for the God of the "man of God" to bless them."

In addition to the above, Togarasei (2005) notes that in one other Pentecostal church, people are graded according to their monetary contributions. In the same line of thought, Fainos Mangena & Samson Mhizha (2013, p. 144) argue that "Seeding to the life of the "Man of God" includes his "Birthday Gift." In one Pentecostal church, members contribute money as a birthday gift for their church leader annually."

The moral blameworthiness of appreciations is best summed up by Kretzschmar (2015, pp. 6-7) who contends that;

> *Those who enter the ministry because they do not know what else to do, see it an opportunity to have a comfortable existence, or exercise power over others. These ought not to be ordained. The church can ill afford ministers who... misuse church money... and... are uncaring and bring the church into disrepute.*

Of all the participants who took part in this study, only two male respondents held different viewpoints on the issue of appreciations. One of the two respondents said "The issue of money is not a problem in the church but how the money is managed." He added that "Appreciations should continue only that they should also be subject to the 50/50 centralization system" [66]. By 50/50 the deacon believed that the proposed centralisation system should only take 50% of the local assembly resources and 50% should remain at the local assembly to cater for the local assembly development.

It is worth noting that although the appreciations were introduced in the AFMZ before the president (2003–2018) came into power, a closer analysis of the data that was collected shows that appreciation was popularised by him in the AFM. It is during his tenure of office that the collection of the appreciation started to be well-organised at the national level where even corporate bodies that exhibited during the national conferences were also expected to take part in giving appreciation [65].

To this end, it can be reiterated that conflict of power which is mainly caused by the need to access appreciations by those who hold or want to assume key positions of influence is rife in the AFM. The conflict of power is also affecting peaceful co-existence in the AFM.

9. Conclusion and recommendation

The question that this article sought to address was how best the AFM in Zimbabwe transfer power and manage appreciations associated with those who occupy leadership positions at the top level in a way that does not engender wide-spread strife? As results indicate, conflict of power in the church under scrutiny altered the traditional model of transferring power which saw old, senior, and mature leaders assuming power at the top level that did not popularise appreciations. The changing of the above-mentioned model saw the church embracing a new model that is associated with the ritual use of elections in the handpicking of preferred successors. This resulted in the election of young leaders at the top level who popularised appreciations. For the church to maintain its unity the transferring of power at the top level and the financial benefits that are raised towards the office and not towards the individual who is holding the office. This article argues that the transferring of power in the church should not be left to chance and there is a need to stick to the traditional model of transferring power and managing appreciations as a way of minimising discord in long-time churches. The AFM must revisit the traditional model of transferring power and also manage the appreciations associated with top leadership offices as a way of uniting the fragmented church. Moreover, based on the biblical texts that value respect for seniority in leadership appointment and equitable distribution of resources, the AFM must revisit its traditional model of transferring power and also manage appreciations responsibly in a manner that does not engender conflict. Given the above, the article suggests that it is imperative for the AFM in Zimbabwe councils to integrate its traditional model of transferring power, as well as the management of appreciations in its constitution. Additionally, its theological education colleges should deliberately integrate leadership succession and financial stewardship courses in their curriculums. The article argues that the traditional model of transferring power and responsible management of appreciations are a valuable tradition for the church and must be respected if the church is going to attain lasting peace, growth, and development. In addition, this study argues that the church is a traditional institution and therefore as much as it wants to keep in step with constantly changing environments, it should endeavour to remain faithful to its tried and tested model of transferring power and also manage its appreciations well as failure to do so will trigger a conflict of power. As alluded to above, one option is to integrate the institutionalised leadership succession trend and responsible management of appreciations in the church's constitution. The advantages of the traditional model of transferring power and responsible management of finances are many. The findings of this study show that both clergy and lay workers have great respect for the traditional model of transferring power and the responsible management of appreciations. This minimises the chances of novices to assume power and power contestations that spill into the courts of law causes strife in the church and it also mitigates the conflict of power that is associated with competition to assume positions of authority that are associated with appreciations.

Author details

Ngoni Chikwanha
Africa University College of Social Sciences, Theology, Humanities, and Education (CSSTHE), Institute of Theology and Religious Studies, Zimbabwe

*Address all correspondence to: ngonichikwanha@gmail.com

References

[1] Duve R, Maitireyi P. Labor arbitration effectiveness in Zimbabwe. 2011. Available from: http://www.accord.org.za/ajcr-issues/%EF%BF%BClabour-arbitration-effectiveness-in-Zimbabwe/ [Accessed: 31 May 2019]

[2] Ndlovu C. The management of the Apostolic Faith Mission in Zimbabwe: A model founded in the apostolic vision, North West: North West University Library [Doctor of Philosophy in Pastoral Studies thesis]. 2018. Available from: https://repository.nwu.ac.za/bitstream/handle/10394/31445/Ndlovu_C.pdf?sequence=1&isAllowed=y [Accessed: 14 April 2019]

[3] Nhumburudzi L. Leadership Succession in Zimbabwe's Pentecostal Churches: The case of the Zimbabwe Assemblies of God Africa (ZAOGA) and the Apostolic Faith Mission in Zimbabwe (AFM). Bindura: BUSE; 2016

[4] Machingura F. A contextual analysis of acts 2:1-13 and the implication in the Apostolic Faith Mission In Zimbabwe (AFM). In: From Text to Practice: The Role of the Bible in daily living of African People Today. Bamberg: University of Bamberg Press; 2011. p. 63

[5] Musariri J. Schism in Pentecostal Churches: A Case of Apostolic Faith Mission in Zimbabwe (2008-2017). Gweru: MSU; 2017. Available from: http://ir.msu.ac.zw:8080/xmlui/bitstream/handle/11408/3413/Final%20Dissertation%20OG.pdf?sequence=1&isAllowed=y [Accessed: 15 April 2019]

[6] Togarasei L. Historicising Pentecostal Christianity in Zimbabwe. Studia Historiae Ecclesiasticae. 2016;**42**:1-13

[7] Chivasa N. Handling of pastoral misconduct and discipline: Evidence from the Apostolic Faith Mission in Zimbabwe church. HTS Teologiese Studies. 2017;**73**(3):1-8. DOI: 10.4102/hts.v73i3.4518

[8] Chivasa N. Instituting dispute resolution procedures in the Apostolic Faith Mission in Zimbabwe church. Skriflig. 2018;**52**(1):1-10. DOI: 10.4102/ids.v52i1.2285 [Accessed: 15 April 2019]

[9] Machingura F. The Pentecostal Understanding of Violence. In: Hunter J, Kügler J, editors. The Bible and Violence in Africa: Papers Presented at the BiAS Meeting 2014 in Windhoek (Namibia), with Some Additional Contributions. Bamberg: Bamberg University Press; 2016. Available from: https://www.academia.edu/21599866/BiAS_20_The_Bible_and_Violence_in_Africa_edited_by_Johannes_HUNTER_and_Joachim_KUEGLER_ [Accessed: 04 September 2018]

[10] Sande N. Contextualising the theology of competition: Towards the nexus of Pentecostal faith, politics and development in Zimbabwe. Afro Asian Journal of Social Sciences. 2017; **VIII**(III Quarter III). ISSN: 2229-5313. p. 1. Available from: https://www.academia.edu/36957504/contextualising_the_theology_of_competition_towards_the_nexus_of_pentecostal_faith_politics_and_development_in_zimbabwe [Accessed: 02 July 2018]

[11] The history of the New Life Assembly of the Apostolic Faith Mission in Chitungwiza, Harare, Zimbabwe. Available from: www.afm-newlifeassembly.org [Accessed: 29 June 2012]

[12] Lovemore. AFM Factions Come Close To Blows In Milton Park. Pindula News. 09 April. 2019,https://news.pindula.co.zw/2019/04/09/afm-factions-come-close-to-blows-in-milton-park/ [Accessed: 31 May 2019]

[13] Chikasha J. AFM Top Brass Suspended. Pindula News. 01 October

2018 https://news.pindula.co.zw/2018/10/01/afm-top-brass-suspended/ [Accessed: 31 May 2019]

[14] AFM leadership wrangle persists. The Herald. 14 May 2018. Available from: https://www.herald.co.zw/afm-leadership-wrangle-persists/ [Accessed: 31 May 2019]

[15] Abigail. WATCH: 'Jambanja MuChurch!'—DRAMA As FIST FIGHT Breaks Out In 'AFM Church' Over Power Struggle. iHarare. 17 November 2018. Available from: https://iharare.com/fist-fight-breaks-out-in-afm-church/ [Accessed: 31 May 2019]

[16] Richard Chidza. AFM power wrangle rages. The News Day. 16 March 2018. Available from: https://www.newsday.co.zw/2018/03/afm-power-wrangle-rages/ [Accessed: 31 May 2019]

[17] AFM church saga deepens. The Standard. 30 September 2018. Available from: https://www.zimbabwesituation.com/news/afm-church-saga-deepens/ [Accessed: 31 May 2019]

[18] Chitemba B. AFM remains in limbo. Nehanda Radio Station. 30 September 2018. Available from: https://nehandaradio.com/2018/09/30/afm-remains-in-limbo/ [Accessed: 27 May 2019]

[19] AFM remains in limbo. The Sunday Mail. 30 September 2018. Available from: https://www.sundaymail.co.zw/afm-remains-in-limbo [Accessed: 31 May 2019]

[20] Staff Reporter. Overstaying AFM leader splits church. 13 April 2015. Available from: www.newzimbabwe.com/news...Overstaying+AFM+leader+splits+church/news.aspxSchellenber [Accessed: 30 May 2017]

[21] AFM church hires NIKUV to rig pastors' elections—Members. 14 April 2015. Available from: https://www.zimeye.net/2015/04/14/nikuv-elections-rip-afm-church-apart-members/ [Accessed: 31 May 2019]

[22] National AFM church in dirty election rigging: Court papers. 13 April 2015. Available from: https://www.zimeye.net/2015/04/13/afm-pastors-contest-churchs-president-election/ [Accessed: 07 July 2017]

[23] Chitemba B. AFM Soap Opera Contiues. Good Morning Zimbabwe. 17 February 2019. Available from: https://gmzimbabwenews.com/index.php/2019/02/17/afm-soap-opera-continues/ [Accessed: 03 June 2019]

[24] AFM total split confirmed. H-Metro. 22 October 2018. Available from: https://www.hmetro.co.zw/afm-total-split-confirmed/ [Accessed: 06 June 2019]

[25] Chikwanha N. Dynamics of power and its implications on leadership succession, governance, and peace building in the Apostolic Faith Mission in Zimbabwe [PhD thesis]. Pietermaritzburg: University of KwaZulu-Natal; 2019

[26] Dr Murefu CM. Mabhonzo Emu AFMZ WhatsApp Social Platform. 4 December 2018

[27] Christian Reus-Smit. (2014).Power, legitimacy, and order, The Chinese Journal of International Politics, 7, 3, 2014, 341-359, https://academic.oup.com/cjip/article/7/3/341/2863858?searchresult=1 [Accessed: 20 November 2018]

[28] Frantz E, Stein EA. Countering coups: Leadership succession rules in dictatorships. Comparative Political Studies. 2016;**50**(7):935-962. DOI: 10.1177/0010414016655538

[29] Mapuranga TP. "Tozeza Baba": Gender-based violence in Oliver Mtukudzi's music. Muziki. 2012;**9**(1):58-70. DOI: 10.1080/18125980.2012.737104

[30] The Cambridge Dictionary. Available from: https://dictionary.cambridge.org/us/dictionary/english/resurrection [Accessed: 31 May 2019]

[31] The Merriam Webster Dictionary. Available from: https://www.merriam-webster.com/dictionary/resurrect [Accessed: 31 May 2019]

[32] Chivasa N. Instituting Dispute Handling Procedures in the Apostolic Faith Mission in Zimbabwe Church. 2018. Available from: https://www.researchgate.net/publication/322906541_Instituting_dispute_resolution_procedures_in_the_Apostolic_Faith_Mission_in_Zimbabwe_church [Accessed: 31 May 2019]

[33] Chivasa N. 2021. Managing Conflict in Faith-based Organizations. Submitted: September 17th, 2020 Reviewed: March 1st, 2021. Published: April 21st, 2021. DOI: 10.5772/intechopen.96932, https://www.intechopen.com/online-first/76373

[34] Interview with Bishop B. Mutare. 31 March 2018

[35] Murefu C. AFMZ WhatsApp social Media Platform

[36] Focus Group Participant. Mutare. 7 July 2018

[37] Focus Group Participant. 7 July 2018

[38] Magaracha TJ, Masengwe G. Power s truggles and cultural identity crises in African Initiated Churches (AICs): Investigating factors and dynamics behind the schism in the African Apostolic Church of Johanne Marange (AACJM). 2013. Available from: https://www.academia.edu/12885873/Power_struggles_and_cultural_identity_crises_in_African_Initiated_Churches_AICs_Investigating_factors_and_dynamics_behind_the_schism_in_the_African_Apostolic_Church_of_Johanne_Marange_AACJM_ [Accessed: 16 July 2018]

[39] Renowned AFM evangelist Chiweshe dies. The Herald. 1 September 2011. Available from: https://www.herald.co.zw/renowned-afm-evangelist-chiweshe-dies/ [Accessed: 08 October 2018]

[40] Conversation with the late Evangelist Chiweshe. AFM MT Carmel Assembly, Chitungwiza. May 2005.

[41] Mupofu M. Chaos as AFM members fight over church finances. My Zimbabwe News. 30 March 2018. Available from: https://www.myzimbabwe.co.zw/news/20414-chaos-as-afm-members-fight-over-church-finances.html [Accessed: 18 May 2019]

[42] Interview with Elder A. Mutare. 15 March 2018

[43] Interview with Elder E. Mutare. 8 June 2018

[44] Interview with Elder. Mutare. 8 June 2018

[45] Interview with Elder 01. Mutare. 8 June 2018

[46] Interview with Elder. Mutare. 31 March 2018

[47] Interview with Elder. Mutare. 15 March 2018

[48] Interview with Pastor. Mutare. 15 March 2018

[49] Interview with Elder. Mutare. 18 March 2018

[50] Interview with Bishop. Mutare. 15 March 2018

[51] Leaky, Wilson D. Strategy and Leadership. Lindon & New York: Routledge; 1993. p. 13

[52] Interview with Bishop. Mutare. 31 March 2018

[53] Govea RM, Holm JD. Crisis, violence and political succession in Africa. Third World Quarterly. 1998;**19**(1):129-148. DOI: 10.1080/01436599814569

[54] Nhariswa N. The Feasibility of Implementing Succession Planning in Mainline Churches: A Case Study of Methodist Church in Zimbabwe. Bindura: BUSE; 2018

[55] Baser B, Ozerdem A. Conflict transformation and asymmetric conflicts: A critique of the failed turkish-kurdish peace process. Terrorism and Political Violence. 2019;**33**:1775-1796. DOI: 10.1080/09546553.2019.1657844

[56] Interview with Pastor B. Mutare. 31 May 2018

[57] Interview with Elder E. Mutare. 08 April 2018

[58] Gathogo J. The challenge of money and wealth in some East African Pentecostal Churches. Studia Historiae Ecclesiasticae. 2011;**37**(2):133-151. Available from: http://uir.unisa.ac.za/handle/10500/5124 [Accessed: 17 September 2020]

[59] Interview with Pastor's Wife. Mutare. 31 March 2018

[60] Interview with Elder. Mutare. 15 May 2018

[61] Interview with Elder F. Mutare. 15 May 2018

[62] Chitando E. In: Chitando E, Gunda MR, Kügler J, editors. Prophets, Profits and Protests Prosperity Theology and Zimbabwean Gospel Music, Prophets, Profits and the Bible in Zimbabwe. Bamberg: University of Bamberg Press. Chapter 6; 2013. pp. 105-107. Available from: https://d-nb.info/1058949144/34 [Accessed: 25 July 2018]

[63] Interview with Pastor. Mutare. 31 May 2018

[64] Obiakor FE. Building patriotic African leadership through African-centered education. Journal of Black Studies. 2004;**34**:402-422. DOI: 10.1177/0021934703258757

[65] Interview with Elder D. Mutare. 8 April 2018

[66] Interview with Deacon. Mutare. 20 May 2018

Single Photon Manipulation

Edited by Keyu Xia

Published in London, United Kingdom

IntechOpen

Supporting open minds since 2005

Single Photon Manipulation
http://dx.doi.org/10.5772/intechopen.83207
Edited by Keyu Xia

Contributors
Constantin Meis, Chandrasekhar Roychoudhuri, Yuanhua Li, Xianfeng Chen, Lei Tang, Keyu Xia, Zhi-Yuan Zhou, Bao-Sen Shi

First published in London, United Kingdom, 2020 by IntechOpen
IntechOpen is the global imprint of INTECHOPEN LIMITED, registered in England and Wales, registration number: 11086078, 5 Princes Gate Court, London, SW7 2QJ, United Kingdom
Printed in Croatia

British Library Cataloguing-in-Publication Data
A catalogue record for this book is available from the British Library

Additional hard and PDF copies can be obtained from orders@intechopen.com

Single Photon Manipulation
Edited by Keyu Xia
p. cm.
Print ISBN 978-1-83880-353-7
Online ISBN 978-1-83880-354-4
eBook (PDF) ISBN 978-1-83880-606-4

For EU product safety concerns:
IN TECH d.o.o., Prolaz Marije Krucifikse Kozulić 3, 51000 Rijeka, Croatia, info@intechopen.com or visit our website at intechopen.com.

Meet the editor

Keyu Xia was awarded his doctoral degree of "Optics" by the Shanghai Institute of Optics and Fine Mechanics, Chinese Academy of Sciences in 2007. He has been a full professor at Nanjing University since 2017. His research interest includes quantum optics and quantum information, in particular, chiral quantum optics. He has published more than 40 peer-reviewed publications. His academic achievements include: (I) proposing the first quantum-state-controlled photon isolator and circulator; (II) proposing a chiral cross-Kerr nonlinear medium to bypass the dynamical reciprocity in nonlinear isolation; (III) experimentally demonstrating the chiral susceptibility-momentum locking as a principle for optical nonreciprocity. Due to his significant contributions to quantum optics and quantum information technology, he was awarded the senior member designation of OSA in 2020.

Contents

Preface

This short book provides readers with some basic concepts of single photons and the latest developments in the field. The book reviews the most important method of generating single photons in experiments and it also introduces an emerging field of single-photon isolation.

The first section provides a very simple picture of the concept of evolution of the photon" from the classical to the quantum formalisms, and the quantization of the light field as a description of the photon. The next section focuses on recent experiments exploiting optical nonlinear processes to generate and manipulate single photons. In the last section, nonreciprocal quantum devices are designed to isolate the backscattering of single photons.

The book aims to present some basic knowledge of single photons to readers in a quick read but with not many details.

Keyu Xia
Professor,
Nanjing University,
Jiangsu, China

Section 1

Basic Concept

Chapter 1

Do We Manipulate Photons or Diffractive EM Waves to Generate Structured Light?

ChandraSekhar Roychoudhuri

Abstract

In the domain of light emissions, quantum mechanics has been an immensely successful guiding tool for us. In the propagation of light and optical instrument design, Huygens-Fresnel diffraction integral (HFDI) (or its advanced versions) and Maxwell's wave equation are continuing to be the essential guiding tools for optical scientists and engineers. In fact, most branches of optical science and engineering, like optical instrument design, image processing, Fourier optics, Holography, etc., cannot exist without using the foundational postulates behind the Huygens-Fresnel diffraction integral. Further, the field of structured light is also growing where phases and the state of polarizations are manipulated usually with suitable classical macro-devices to create wave fronts that restructured through light-matter interactions through these devices. Mathematical modeling of generating such complex wave fronts generally follows classical concepts and classical macro tools of physical optics. Some of these complex light beams can impart mechanical angular momentum and spin-like properties to material particles inserted inside these structured beams because of their electromagnetic dipolar properties and/or structural anisotropy. Does that mean these newly structured beams have acquired new quantum properties without being generated through quantum devices and quantum transitions? In this chapter, we bridge the classical and quantum formalism by defining a hybrid photon (HP). HP is a quantum of energy, $h\nu$, at the initial moment of emission. It then immediately evolves into a classical time-finite wave packet, still transporting the original energy, $h\nu$, with a classical carrier frequency ν (oscillation of the E-vector). This chapter will raise enquiring questions whether all these observed "quantum-like" behaviors are manifestations of the joint properties of interacting material particles with classical EM waves or are causal implications of the existence of propagation of "indivisible light quanta" with exotic properties like spin, angular momentum, etc.

Keywords: structured light, hybrid photon, non-interaction of light (NIW), Huygens principle, photoelectric effect, semiclassical model

1. Introduction

Structured light is a matured applied field of study. It has been steadily inventing many new tools and techniques to manipulate and study, from nanoparticles to molecules to atoms. Other chapters of this book have described these developments.

The purpose of this chapter is to promote the development of out-of-box enquiring questions in physics leveraging the topic of structured light. It is a complex thinking and analytical process to describe a physical phenomenon simply based upon reproducible experimental data. This is because experimental data generation requires detector and deductee to undergo some physical transformation in their relevant parameters after exchanging some energy guided by some allowed force of interaction between them. Since we cannot directly observe the details of the physical interaction process, we cannot be certain from the properties of the measured data as to which property belongs to the detector and which belongs to the deductee. We have not been addressing this important enquiring question explicitly in physics. The field of structured light is a good test optical phenomenon to explore this enquiring question.

Beams of structured light are generated by using classical optical components and the analytical tools of classical optics, which are Maxwell's wave equation and Huygens-Fresnel diffraction integral (or its advanced versions). Then, the concept of "indivisible light quanta" must have come from Einstein's paper on photoelectric effect [1]. However, Lamb et al. [2–4] have clearly shown that the use of semiclassical model, classical light, and quantized atoms yields a much more causal and self-consistent model for light-matter interactions. This chapter, therefore, strengthens this concept behind the semiclassical model by underscoring some neglected but fundamental nature of light from two fundamental angles—"We never see light" (Section 2) and "Light does not see light" (Section 3). Then we discuss the consequences of assigning detector's intrinsic quantum properties to the energy donating classical and Maxwellian light waves as we do for the photoelectric effect (Section 4). Next, in Section 5, we discuss the consequences of ignoring interaction process visualization, which guides us to accept the necessity of introducing the concept of hybrid photon model. Hybrid photon model eliminates the need for accepting the postulate of "wave-particle duality." This duality postulate actually originated in late 1600s during debate between Newton ("corpuscular") and Huygens ("secondary wavelets"), and they agreed that their debate arose out of their ignorance about the deeper structure of light. Unfortunately, founders of mathematical formalism of quantum have promoted the "wave-particle duality" as the new confirmed knowledge. In reality, this postulate should energize us to keep exploring the deeper issues behind quantized emission and absorption of light and classical propagation properties of light. The last section on discussion underscores that we should always try to reevaluate working theories beyond its prevailing successes so we can advance our current understanding. Then discover new phenomena and then invent new tools and technologies.

2. We never "see" light

We only perceive or measure the physical transformation induced by light energy in material bodies, which have their own unique response characteristics due to their unique response properties to light. Therefore, assigning any new physical property, to a physical entity under study, should be done carefully to ascertain that the observed (measured) property is not that of the detecting entity. This is especially important for light. We always infer the incidence (presence) of light after observing (or perceiving) some physical transformation in the detecting element. It could take place through a wide variety of already known phenomena like photoelectric effect, photochemical effect, photothermal effect, photo-acoustic effect, etc. In all such cases, a finite amount of energy from the EM wave is absorbed by the detecting element to undergo some quantitative physical transformation, which becomes our data. If the detecting element is inherently quantum mechanical in nature, then the amount of energy $\Delta E_{mn} = h\nu_{mn}$ is absorbed by the detector out of the EM waves and will correspond to the specific quantum transition. However, all light-matter interactions are frequency dependent since all materials are individual dipolar atoms and molecules or their assemblies in solid or liquid states. X-rays and γ-rays do not interact with quantum mechanical Si-photoelectric detectors or classical photothermal detectors. We need appropriate materials where X-rays can stimulate the electrons in the inner shells of atoms and γ-rays can stimulate the nuclear energy levels at the core of atoms.

The strength of the *evidence-based science* lies with the corroboration of evidences with a suitable mathematical model. The model must help us to *visualize the interaction processes* that give rise to measurable data (evidence). This is the foundation of our causal approach to explore the laws of nature. This causal approach allows us to keep refining both the measurements and the modeling as we keep integrating diverse observations into a broader and well-validated theory. This is how our scientific advances have been continuing for centuries. Therefore, let us explore the physical process steps behind the generic detection/interaction processes (Ch. 12, in [5]):

1. All measured *data* are some quantitative *physical transformations* in some detector element induced by a deductee-element.

2. All physical transformations must be triggered by some physical interaction (stimulation) process, followed by energy exchange between the detector and the deductee. Discouraging the visualization of such invisible interaction processes has been the key mystifying reason behind our “working” theories, whose purpose has been limited to validate only the measurable data.

3. All energy exchange must be guided (allowed) by some specific and allowed force of interaction existing between the detector and the deductee. Our continuing failure to understand the origin of all forces and unify them is the key bottlenecks behind the causal advancement in modern physics.

4. All forces, short or long range, have finite physical ranges. Therefore, all interactions are fundamentally “local” or physical range dependent.

Thus, we cannot generate observable (measurable) data without some physical transformation in an interactant (detector) whose intrinsic physical properties dictate its specific response characteristics to one or the other force to participate in any interaction, leading to a specified amount of energy exchange leading to the observable transformation. Obviously, recordable data generation is not possible if the interactants are physically beyond the range of their mutual force of interaction. Causal physics require that the interactants recognize each other through their mutually allowed force of interaction. Without a direct hit of a well-collimated laser beam within the active area of a detector of a power meter, we cannot ascertain the energy of the laser beam. Interaction-free data generation cannot take place in the causal world. “Spooky action at a distance” is an unfortunate cultural phenomenon that wants to mystify physics. Nature is systematically causal. That is why our “cause-effect” inter-relating causal mathematical equations, through centuries, have remained the key guiding tool to explore nature. Nature is not mystical.

Measured and analyzed “elliptical polarization” does not imply that the resultant electrical vector of the light beam is rotating circularly as the composite light beam (two collinear, phase-steady, and orthogonally polarized beams with 90° relative phase delay) is propagating with the resultant E-vector helically rotating around the Poynting vector. In this assumed and imaginary model, the energy of the composite light beam would have been also oscillating due to time-varying resultant amplitude of the E-vector. This would have implied that nature is violating the law of conservation of energy. Fortunately, in this case, our mathematics has been guiding us along the correct and causal path. Jones' matrix has been constructed to find the final energy of a composite light beam as the sum of the two separate energies contained in each of the two orthogonal polarization. The energy in each of the two orthogonal components is the square modulus of the sum of the X-component amplitudes and the Y-component amplitudes, carried out separately. Interested readers should consult Ch. 9 on polarization phenomenon in Ref. [5]. The chapter underscores, using elementary mathematics and the bulk dipolar polarizability χ, that without explicitly inserting this light-matter interaction parameter, the understanding of the ongoing physical process becomes difficult and confusing.

3. Light does not "see" light

The light wave amplitudes cross propagate and co-propagate through each other in the absence of interacting materials. This is why experimental astrophysics can image and analyze individual distant galaxies or stars even though the light selected by a telescope has crossed through the light beams of innumerable galaxies and/or stars. This is the same physical reason why we can see (recognize) each other from a distance, even though the scattered light beams from innumerable other faces and objects are crossing through each other. Alhazen experimentally validated this non-interaction of waves, or NIW, about a thousand years ago [6]. This brilliantly simple experiment is sketched in **Figure 1**.

Alhazen generated the inverted images of a set of candles through a pinhole camera. He found that blocking anyone or more candles does not create any changes in the images of the other candles. Inverted images clearly underscored that the light from all the candles were crossing through each other at the tiny pinhole. Alhazen underscored that he did not understand the deeper nature of light. He was humble.

Much later, Huygens formally postulated NIW in his 1690 book [7] when he presented his principle of wave propagation visualizing the process as the perpetual generation of innumerable secondary wavelets out of every point on the wave front. This also implied that the space is an energetic tension field to be able to support the perpetual wavelet generation and propagation (Ch. 11 in [5, 8–10]). Huygens explicitly articulated non-interaction of waves (**Figure 2**):

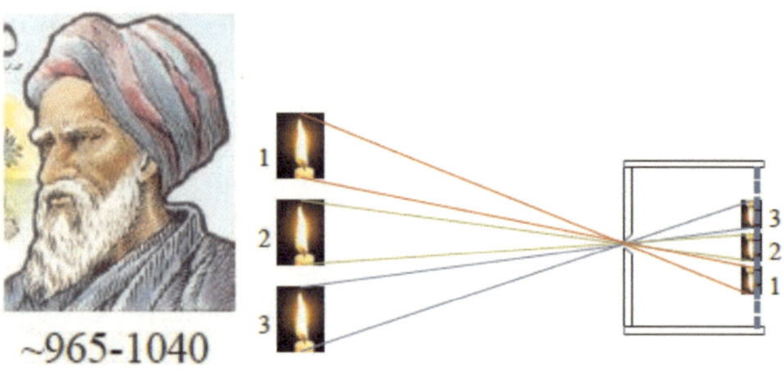

Figure 1.
Alhazen's ancient experiment forced him to conclude that light does not interact with light. We still are struggling with the wave-particle duality [5].

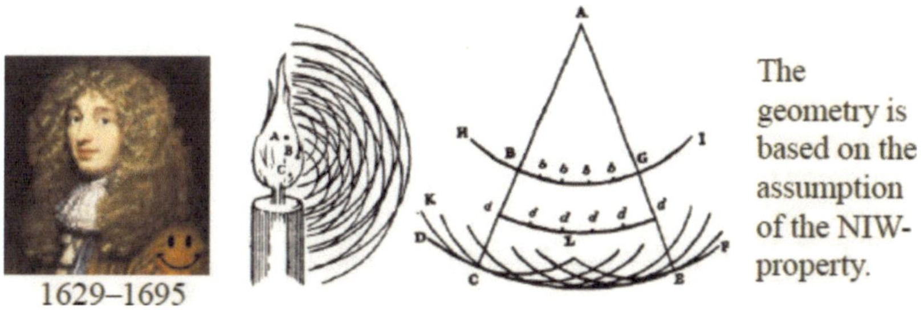

Figure 2.
Huygens' visualization of the wave propagation process through indefinite number of secondary wavelets, diffractively evolving through each other, "unperturbed by each other, cross one another without hindering one another in any way" [7]. This is non-interaction of waves (NIW) [5].

> *For I do not find that any one has yet given a probable explanation of the first and most notable phenomena of light, namely ......how visible rays, coming from an infinitude of diverse places, cross one another without hindering one another in any way. From p. 2 in [7].*

In p. 4 of his 1690 book, Huygens clearly anticipated the existence of a universal tension field, like pressure tension of air, but without any material particles, which facilitates the perpetual propagation of waves, as sound does in the air.

In 1817, Fresnel gave the mathematical structure to the Huygens principle in which NIW was automatically built in Huygens-Fresnel diffraction integral (HFDI). The integral literally propagates innumerable spherical wavelets that keep evolving through each other while diffractively evolving as co-propagating and cross propagating through each other [11]. $E(P_{\text{det.}})$ is the resultant amplitude:

$$E(P_{\text{det.}}) = \frac{-i}{\lambda} \iint_{\Sigma} U(P_{source.}) \frac{\exp\left(ikr_{s\to d}\right)}{r_{s\to d}} \cos\theta \, ds \tag{1}$$

Notice that the above HFDI propagates all spherical wave fronts out of every source point to the detector plane, irrespective of its distance $r_{s\to d}$ from the source plane. These amplitude wave fronts evolve through each other completely independent of each other irrespective of how far they are propagating. In other words, the HFDI has automatically incorporated the NIW property of the waves.

After Maxwell's wave equation was developed (1867), it was found that HFDI is a solution to Helmholtz equation, a time-independent form of Maxwell's generalized wave equation. Maxwell's wave equation accepts any linear superposition of wave amplitudes as its solution. The physical meaning, in the context of NIW, is that wave properties of the individual propagating wave remain unaltered as they cross propagate and/or co-propagate through each other. In other words, light does not interfere with light in the absence of interacting material, which we have logically derived in section on "We do not see light," except through the "eyes" of interacting materials.

It is then obvious that the generation and spatial superposition of multiple complex light wave fronts will continue to diffractively evolve and co-propagate as independent beams. However, when they finally interact with some materials, the energy transfer to any interacting material will be the square modulus of the sum of the finally evolved "local" wave front incident on the material. If the material is an anisotropic polarized detector, it will respond to the square modulus of the sum of all the amplitude components projected on to its polarization axis. If it is a very small-suspended anisotropic particle and the state of polarization is rotating slowly in time and if the inertia permits, the anisotropic particle will rotate with the rotating polarizing field since most materials strongly respond to the resultant E-vector. However, the original set of multiple co-propagating wave amplitudes does not reorganize themselves into a single composite wave front because of the overriding NIW property of waves.

4. Consequences of assigning detector's properties to the energy donating entity

Can we logically confirm that the emission of a single photoelectron proves the existence of light as "indivisible light quanta"? We should recognize that the individual "clicks," which we register in photon counting electronics, are actually a brief current pulse, probably, consisting of billions of amplified electrons. It may not be difficult to validate that this highly amplified current pulse has been originally triggered by a single photoelectron. However, releasing a quantum-mechanically bound electron does not necessarily require the presence of a quantum photon of energy $h\nu_{mn} = \Delta E_{mn}$. The quantum cupful of energy ΔE_{mn} can be acquired by a quantum entity from almost any source of energy under appropriate condition of interactions. Ancient humans used to create fire by using sparks generated by fast mechanical collisions between a pair of stones. They had no idea that they were inducing quantum transitions in the molecules of the stones while transferring the classical kinetic energy out of their moving hands! This is why the quantum formalism does not require any quantum postulate that energy providers to induce quantum transitions have to have energy-matching quantum states. In fact, Boltzmann's classical statistical thermal population density formula has been co-opted by the quantum mechanics. Un-quantized thermal energy can be absorbed during thermal collisions by quantum entities to fill up their quantum cups while accepting only that much of energy that fills up their quantum cups [12].

Toward the end of his life, Einstein, the originator of the concept of "indivisible light quanta," clearly stated that even after "50 years of brooding," he still did not understand "what are light quanta" [13]. Author was inspired by Einstein's doubt and delved into exploring the nature of light for many decades [14–16].

In the section on "We do not see light," we have underscored that detectors see light based on their internal physical properties. This is why visual observation of classical interferometry never pointed us to the quantumness of light. In fact, Newton was the first inventor of two-beam interferometry. He measured the radius of curvature of his plano-convex lens by putting it on a flat mirror and shining light from the top. Note that the debate over wave-particle duality started long time ago during late 1600 by Newton ("corpuscular") and Huygens ("wavelet"). Nevertheless, they recognized that their debate represented their deeper ignorance about the fundamental nature of light. We still have not fully understood the deeper nature of light. Therefore, we should not make the "wave-particle duality" as our confirmed new knowledge. We should humbly continue to explore the deeper nature of light. That is the purpose of this chapter.

The first solid reasoning behind theorizing emission and absorption of light from materials in discrete energy packets was presented by Planck in 1900 to match analytically the already measured blackbody radiation curve. However, Planck maintained his understanding that the quantum processes are real only during the instants of emission and absorption. After emission, the EM energy packet immediately evolves into Huygens' diffractive wavelets. This is how the diffractive radiation achieves the state of equilibrium energy density within the enclosed blackbody cavity [14].

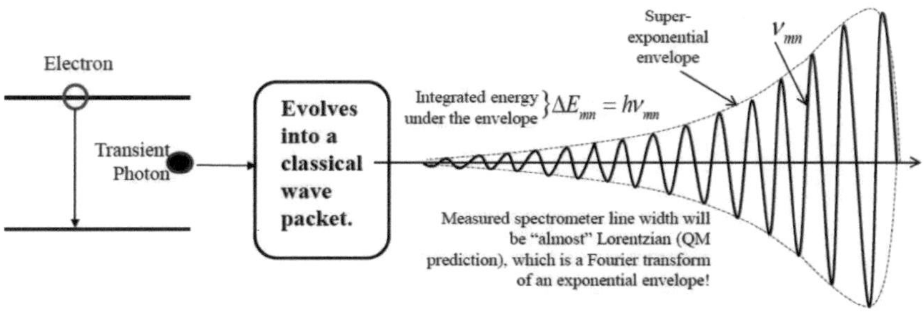

Figure 3.
Transient quantum photon, immediately after emission from an atom, evolves into a diffractively spreading classical wave packet with quasi-exponential temporal envelope. All the quantum predictions are preserved. The total energy carried by the wave packet is $\Delta E_{mn} = h\nu_{mn}$ with the unique carrier frequency ν_{mn}. The Fourier transform of the quasi-exponential envelope gives a spectral line width close to Lorentzian, which is the normal spectral line width of spontaneous emissions.

However, during very late 1800, emission of photoelectrons from photocathode showed some uniqueness. Below some optical frequency, there was no photoelectron emission in spite of increasing the radiation density. Young Einstein correctly surmised that there is some "quantumness" hidden behind this frequency dependence and no electron emission after a cutoff frequency. Unfortunately, Einstein assigned this quantumness to light, instead of to the electrons. However, we now know that electrons are always bound quantum mechanically in all materials, even when they are bound collectively in quantum energy bands in solid state [15]. Here, we must recognize that Bohr atom was formulated in 1913 and Quantum Mechanics was formulated in 1925, many years after the 1905 paper by Einstein on the photoelectric effect. However, had Einstein correctly assigned the quantumness, observed in photoelectric effect, to electrons instead of to light, he would have been able to formulate quantum mechanics the Einsteinian way some 20 years earlier.

We believe that Planck's view of light is correct. EM waves are classical waves, solutions of Maxwell's equation, and propagates following Huygens secondary wavelets. In fact, Refs. [2–4] have derived the equation for photoelectric emission using the semiclassical method. Here, we present a heuristic approach to present the hybrid photon model that is a quantum at the moment of emission but a classical wave packet with a quasi-exponential temporal envelope. The total energy under the envelope corresponds to the QM predictions: (i) total energy of the wave packet is $\Delta E_{mn} = h\nu_{mn}$, and (ii) the quasi-exponential envelope assures the observed spontaneous emission line width as very close to Lorentzian, the Fourier transform of the amplitude envelope of the light pulse (see **Figure 3**).

5. Consequences of ignoring interaction process visualization: the necessity of the hybrid photon model

Let us first recognize that Einstein's photoelectric equation is an energy-balancing equation to match the observed data. This is measurable data modeling epistemology (MDM-E). We need to incorporate interaction process mapping epistemology (IPM-E) over and above MDM-E. Einstein's formulation did not embody light-matter interaction process, as we have underscored in the section on "Light does not see light." For accurate semiclassical derivation of the photoelectric effect, the readers should consult the following references [2–4]. We will present here only a heuristic derivation of Einstein's energy-balancing photoelectric equation, but starting from light-matter amplitude-amplitude stimulation, the E-vector of light

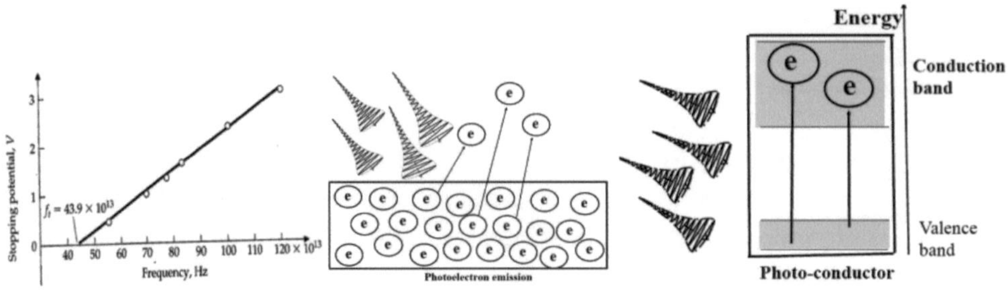

Figure 4.
Left diagram: Emission of photoelectrons from a given material stops at a fixed specific frequency [16]. Middle diagram: Photoelectron emission from photocathode. Right diagram: Photoelectron transfer from valence to conduction band.

stimulating the dipoles as $\chi(\nu_q)E(\nu_q)$, containing the bound electrons, where $\chi(\nu_q)$ is the polarizability, or the light-matter *interaction parameter*. Since semiclassical thermal radiation consists of random wave groups emitted spontaneously with random phases, the total dipolar amplitude-amplitude stimulation of a bound electron can be expressed as

$$\Psi = \sum\nolimits_q \psi_q = \sum\nolimits_q \chi(\nu_q)E(\nu_q) \qquad (2)$$

The bound electron system must absorb the necessary amount of quantum-cup-filling energy, before the electron can be released to the conduction band or become a free-space electron. This energy exchange is a quadratic process:

$$|\Psi|^2 = \left|\sum\nolimits_q \chi(\nu_q)E(\nu_q)\right|^2 \propto h\nu_q \qquad (3)$$

For any quantum system, we must take the ensemble average. A single event (data point), as in Eq. (3), is never sufficient to verify a theory:

$$\left\langle|\Psi|^2\right\rangle = \left\langle\left|\sum\nolimits_q \chi(\nu_q)E(\nu_q)\right|^2\right\rangle \Leftrightarrow \langle h\nu_q\rangle = \left\langle \phi_{work\ fn.} + (1/2)m\mathrm{v}_{el.}^2\right\rangle \qquad (4)$$

In the right segment of Eq. (4), we have "recovered" Einstein's photoelectric energy-balancing equation out of dipole amplitude stimulations due to multitudes of waves. The left curve in **Figure 4** represents the photoelectric current [15]. Waves only fill up the quantum cups with the necessary energy if the dipoles are resonant to the frequency ν of the incident waves.

6. Discussions

Visible light is always generated through orbital quantum electron transition processes in atoms. We have presented our *hybrid photon* model where light is released as a quantum energy packet, $h\nu$, as required by quantum formalism. Then we posit that immediately after the release of the $h\nu$ packet, it evolves into a classical wave packet and follows Maxwell's wave equation and Huygens-Fresnel diffraction integral. We generate structured light using classical optical components and classical optical analytical tools. The possibility of introducing any quantumness in classical light during this process is difficult to imagine. The author is suggesting that we should explore the physical response properties of the material particles that are inserted into the structured beams and try to visualize the light-matter dipolar interaction processes. This would be a better system-engineering approach to understand different optical phenomena [17, 18].

The key point of the author is that our unquestioned acceptance of the wave-particle duality has been hindering our deeper enquiry into the ultimate nature of light. The author has been attempting to inspire this process over decades by organizing special publications [13] and special conference series at SPIE from 2005 to 2015 [19], publishing experimental papers [20], and writing books [5, 21]. During this long arduous process, the author has recognized that Huygens principle (HP) of "secondary wavelets" has deeper enduring value for physics. HP requires space to be a physical tension field, a complex tension filed or CTF, to facilitate the perpetual and well-defined velocity of light. CTF possesses the necessary characteristic properties, which facilitates the perpetual velocity of light, $c = \left(\varepsilon_0^{-1}/\mu_0\right)^{1/2}$, through the entire cosmic space. CTF must also possess other physical attributes that we have not been exploring actively. Thus, CTF could have serious implications in guiding us to reorganize our investigations to fulfill Einstein's dream of defining a unified field. CTF could be behind the emergence of both the EM waves and the particles as different kinds of oscillations of the same CTF, which holds 100% of the energy of our cosmic system (Ch. 11 in [5, 8, 17]).

Optical physicists should note that the two major "successful theories" for gravity, those of Newton and of Einstein, have been unable to explain the velocity distribution curves measured for a couple hundred galaxies. Therefore, theoretical physicists have proposed unnecessary postulates of the existence of Dark Matter and Dark Energy, neither of whose existence has been confirmed over the last

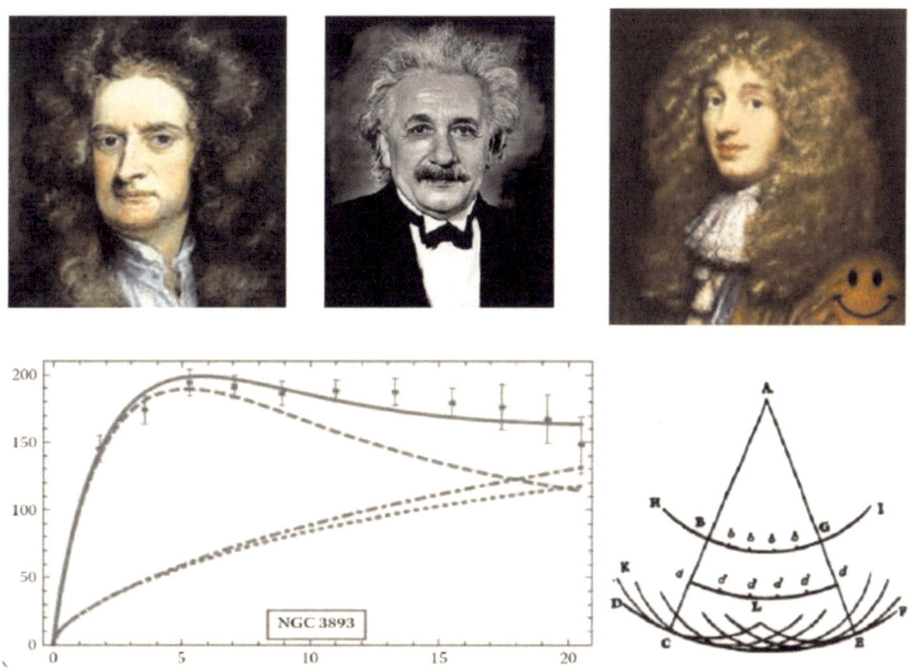

Figure 5.
Left-bottom curves [22]: Gravity theories of Newton and Einstein cannot match the measured velocity distribution of stars in one particular galaxy. This phenomenon turns out to be true for a couple of hundreds of galaxies. These two theories are very accurate for our solar system, but not good at the galactic scale. Bottom right: Huygens 1690 postulate of secondary wavelets [7], framed into Huygens-Fresnel diffraction integral, is still the core guiding analytical equation for the broad field of physical optics, including generating structured light.

several decades. These theories are definitely not wrong. Those who have been successfully launching and manipulating artificial satellites in our solar system rarely need to go beyond the mechanics of Newtonian gravity. Einstein's gravity correctly predicts the precession of the perihelion of Mercury. However, these two theories must be limited in capability to model gravity in the galactic scale (**Figure 5**).

In contrast, in spite of subtle mathematical issues behind the Huygens postulate [23] of secondary wavelets, it remains the key foundational guide to propagate light through free space and non-interacting materials. To model light-matter interaction, Maxwell's equations have remained quite successful. In the history of physics, all theories eventually yield to new and better theories. Our attempts should be directed along these lines. We should not try to keep promoting the general validity of all working theories.

Optical physicists should explore the *deeper enduring values* behind the Huygens principle and find the limits of its application in different optical phenomena to advance further optical physics. Studies in optical phenomena have been guiding major advances in physics since ancient times. Starting from the 1600s to 1800s, advancements in physics were predominantly pioneered by scientists studying the broad field of optical sciences. However, starting from the early 1900s, this pioneering role has been shifted from guiding fundamental physics to finding only novel technical applications of optics. It is time for optical physicists to pick up more proactive roles in guiding the development of fundamental physics [24].

Author details

ChandraSekhar Roychoudhuri
Department of Physics, University of Connecticut, Storrs, CT, USA

*Address all correspondence to: chandra.roychoudhuri@uconn.edu

References

[1] Einstein A. Concerning a heuristic point of view about the creation and transformation of light. Annalen der Physik. 1905;**17**:132-148

[2] Lamb WE, Scully MO. Polarization, matter and radiation, Jubilee volume in honor of Alfred Kastler. In: Photoelectric Effect without Photons. Paris: Presses Universitaires de France; 1969. pp. 363-369

[3] Grynberg G, Aspect A, Fabre C. Introduction to Quantum Optics: From the Semi-Classical Approach to Quantized Light. Cambridge University Press; 2010

[4] Stroud CR, Jaynes ET. Long-term solutions in semi-classical radiation theory. Physical Review A. 1970;**1**(1): 106-121

[5] Roychoudhuri C. Causal Physics: Photon by Non-Interaction of Waves. Boca Raton: Taylor & Francis; 2014

[6] Ronchi V. Nature of Light. Cambridge: Harvard University Press; 1970. p. 53

[7] Huygens C. Treatise on Light, drafted in 1678. English translation. Chicago: University of Chicago Press; 2005 Project Gutenberg Edition: Available from: http://www.gutenberg.org/ebooks/14725

[8] Roychoudhuri C. Next frontier in physics—Space as a complex tension field. Journal of Modern Physics. 2012

[9] Roychoudhuri C. Could space be considered as the inertial rest frame? In: Proc. SPIE. Vol. 9570-30; 2015

[10] Roychoudhuri C. The concept of "fundamental" must keep evolving, FQXi essay competition. 2015. Available from: https://fqxi.org/data/essay-contest-files/Roychoudhuri_180121_Fundame.pdf

[11] Born M, Wolf E. Principles of Optics. 6th ed. Cambridge University Press; 1980

[12] Roychoudhuri C. Hybrid photon model bridges classical and quantum optics.In: JW3A.32-1, OSA Annual Conference; 2017

[13] Roychoudhuri C, Roy R, editors. The nature of light. What is a photon? Optics & Photonics News (OSA). 2003. Available from: https://www.osa-opn.org/opn/media/Images/PDFs/3185_6042_30252.pdf?ext=.pdf

[14] Planck M. The Theory of Heat Radiation. Blakistons Son & Co.; 1914. Free download from Gutenberg eBooks

[15] Hufner S. Photoelectron Spectroscopy: Principles and Applications. Springer; 2010

[16] Bernstein J, Fishbane PM, Gasiorowicz S. Modern Physics. Prentice Hall; 2000

[17] Roychoudhuri C. Urgency of evolution process congruent thinking in physics. In: An advocacy to elevate the prevailing abstract physics—Thinking towards a functionally useful reverse-engineering thinking, Proc. SPIE. Vol. 9570; 2015

[18] Roychoudhuri C. Consequences of repeated discovery and benign neglect of non-interaction of waves (NIW). In: Proc. SPIE. Vol. 10452 1045215; 2017. Available from: https://spie.org/Publications/Proceedings/Paper/10.1117/12.2266216

[19] Roychoudhuri C. et al. Key organizer of the conference series: Nature of light: What (is) are photons? In: Proc. SPIE Vol. 5866, 2005; Proc. SPIE Vol. 6664, 2007; Proc. SPIE Vol. 7421, 2009; Proc. SPIE Vol. 8121, 2011; Proc. SPIE Vol. 8832, 2013; Proc. SPIE Vol. 9570, 2015

[20] Roychoudhuri C. Most of the author's papers and presentations for workshop, etc. Available from: http://www.natureoflight.org/CP/

[21] Roychoudhuri C, Kracklauer AF, Creath K. The Nature of Light: What Is a Photon? Boca Raton: Taylor & Francis; 2008

[22] Mannheim PD, O'Brian JG. Fitting galactic rotation curves with conformal gravity and a global quadratic potential. Physical Review D. 2012;**85**:124020

[23] Goodman J. Fourier Optics. W. H. Freeman; 2017

[24] Roychoudhuri C, Tirfessa N. Bringing reality in physics: System engineering approach to optical phenomena following Huygens' Principle. In: Proc. SPIE 11143; 2019. DOI: 10.1117/12.2523602. Available from: https://www.spiedigitallibrary.org/conference-proceedings-of-spie on 08 Jul 2019

Chapter 2

Quantized Field of Single Photons

Constantin Meis

Abstract

We present theoretical developments expressing the physical characteristics of a single photon in conformity with the experimental evidence. The quantization of the electromagnetic field vector potential amplitude is enhanced to a free of cavity photon state. Coupling the Schrödinger equation with the relativistic massless particle Hamiltonian to a symmetrical vector potential relation, we establish the *vector potential - energy* equation for the photon expressing the simultaneous *wave-particle* nature of a single photon, an intrinsic physical property. It is shown that the vector potential can be naturally considered as a real wave function for the photon entailing a coherent localization probability. We deduce directly the electric and magnetic field amplitudes of the cavity-free single photon, which are revealed to be proportional to the square of the angular frequency. The zero-energy electromagnetic field ground state (EFGS), a quantum vacuum real component, issues naturally from Maxwell's equations and the vector potential quantization procedure. The relation of the quantized amplitude of the photon vector potential to the electron-positron charge results directly showing the physical relationship between photons and electrons-positrons that might be at the origin of their mutual transformations. It becomes obvious that photons, as well as electrons-positrons, are issued from the same quantum vacuum field.

Keywords: single photon, vector potential, photon wave-particle equation, photon wave function, photon electric field, electromagnetic field ground state, electron-positron charge

1. Introduction

During the last decades, an impressive technological development has been achieved permitting the manipulation of single photons with a high degree of statistical accuracy. However, despite the significant experimental advances, we still do not have a clear physical picture of a single photon state universally accepted by the scientific community, especially involved in quantum electrodynamics. In this chapter, based on the present state of knowledge, we make a synthesis of the physical characteristics of a single photon put in evidence by the experiments, and we advance theoretical developments for its representation. Accordingly, the concept of the wave-particle nature of a single photon becomes physically comprehensive and in agreement with the experimental evidence.

However, before advancing in the theoretical developments, we consider that it is important starting with a brief historical review on the efforts carried out previously for understanding the nature of light while simultaneously making a synthesis of the main experimental results which are of crucial importance for the comprehension of the birth of the photon concept.

The very first scientific publications on the nature of light are due to ancient Greeks who believed light is composed of corpuscles [1, 2]. Around 300 BC Euclid published the book *Optica* in which he developed the laws of reflection based on the rectilinear propagation of light. Two centuries later, Ptolemy of Alexandria published the book *Optics*, in which he included extensively all the previous knowledge on light. In this book, colours as well as refraction of the moonlight and sunlight by the earth's atmosphere were analysed. After Ptolemy of Alexandria, almost no progress has been reported until the seventeenth century.

In the year of 1670, Newton revived the ideas of ancient Greeks and advanced the theory following that light is composed of corpuscles that travel rectilinearly [3]. Ten years later, Huygens developed the principles of the wave theory of light [1, 4, 5]. Huygens' wave theory was a hard opponent to Newton's corpuscle concept. In the beginning of the nineteenth century, Young obtained experimentally interference patterns using different sources of light and explained some polarisation observations by assuming that light oscillations are perpendicular to the propagation axis [1, 6]. Euler and Fresnel explained the diffraction patterns observed experimentally by applying the wave theory [6]. In 1865, Maxwell published his theory on the electromagnetic waves establishing the relations between the electric and magnetic fields and showing that light is composed of electromagnetic waves [7]. A few years later, Hertz confirmed Maxwell's theory by discovering the long-wavelength electromagnetic radiation [1, 7]. Thus, at the end of the nineteenth century, the scientific community started to accept officially the wave nature of light replacing Newton's theory.

Nevertheless, new events supporting the particle nature of light occurred in the beginning of the twentieth century. Stefan and Wien discovered the direct relationship between the thermal radiation energy and the temperature of a black body [8, 9]. However, the emitted radiation energy density as a function of the temperature calculated by Rayleigh failed to describe the experimental results at short wavelengths. Scientists had given the name "UV catastrophe" to this problem revealing the necessity of a new theoretical approach. Planck managed to establish the correct energy density expression for the radiation emitted by a black body with respect to temperature, in excellent agreement with the experiment [8]. For that purpose, he assumed that the bodies are composed of "oscillators" which have the particularity of emitting the electromagnetic energy in "packets" of $h\nu$, where ν is the frequency and h is a constant that was later called Planck's constant. During the same period, the experiments carried out by Michelson et al. [10] demonstrated that the speed of light in vacuum is a universal physical constant corresponding to the product of the frequency ν times the wavelength λ, that is, $c = \lambda \nu$.

In 1902, Lenard pointed out that the photoelectric effect, discovered by Hertz 15 years earlier [11], occurs beyond a threshold frequency of light and the kinetic energy of the emitted electrons does not depend on the incident light intensity. Based on Planck's works, Einstein proposed a simple interpretation of the photoelectric effect assuming that the electromagnetic radiation is composed of quanta with energy $h\nu$ [12]. He advanced that *the energy of a light ray when spreading from a point consists of a finite number of energy quanta localised in points in space, which move without dividing and are only absorbed and emitted as a whole.* Although that was a decisive step towards the particle theory of light, the concept of the light quanta was still not generally accepted, and Bohr, who was strongly opposed to the particle concept of light [13], announced in his Nobel lecture (1922) that *the light quantum hypothesis is not compatible with the interference phenomena and consequently it cannot throw light in the nature of radiation.* Bohr's statement was rather surprising because Taylor's experiments, consisting of repeating Young's double slit diffraction at extremely low light intensities, had already demonstrated since 1909 that light rays are composed of discrete parts whose spots compose the diffraction patterns by gradual accumulation on the detection screen [14]. Compton published his studies on X-rays scattered by free electrons in 1923 advancing that the experimental results could only be interpreted based on the light quanta model [15].

Thus, the photoelectric effect and Compton scattering have been initially considered as the undoubtable demonstrations of the particle nature of light and historically were the strongest arguments in favour of the light quanta concept, which started to be universally accepted, and Lewis introduced the word "photon", from the Greek word *phos* (Φωs, which means light) [1, 4].

Therein, it is extremely important to mention that Wentzel in 1926 [16] and Beck in 1927 [17], as well as much later Lamb and Scully in the 1960s [18], demonstrated that the photoelectric effect can be interpreted remarkably well by only considering the wave nature of light, without referring to photons at all [19]. Furthermore, the Compton scattering has been fully interpreted by Klein and Nishina in 1929 [20] also by considering the electromagnetic wave nature of light without invoking the photon concept. On the other hand, Young's experiment, initially presented as the most convincing argument for the wave nature of light, was applied by Taylor at very low intensities to demonstrate the particle concept of light [14]. Indeed, much later Jin et al. [21] published an excellent theoretical interpretation of Young's diffraction experiments based only on the particle representation of light.

Thus, the picture on the nature of light in the 1930s was rather confusing since both opposite sides defending the wave or the particle nature advanced equally strong arguments. Hence, Bohr, inspired by de Broglie's thesis on the simultaneous wave character of particles, announced the *complementarity principle* according to which *light has both wave and particle natures appearing mutually exclusively in each specific experimental condition* [1, 2, 19].

The development of lasers [22] in the 1960s and the revolutionary parametric down-convertion techniques [23, 24] in the 1970s, have made it possible to realise conditions in which, with a convenient statistical confidence, only a single photon may be present in the experimental apparatus. In this way, the double-prism experiment [25] realised in the 1990s contradicted for the first time Bohr's *mutual exclusiveness* demonstrating that a *single photon exhibits both the wave and particle natures in the same experimental conditions*.

According to the experimental investigations, it has been always stated that a photon has circular, left or right, polarisation with spin $\pm h/2\pi$ and cannot be conceived along the propagation axis within a length shorter than its wavelength [26]. Indeed, since Mandel's experiments in the 1960s [27, 28], all the efforts to localise precisely a single photon remained fruitless yielding the conclusion is that a photon cannot be better localised than within a volume of the order of the cube of its wavelength [29, 30]. Furthermore, Grangier et al. demonstrated experimentally the indivisibility of photons [19, 31], while in recent years the entangled state experiments [29, 30] have shown that the photon should be locally an integral entity during the detection procedure but with a real non-local wave function.

The lateral expansion of a single photon, considered locally as an indivisible entity, was always an intriguing part of physics. With the purpose of studying the lateral expansion of the electromagnetic rays, Robinson in 1953 [32] and Hadlock in 1958 [33] carried out experiments using microwaves crossing small apertures and deduced that no energy is transmitted through apertures whose dimensions are smaller than roughly $\sim\lambda/4$. In 1986, for the same purpose, Hunter and Wadlinger [34, 35] used X-band microwaves with λ = 28.5 mm and measured the transmitted power through rectangular or circular apertures of different dimensions. They concluded that no energy is transmitted when the apertures are smaller than $\sim\lambda/\pi$ confirming that the lateral expansion of the photons is a fraction of the wavelength.

Thus, the experiments have shown that the single photon is not a point and cannot be localised at a coordinate, as stated by Einstein, while it can exhibit both the wave and particle natures in the same experimental conditions contradicting Bohr's mutual exclusiveness. However, quantum electrodynamics (QED) has been developed during the 1930s to 1960s based upon the point particle model for the photon [36–39]. In fact, the point photon concept has permitted to establish an efficient mathematical approach for describing states before and after an interaction processes [19, 39–41], but it is naturally inappropriate for the description of the real nature of a single photon.

Finally, what we can essentially draw out by summing up the experimental evidence is that a single photon is a minimum, local, indivisible part of the electromagnetic field with precise energy $h\nu$ and momentum $h\nu/c$, having circular left or right polarisation with spin $\pm h/2\pi$, respectively. It is not a point particle since it expands over a wavelength λ along the propagation axis and is detectable within a volume of the order of λ^3 entailing that its lateral expansion is a fraction of its wavelength. Hence, it appears to be a local "wave-corpuscle" guided by a non-local wave function, absorbed and emitted as a whole and capable of interacting with charges increasing or decreasing its frequency and consequently its energy.

In what follows, we present first the standard theoretical representation of the electromagnetic field quantization resulting in photons, and next we proceed to recent advances based on the vector potential quantization enhanced to a single photon state.

2. The electromagnetic field vector potential

2.1 Reality of the vector potential

Since the formulation of Maxwell's equations, the vector potential $\vec{A}\left(\vec{r},t\right)$ was considered as a pure mathematical artefact [4, 5, 7] used to calculate the electric field:

$$\vec{E}\left(\vec{r},t\right) = -\partial\vec{A}\left(\vec{r},t\right)/\partial t - \vec{\nabla}\Phi\left(\vec{r},t\right) \tag{1}$$

where $\Phi\left(\vec{r},t\right)$ is the scalar potential, as well as the magnetic field:

$$\vec{B}\left(\vec{r},t\right) = \vec{\nabla} \times \vec{A}\left(\vec{r},t\right) \tag{2}$$

In 1949, Ehrenberg and Siday were the first to put in evidence the influence of the vector potential on charged particles [42] deducing that it is a real physical field. Ten years later, Aharonov and Bohm re-infirmed the influence of the vector potential on electrons in complete absence of electric and magnetic fields [43]. That was confirmed experimentally by Chambers [44], Tonomura et al. [45], and Osakabe et al. [46] demonstrating without any doubt the reality of the vector potential field end its direct influence on charges.

From a theoretical point of view [43], the behaviour of a particle with charge q and mass m in the vicinity of a solenoid where the vector potential is present is described by the Hamiltonian:

$$H = \frac{1}{2m}\left(-i\hbar\vec{\nabla} - q\vec{A}\left(\vec{r},t\right)\right)^2 + q\Phi\left(\vec{r},t\right) \tag{3}$$

with $\hbar = h/2\pi$ as Planck's reduced constant.

If the solenoid is extremely long along the z axis, then the magnetic field is uniform in the region inside and zero outside. The scalar potential Φ can be put to zero by assuming that the solenoid is not charged. In this case, in the outside region, the electric and magnetic fields are zero, but the vector potential is not zero and depends on the magnetic field flux in the solenoid:

$$\vec{A} = \frac{1}{2\pi r}\int_s \vec{B}\cdot d\vec{S}\,\hat{e}_\theta \tag{4}$$

where r is the radial distance from the z axis of the solenoid, S is the surface of the circle with radius r perpendicular to z, and $\hat{e}_\theta$ is the angular unit vector in cylindrical coordinates.

The Schrödinger equation for a charged particle outside the solenoid, where the vector potential is not zero, writes in complete absence of any other external potential:

$$i\hbar\frac{\partial}{\partial t}\Psi\left(\vec{r},t\right) = \frac{1}{2m}\left(i\hbar\vec{\nabla} + q\vec{A}\right)^2\Psi\left(\vec{r},t\right) \tag{5}$$

with $\vec{A}$ given by Eq. (4). The solutions of the last equation are the wave functions:

$$\Psi\left(\vec{r},t\right) = \Psi_p\left(\vec{r},t\right)e^{\frac{iq}{\hbar}\int_0^{\vec{r}}\vec{A}\left(\vec{r}'\right)\cdot d\vec{r}'} \tag{6}$$

where $\Psi_p\left(\vec{r},t\right)$ is the solution of Schrödinger's equation in absence of the vector potential:

$$i\hbar\frac{\partial}{\partial t}\Psi_p\left(\vec{r},t\right) = -\frac{\hbar^2}{2m}\vec{\nabla}^2\Psi_p\left(\vec{r},t\right) \tag{7}$$

The exponential part of the wave function of Eq. (6) entails that two particles have equal charge and mass moving both outside the solenoid at the same distance from the axis, but the first in the same direction with the vector potential $\vec{A}$ and the second in the opposite direction will suffer a phase difference:

$$\delta\Theta = \frac{q}{\hbar}\int_s \vec{B}\cdot d\vec{S} \tag{8}$$

Interference patterns for electrons in analogue conditions have been observed experimentally [44–46] demonstrating that the vector potential is a real physical field and interacts directly with charged particles in complete absence of magnetic and electric fields and of any other potential.

2.2 The radiation vector potential: classical to quantum link

The vector potential, being a real field, is considered as the fundamental link between the electromagnetic wave theory issued from Maxwell's equations and the particle concept in quantum electrodynamics (QED) [19, 36, 39]. We will show analytically how this link is established.

In the classical theory [5, 7], the energy density of a mode k of the electromagnetic wave writes:

$$W_k\left(\vec{r},t\right) = \frac{1}{2}\left(\varepsilon_0\left|\vec{E}_k\left(\vec{r},t\right)\right|^2 + \frac{1}{\mu_0}\left|\vec{B}_k\left(\vec{r},t\right)\right|^2\right) \tag{9}$$

where ε_0 and μ_0 are the electric permittivity and magnetic permeability of the vacuum, respectively, related to the speed of light in vacuum c by $\varepsilon_0\mu_0 c^2 = 1$.

In the case of a monochromatic plane wave with angular frequency ω_k, the electric $\vec{E}_k\left(\vec{r},t\right)$ and magnetic $\vec{B}_k\left(\vec{r},t\right)$ fields are proportional to the vector potential amplitude $A_{0k}(\omega_k)$:

$$\vec{E}_k\left(\vec{r},t\right) = -2\omega_k A_{0k}(\omega_k)\hat{\varepsilon}\,\sin\left(\vec{k}\cdot\vec{r} - \omega_k t\right) \tag{10}$$

$$\vec{B}_k\left(\vec{r},t\right) = -\frac{1}{c}2\omega_k A_{0k}(\omega_k)\left(\hat{k}\times\hat{\varepsilon}\right)\sin\left(\vec{k}\cdot\vec{r} - \omega_k t\right) \tag{11}$$

where $\hat{\varepsilon}$ is a unit vector perpendicular to the propagation axis, $\left|\vec{k}\right| = 2\pi/\lambda_k$ is the wave vector along the propagation axis, and λ_k is the wavelength of the mode k.

Introducing Eqs. (10) and (11) in Eq. (9), the energy density now depends on the square of the vector potential amplitude:

$$W_k\left(\vec{r},t\right) = 4\varepsilon_0\omega_k^2|A_{0k}(\omega_k)|^2\sin^2\left(\vec{k}\cdot\vec{r} - \omega_k t\right) \tag{12}$$

The mean value over a period, thus over a wavelength, is time independent:

$$W_k = 2\varepsilon_0\omega_k^2|A_{0k}(\omega_k)|^2 \tag{13}$$

Note that the last equation expressing the mean energy density over a period of the mode k of the electromagnetic wave is independent on any external volume yielding that in the classical description, a free of cavity electromagnetic radiation mode expands naturally within a minimum volume. In a given cavity, this volume corresponds roughly to that imposed by the boundary conditions and the cut-off wave vectors [4, 5, 7].

On the other hand, in the quantum description, the energy density for a number $N(\omega_k)$ of k-mode photons with angular frequency ω_k and energy $\hbar\omega_k$ in a volume V writes simply:

$$W_k = \frac{N(\omega_k)\hbar\omega_k}{V} \tag{14}$$

In order to link the classical to the quantum description [4, 9, 19], the classical mean energy density over a period, expressed by Eq. (13), is imposed to be equivalent to the quantum mechanics expression of Eq. (14) for $N(\omega_k) = 1$ getting the vector potential amplitude for a single k-mode photon:

$$|A_{0k}(\omega_k)| = \sqrt{\frac{\hbar}{2\varepsilon_0\omega_k V}} \tag{15}$$

The last relation is the fundamental link between the classical and quantum theory of light which is used to define in QED the vector potential amplitude operators for a single photon [19, 26, 29, 36–41]:

$$\tilde{A}_{k\lambda} = \sqrt{\frac{\hbar}{2\varepsilon_0\omega_k V}}a_{k\lambda} \qquad \tilde{A}^*_{k\lambda} = \sqrt{\frac{\hbar}{2\varepsilon_0\omega_k V}}a^+_{k\lambda} \tag{16}$$

where $a_{k\lambda}$ and $a^+_{k\lambda}$ are, respectively, the annihilation and creation non-Hermitian operators for a k-mode and λ-polarisation photon.

Therein, it is worth noting that an external arbitrary volume parameter V appears in the vector potential amplitude of the single photon, expressed by Eq. (15), which is supposed to be an intrinsic physical property. This could entail the unphysical interpretation that a single photon in an infinite cavity has zero vector potential, thus zero electric and magnetic fields and consequently zero energy. This ambiguity, which is scarcely quoted in the literature, is lifted by considering that, in the case of a single photon, the volume V in Eq. (15) is equivalent to that defined by the boundary conditions in a cavity for the single radiation mode k.

3. Electromagnetic field quantization and the photon description

3.1 Harmonic oscillator representation of the electromagnetic field

The energy of the electromagnetic field in a volume V considered as a superposition of different k-modes and λ-polarisations is obtained directly from Eq. (13):

$$E_{EM} = 2\varepsilon_0 V\sum_{k,\,\lambda}\omega_k^2|A_{k\lambda}(\omega_k)|^2 \tag{17}$$

where the summation over the λ-polarisations takes only two values corresponding to circular left and right [19, 36–41].

Replacing in Eq. (17) the vector potential amplitude and its conjugate by the relations of the vector potential amplitude operators defined in Eq. (16), we get the "normal ordering" radiation Hamiltonian corresponding to the order $a^+_{k\lambda}a_{k\lambda}$ of the creation and annihilation operators:

$$\tilde{H}_{NO} = \sum_{k,\,\lambda} a^+_{k\lambda}a_{k\lambda}\hbar\omega_k \tag{18}$$

and the "anti-normal ordering" Hamiltonian corresponding to the order $a_{k\lambda}a^+_{k\lambda}$

$$\tilde{H}_{ANO} = \sum_{k,\,\lambda}\left(a^+_{k\lambda}a_{k\lambda} + 1\right)\hbar\omega_k \tag{19}$$

where we have used the fundamental commutation relation in quantum electrodynamics:

$$\left[a_{k\lambda}, a^+_{k\lambda}\right] = 1 \tag{20}$$

In Dirac's representation the eigenfunctions take the simple expression $|n_{k\lambda}\rangle$, and the action of the creation and annihilation operators of a single k-mode and λ-polarisation photon writes:

$$a^{+}_{k\lambda}|n_{k\lambda}\rangle = \sqrt{n_{k\lambda}+1}\,|n_{k\lambda}+1\rangle; \quad a_{k\lambda}|n_{k\lambda}\rangle = \sqrt{n_{k\lambda}}\,|n_{k\lambda}-1\rangle \tag{21}$$

The successive action of both operators in the normal order corresponds to the photon number Hermitian operator $\tilde{n}_{k\lambda} = a^{+}_{k\lambda}a_{k\lambda}$ having the eigenvalue $n_{k\lambda}$ representing the number of k-mode and λ-polarisation photons:

$$a^{+}_{k\lambda}a_{k\lambda}|n_{k\lambda}\rangle = \tilde{n}_{k\lambda}|n_{k\lambda}\rangle = n_{k\lambda}|n_{k\lambda}\rangle \tag{22}$$

In this representation the normal and anti-normal ordering radiation Hamiltonians write, respectively:

$$\tilde{H}_{NO} = \sum_{k,\,\lambda} \tilde{n}_{k\lambda}\hbar\omega_k; \quad \tilde{H}_{ANO} = \sum_{k,\,\lambda} (\tilde{n}_{k\lambda}+1)\hbar\omega_k \tag{23}$$

We obtain a harmonic oscillator Hamiltonian for the electromagnetic field by considering the mean value of the normal ordering and anti-normal ordering Hamiltonians:

$$\tilde{H}_{EM} = \frac{1}{2}\left(\tilde{H}_{NO} + \tilde{H}_{ANO}\right) = \sum_{k,\,\lambda}\left(\tilde{n}_{k,\,\lambda} + \frac{1}{2}\right)\hbar\omega_k \tag{24}$$

Thus, in QED the electromagnetic field is considered to be an ensemble of harmonic oscillators each represented by a point particle, the photon, whose eigenfunction is denoted simply by $|1_{k\lambda}\rangle$ [19, 39, 41].

Although we have no experimental facts showing the harmonic oscillator nature of a single photon, this representation has been adopted since the 1930s [37].

In a different way, a harmonic oscillator representation for the electromagnetic field can be obtained by the intermediate of the canonical variables of position $Q_{k\lambda}$ and momentum $P_{k\lambda}$. For that purpose we introduce the definitions expressing the vector potential amplitude and its complex conjugate with respect to $Q_{k\lambda}$ and $P_{k\lambda}$ [19, 29, 41]:

$$A_{k\lambda} = \frac{(\omega_k Q_{k\lambda} + iP_{k\lambda})}{2\omega_k\sqrt{\varepsilon_0 V}}; \quad A^{*}_{k\lambda} = \frac{(\omega_k Q_{k\lambda} - iP_{k\lambda})}{2\omega_k\sqrt{\varepsilon_0 V}} \tag{25}$$

Introducing the last expressions in Eq. (17), we get the electromagnetic field energy:

$$E_{EM} = \frac{1}{2}\sum_{k,\,\lambda}\left(P^2_{k\lambda} + \omega^2_k Q^2_{k\lambda}\right) \pm i\omega_k[Q_{k\lambda}, P_{k\lambda}] \tag{26}$$

where the (+) sign is obtained when Eq. (17) is considered initially to be in the "normal order", $A^{*}_{k\lambda}A_{k\lambda}$, and the (−) one when in the "anti-normal order" $A_{k\lambda}A^{*}_{k\lambda}$.

With the purpose of establishing a harmonic oscillator representation for the electromagnetic field, it is generally considered that $[Q_{k\lambda}, P_{k\lambda}] = 0$ in Eq. (26), because $Q_{k\lambda}$ and $P_{k\lambda}$ are simply canonical variables, getting the energy of an ensemble of harmonic oscillators:

$$E_{EM} = \frac{1}{2}\sum_{k,\,\lambda}\left(P_{k\lambda}^2 + \omega_k^2 Q_{k\lambda}^2\right) \tag{27}$$

Replacing in the last equation the classical canonical variables of position and momentum with the corresponding Hermitian operators [19, 29, 41]:

$$\tilde{P}_{k\lambda} = i\sqrt{\frac{\hbar\omega_k}{2}}\left(a_{k\lambda}^+ - a_{k\lambda}\right); \quad \tilde{Q}_{k\lambda} = \sqrt{\frac{\hbar}{2\omega_k}}\left(a_{k\lambda}^+ + a_{k\lambda}\right) \tag{28}$$

and putting $a_{k\lambda}^+ a_{k\lambda} = \tilde{n}_{k\lambda}$, one gets the harmonic oscillator Hamiltonian for the radiation field:

$$\tilde{H}_{EM} = \sum_{k,\,\lambda}\left(\tilde{n}_{k,\,\lambda} + \frac{1}{2}\right)\hbar\omega_k \tag{29}$$

At that level it is important to note that, for a harmonic oscillator of a particle with mass m and momentum $\vec{p} = m d\vec{q}/dt$, with canonical variables of position $Q = \left|\vec{q}\right|\sqrt{m}$ and momentum $P = \left|\vec{p}\right|/\sqrt{m}$, the transition from the classical expression of energy:

$$E = \frac{1}{2}\left(P^2 + \omega^2 Q^2\right) \tag{30}$$

to the quantum mechanics Hamiltonian:

$$\tilde{H} = \frac{1}{2}\left(\tilde{P}^2 + \omega^2\tilde{Q}^2\right) = \left(a^+a + \frac{1}{2}\right)\hbar\omega = \left(\tilde{n} + \frac{1}{2}\right)\hbar\omega \tag{31}$$

where $\tilde{P} = i\sqrt{\frac{\hbar\omega}{2}}(a^+ - a)$, $\tilde{Q} = \sqrt{\frac{\hbar}{2\omega}}(a^+ + a)$, and $\tilde{n} = a^+a$ is direct and needs no commutation operations between the canonical variables P and Q [19, 39].

Consequently, the harmonic oscillator Hamiltonian for a particle of mass m expressed by Eq. (31) is a quite physical result (e.g., phonons in solid-state physics) obtained with a perfect correspondence between the classical canonical variables of momentum and position P and Q, respectively, and the corresponding Hermitian operators $\tilde{P}$ and $\tilde{Q}$.

Conversely, this is not the case for the electromagnetic field [19, 29, 39] because commutations between the canonical variables $Q_{k\lambda}$ and $P_{k\lambda}$ occur during the mathematical transition from Eq. (17) to Eq. (26). It is then considered that $[Q_{k\lambda}, P_{k\lambda}] = 0$ in order to obtain Eq. (27) just before replacing the canonical variables by the corresponding quantum mechanics operators. Therein, it is important to remark that Heisenberg's commutation relation $\left[\tilde{Q}_{k\lambda}, \tilde{P}_{k'\lambda'}\right] = i\hbar\delta_{kk'}\delta_{\lambda\lambda'}$ is a fundamental concept of quantum mechanics, which should not be ignored when replacing classical variables by the corresponding quantum mechanics operators [19]. In fact, without dropping $[Q_{k\lambda}, P_{k\lambda}]$ in Eq. (26) and replacing the canonical variables by the corresponding quantum operators of Eq. (28), we get naturally the same normal ordering and anti-normal ordering radiation Hamiltonians as in Eq. (23):

$$\begin{pmatrix} \tilde{H}_{EM}^{(+)} = \frac{1}{2}\sum_{k,\lambda}\left(\tilde{P}_{k\lambda}^{2} + \omega_k^2\tilde{Q}_{k\lambda}^{2}\right) + i\omega_k\left[\tilde{Q}_{k\lambda}, \hat{P}_{k'\lambda'}\right] \\ \tilde{H}_{EM}^{(-)} = \frac{1}{2}\sum_{k,\lambda}\left(\tilde{P}_{k\lambda}^{2} + \omega_k^2\tilde{Q}_{k\lambda}^{2}\right) - i\omega_k\left[\tilde{Q}_{k\lambda}, \tilde{P}_{k'\lambda'}\right] \end{pmatrix} = \begin{pmatrix} \tilde{H}_{NO} = \sum_{k,\lambda}\tilde{n}_{k\lambda}\hbar\omega_k \\ \tilde{H}_{ANO} = \sum_{k,\lambda}(\tilde{n}_{k\lambda} + 1)\ \hbar\omega_k \end{pmatrix} \tag{32}$$

Obviously, as frequently quoted [2, 19, 39], the fundamental mathematical ambiguity consisting of cancelling the commuting classical variable term $[Q_{k\lambda}, P_{k\lambda}] = 0$ before the substitution by non-commuting quantum mechanics operators $\left[\tilde{Q}_{k\lambda}, \tilde{P}_{k'\lambda'}\right] = i\hbar\delta_{kk'}\delta_{\lambda\lambda'}$ leads to the harmonic oscillator Hamiltonian for the electromagnetic field.

In fact, since no experiment has yet demonstrated that a single photon is a harmonic oscillator, the main reason for considering the electromagnetic field as an ensemble of harmonic oscillators lies in the importance of the zero-point energy (ZPE) issued in absence of photons from the eigenvalue $n_{k\lambda} = 0$ of Eq. (29) corresponding to the vacuum energy:

$$E_{ZPE} = \sum_{k,\lambda}\frac{1}{2}\hbar\omega_k \tag{33}$$

The summation of the last expression over all modes and polarisations is infinite and represents the principal singularity in the QED formalism [19, 26, 29, 36, 39].

Nevertheless, the zero-point energy is very important because it is considered to be the basis for the explanation of the vacuum effects such as the spontaneous emission, the Lamb shift and the Casimir effect. However, as pointed out by many authors [19, 26, 39, 41], it is important to underline that the explanation of the spontaneous emission and the Lamb shift in QED is not due to Eq. (33) but precisely to the commutation properties of the photon creation and annihilation operators, $a_{k\lambda}^{+}$ and $a_{k\lambda}$, respectively. It has to be emphasized that in quantum mechanics theory Eq. (33), being a constant, commutes with all Hermitian operators corresponding to physical observables and consequently has absolutely no influence to any quantum process.

Conversely, the zero-point energy expressed by Eq. (33) is useful for the explanation of the spontaneous emission and the Lamb shift in the classical description of radiation [2, 39, 47].

Regarding the Casimir effect, it is often commented that caution has to be taken concerning the interpretation of its physical origin because it has been demonstrated by different methods [48–50] that it can be easily explained using classical electrodynamics without invoking at all the zero-point energy.

Hence, in view of the above, the normal ordering Hamiltonian is the one mainly used in QED, casting aside the vacuum singularity issued from the harmonic oscillator formalism, while the zero-point energy issued from the harmonic oscillator Hamiltonian is principally useful in the classical formalism for the interpretation of the vacuum effects [2, 19, 39, 47].

3.2 Electromagnetic field vector potential quantization in QED

We have analysed in Section 3.1 the electromagnetic field energy quantization according to the harmonic oscillator representation. Now, we will analyse the vector potential field quantization following the second quantisation process.

Considering the natural units ($\hbar = c = 1$), the radiation vector potential writes within the frame of the quantum field theory (QFT) [26, 38]:

$$\vec{A}(x) = \int \frac{d^3k}{(2\pi)^3 2k_0} \sum_{\lambda=1}^{2} \hat{\varepsilon}_{k\lambda} \left[\alpha^{(\lambda)}(k) e^{-ikx} + \alpha^{(\lambda)+}(k) e^{ikx} \right] \tag{34}$$

with

$$\left[\alpha^{(\lambda)}(k), \alpha^{(\lambda')+}(k') \right] = 2k_0 (2\pi)^3 \delta_{\lambda\lambda'} \delta^3 \left(\vec{k} - \vec{k}' \right) \tag{35}$$

where $\delta_{\lambda\lambda'}$ is the Kronecker delta, $\delta^3\left(\vec{k} - \vec{k}'\right)$ is the Dirac delta function, and

$$\alpha^{(\lambda)}(k) = (2k_0)^{1/2} (2\pi)^{3/2} \alpha_{k\lambda}; \quad \alpha^{(\lambda)+}(k) = (2k_0)^{1/2} (2\pi)^{3/2} \alpha_{k\lambda}^{+} \tag{36}$$

Using Eq. (36) in Eq. (34), the vector potential becomes:

$$\vec{A}(x) = \int \frac{d^3k}{(2\pi)^{3/2} (2k_0)^{1/2}} \sum_{\lambda=1}^{2} \hat{\varepsilon}_{k\lambda} \left[\alpha_{k\lambda} e^{-ikx} + \alpha_{k\lambda}^{+} e^{ikx} \right] \tag{37}$$

with $\omega_k = \left(\vec{k}^2 + l^2 \right)^{1/2}$ and $k^2 = k_0^2 - \left(\vec{k} \right)^2 = l^2$.

For $k = l = 0$ then $k_0 = \left| \vec{k} \right| = \omega_k$ and Eq. (37) writes:

$$\vec{A}(x) = \int \frac{d^3k}{(2\pi)^{3/2}} \sqrt{\frac{1}{2\omega_k}} \sum_{\lambda=1}^{2} \hat{\varepsilon}_{k\lambda} \left[\alpha_{k\lambda} e^{-ikx} + \alpha_{k\lambda}^{+} e^{ikx} \right] \tag{38}$$

Suppressing the natural units (i.e., introducing c and $\hbar$) and transforming the last equation in the SI system, which is generally used in QED, we get [38, 41, 51].

$$\vec{A}(x) = \int \frac{d^3k}{(2\pi)^{3/2}} \sqrt{\frac{\hbar}{2\varepsilon_0 \omega_k}} \sum_{\lambda=1}^{2} \hat{\varepsilon}_{k\lambda} \left[\alpha_{k\lambda} e^{-ikx} + \alpha_{k\lambda}^{+}(k) e^{ikx} \right] \tag{39}$$

On the basis of the density of state theory, the quantization of a field in a cavity of volume V permits to transform the continuous summation over the modes to a discrete one [19, 51]:

$$\int \frac{d^3k}{(2\pi)^{3/2}} = \sqrt{\frac{1}{V}} \sum_k \tag{40}$$

The last transformation is only valid for an ensemble of modes k whose wavelengths λ_k are much shorter than the characteristic dimensions of the volume V [19, 29, 39, 41].

Switching now to Heisenberg's representation:

$$\alpha_{k\lambda}(t) = \alpha_{k\lambda} e^{-i\omega_k t} \quad ; \quad \alpha_{k\lambda}^{+}(t) = \alpha_{k\lambda}^{+} e^{i\omega_k t} \tag{41}$$

Generalizing the coordinate system, adapting the phase and using Eq. (40), the vector potential of the electromagnetic field writes in QED [19, 29, 39, 41, 51]:

$$\vec{A}\left(\vec{r},t\right)=\sum_{k}\sqrt{\frac{\hbar}{2\varepsilon_0\omega_k V}}\sum_{\lambda=1}^{2}\hat{\varepsilon}_{k\lambda}\left[\alpha_{k\lambda}e^{i\left(\vec{k}\cdot\vec{r}-\omega_k t\right)}+\alpha_{k\lambda}^{+}e^{-i\left(\vec{k}\cdot\vec{r}-\omega_k t\right)}\right] \quad (42)$$

Considering the scalar potential to be constant, the electric field is:

$$\vec{E}\left(\vec{r},t\right)=i\sum_{k}\sqrt{\frac{\hbar\omega_k}{2\varepsilon_0 V}}\sum_{\lambda=1}^{2}\hat{\varepsilon}_{k\lambda}\left[\alpha_{k\lambda}e^{i\left(\vec{k}\cdot\vec{r}-\omega_k t\right)}-\alpha_{k\lambda}^{+}e^{-i\left(\vec{k}\cdot\vec{r}-\omega_k t\right)}\right] \quad (43)$$

The last expressions represent in a given volume V the quantized vector potential and the electric field of the electromagnetic radiation composed of a large number of modes k each with angular frequency ω_k and wavelength $\lambda_k=2\pi c/\omega_k$ much smaller than $V^{1/3}$:

$$\lambda_k \ll V^{1/3} \quad (\forall k) \quad (44)$$

The amplitudes in Eqs. (42) and (43) have been obtained using the density of state theory and are valid only on the condition of Eq. (44). Furthermore, the boundary conditions of the electromagnetic waves considered in cavities and waveguides impose the wave vectors k of the modes to be higher than a characteristic cut-off value $k>k_{cut-off}$ $\left(\lambda_k<\lambda_{cut-off}\right)$ depending on the dimensions and the shape of the volume containing the radiation field [4–7]. Consequently, for a volume V with finite dimensions, the summation in Eqs. (42) and (43) runs only over the modes k with wave vectors higher than the minimum cut-off value $k_{cut-off}(V)$ imposed by the shape and dimensions of V so that we can write more precisely:

$$\vec{A}\left(\vec{r},t\right)=\sum_{k>k_{cut-off}(V)}\sqrt{\frac{\hbar}{2\varepsilon_0\omega_k V}}\sum_{\lambda=1}^{2}\hat{\varepsilon}_{k\lambda}\left[\alpha_{k\lambda}e^{i\left(\vec{k}\cdot\vec{r}-\omega_k t\right)}+\alpha_{k\lambda}^{+}e^{-i\left(\vec{k}\cdot\vec{r}-\omega_k t\right)}\right] \quad (45)$$

$$\vec{E}\left(\vec{r},t\right)=i\sum_{k>k_{cut-off}(V)}\sqrt{\frac{\hbar\omega_k}{2\varepsilon_0 V}}\sum_{\lambda=1}^{2}\hat{\varepsilon}_{k\lambda}\left[\alpha_{k\lambda}e^{i\left(\vec{k}\cdot\vec{r}-\omega_k t\right)}-\alpha_{k\lambda}^{+}e^{-i\left(\vec{k}\cdot\vec{r}-\omega_k t\right)}\right] \quad (46)$$

The last equations represent the vector potential and the electric field of a large number of modes k of the quantized electromagnetic field in a finite volume V with $\lambda_k \ll V^{1/3}\,(\forall k)$.

4. Quantized vector potential of a single photon

We have seen in Section 3.1 that according to the energy quantization procedure, a k-mode and λ-polarisation photon is considered to be a point harmonic oscillator represented by the simplified eigenfunction $|1_{k\lambda}\rangle$. On the other hand, following the field quantization procedure in Section 3.2, it appears clearly that the established vector potential and electric field expressions in Eqs. (42) and (43), under the condition of Eq. (44), concern a large number of modes in a considerably big volume compared to their wavelengths. Thus, with the aim of obtaining a clearer picture of the single photon, we will now complement the previous descriptions by enhancing the vector potential amplitude quantization to the photon level.

4.1 Photon vector potential amplitude and quantization volume

As mentioned in Section 2.2, the classical expression of the mean energy density over a period for a single electromagnetic mode k, represented by Eq. (13), can be considered equivalent to that for a single photon in the quantum representation, given by Eq. (14) for $N(\omega_k) = 1$, on the condition that the volume V is not arbitrary but corresponds to that defined by the boundary conditions in a cavity for the considered electromagnetic mode. In fact, the physical properties of a free photon are independent on any surrounding volume unless the characteristic dimensions of the last one are of the order of the photon wavelength [52].We recall again that the experimental evidence has shown [19, 27, 29, 51] that a single photon with angular frequency ω_k and wavelength $\lambda_k = 2\pi c/\omega_k$ can only be localised within a volume V_k whose dimensions are roughly the cube of its wavelength:

$$V_k \propto \lambda_k^3 \qquad \Rightarrow \qquad V_k \propto \omega_k^{-3} \tag{47}$$

From a theoretical point of view, this is also compatible with the density of state theory according to which the spatial volume corresponding to a single state of the quantized field is proportional to ω_k^{-3} [19, 29, 39, 41].

On the other hand, the dimension analysis of the vector potential issued from the general solution of Maxwell's equations yields that it is proportional to an angular frequency [5, 7, 9]:

$$\vec{A}\left(\vec{r},t\right) = \frac{\mu}{4\pi}\int \frac{\vec{J}\left(\vec{r}\,',t - \frac{|\vec{r}-\vec{r}\,'|}{c}\right)}{|\vec{r} - \vec{r}\,'|} d^3r' \quad \propto \quad \omega \tag{48}$$

where J is the current density ($C\,m^{-2}\,s^{-1}$) and μ the magnetic permeability.

Indeed, it is well established experimentally that the energy density radiated by a dipole is proportional to ω^4 entailing from Eq. (12) that the vector potential amplitude is normally proportional to ω [4, 5, 7].

This result is gauge independent since it concerns the natural units of the vector potential.

According to the previous considerations, for a free single k-mode photon with λ-polarisation (left or right circular), the vector potential can be written in quantum and classical formalism:

$$\begin{aligned} \tilde{\alpha}_{k\lambda}\left(\vec{r},t\right) &= \alpha_{0k}(\omega_k)\left[\hat{\varepsilon}_{k\lambda}\alpha_{k\lambda}e^{i\left(\vec{k}\cdot\vec{r}-\omega_k t\right)} + \hat{\varepsilon}_{k\lambda}^{*}\alpha_{k\lambda}^{+}e^{-i\left(\vec{k}\cdot\vec{r}-\omega_k t\right)}\right] \\ \vec{\alpha}_{k\lambda}\left(\vec{r},t\right) &= \alpha_{0k}(\omega_k)\left[\hat{\varepsilon}_{k\lambda}e^{i\left(\vec{k}\cdot\vec{r}-\omega_k t\right)} + \hat{\varepsilon}_{k\lambda}^{*}e^{-i\left(\vec{k}\cdot\vec{r}-\omega_k t\right)}\right] \end{aligned} \tag{49}$$

where, following to the above analysis, the amplitude writes:

$$\alpha_{0k}(\omega_k) = |\xi|\omega_k \tag{50}$$

with ξ being a constant [2, 53–55].

We can evaluate ξ [2, 53] by using Eqs. (49) and (50) in Eq. (13) and normalising the energy to that of a single photon, $\hbar\omega_k$, by integrating over a wavelength along the propagation direction while taking into account the experimental results on the lateral expansion of the photon [32–35, 56]. We get:

$$|\xi| = \left|\frac{1}{(2\pi)^{3/2}}\sqrt{\frac{\hbar}{8\alpha\varepsilon_0 c^3}}\right| = \left|\frac{\hbar}{4\pi e c}\right| = 1.747 \quad 10^{-25} \ Volt \ m^{-1} s^2 \tag{51}$$

where $\alpha = e^2/4\pi\varepsilon_0\hbar c \approx 1/137.036$ is the fine structure constant and e is the electron charge. Obviously, when introducing Eq. (50) in Eq. (17) for a single k-mode photon, an appropriate volume V_k has to be considered for the equation to hold:

$$E_k = \hbar\omega_k = 2\varepsilon_0 V_k \xi^2 \omega_k^4 \tag{52}$$

Thus, the characteristic volume of a free single photon writes in agreement with Eq. (47):

$$V_k = \left(\frac{\hbar}{2\varepsilon_0 \xi^2}\right)\omega_k^{-3} \tag{53}$$

Replacing ξ expressed by Eq. (51) in Eq. (53), we obtain the photon quantization volume:

$$V_k \approx 4\alpha\lambda_k^3 \tag{54}$$

Equations (50) and (53) express the quantized vector potential amplitude and the spatial extension of a single photon with the constant ξ evaluated to be $|\xi| = \hbar/4\pi|e|c$.

4.2 Photon classical-quantum (wave-particle) physical properties

For a free k-mode photon, the volume V_k corresponds to the space in which the quantized vector potential oscillates at the angular frequency ω_k over a period along the propagation axis generating orthogonal electric and magnetic fields whose amplitudes are, respectively:

$$\left|\vec{\varepsilon_k}\right| = \left|-\partial\vec{\alpha_{k\lambda}}\left(\vec{r},t\right)/\partial t\right| \propto |\xi|\omega_k^2; \qquad \left|\vec{\beta_k}\right| \propto \sqrt{\varepsilon_0\mu_0}|\xi|\omega_k^2 \tag{55}$$

which are independent on any external arbitrary volume parameter and are directly proportional to the square of the angular frequency [2, 54, 55].

We can now express the quantum properties of the photon, energy, momentum, and spin by integrating the classical electromagnetic expressions over the volume V_k and by using the vector potential amplitude obtained in Eq. (50), linking in this way the classical (wave) to the quantum (particle) representations [2]. The energy writes:

$$E_k = \int_{V_k} 2\varepsilon_0 \alpha_{0k}^2 \omega_k^2 d^3r = \int_{V_k} 2\varepsilon_0 \xi^2 \omega_k^4 d^3r = 2\varepsilon_0 \xi^2 \omega_k^4 V_k = \hbar\omega_k \tag{56}$$

With the same token considering circular polarisation [4, 5, 7, 9] for the amplitudes of the electric and magnetic fields in Eq. (55), the momentum is:

$$\vec{p_k}= \int_{V_k} \varepsilon_0 \vec{\varepsilon_{k\lambda}} \times \vec{\beta_{k\lambda}}\, d^3r = \varepsilon_0 \left(\sqrt{2}\omega_k \alpha_{0k}\right)\left(\sqrt{2}\omega_k \alpha_{0k}/c\right) V_k\, \vec{k} \,/\left|\vec{k}\right| = \hbar\, \vec{k} \quad (57)$$

According to the classical electromagnetic theory, the spin can be written through the electric and magnetic field components; hence, using again the circular polarisation, we get:

$$\left|\vec{S}\right| = \int_{V_k} \varepsilon_0 \left|\vec{r} \times \left(\vec{\varepsilon_{k\lambda}} \times \vec{\beta_{k\lambda}}\right)\right| d^3r = \varepsilon_0 (c/\omega_k)\left(\sqrt{2}\omega_k \alpha_{0k}\right)\left(\sqrt{2}\omega_k \alpha_{0k}/c\right) V_k = \hbar \quad (58)$$

where we have taken the mean value $<\left|\vec{r}\right|>_k = c/\omega_k$ obtained for a single photon state [57].

The fact that the quantum properties, energy, momentum, and spin, of the photon can be expressed through the classical electromagnetic fields integrated over the volume V_k signifies that the photon has naturally a spatial extension, and consequently when employing the term “wave-particle”, one must have in mind that a single photon is a “three-dimensional particle”.

We can now obtain Heisenberg’s uncertainty relation for position and momentum using V_k. Indeed, replacing V in Eq. (16) by V_k, we get the photon vector potential amplitude operators:

$$\tilde{\alpha}_{0k\lambda} = |\xi|\, \omega_k a_{k\lambda}\, ; \qquad \tilde{\alpha}^*_{0k\lambda} = |\xi|\, \omega_k a^+_{k\lambda} \quad (59)$$

The corresponding position $\tilde{Q}_{k\lambda}$ and momentum $\tilde{P}_{k\lambda}$ Hermitian operators [19, 29, 51] write:

$$\tilde{Q}_{k\lambda} = \sqrt{\varepsilon_0 V_k}\left(\tilde{\alpha}_{0k\lambda} + \tilde{\alpha}^*_{0k\lambda}\right); \quad \tilde{P}_{k\lambda} = -i\omega_k \sqrt{\varepsilon_0 V_k}\left(\tilde{\alpha}_{0k\lambda} - \tilde{\alpha}^*_{0k\lambda}\right) \quad (60)$$

Thus, introducing Eq. (59) in Eq. (60) and using Eq. (20) with Eq. (53), Heisenberg’s commutation relation, a fundamental concept in quantum theory, results directly [2]:

$$\left[\tilde{Q}_{k\lambda}, \tilde{P}_{k'\lambda'}\right] = -i\varepsilon_0 \omega^2_{k'} \omega_k \sqrt{V_k V_{k'}}\left[\left(\xi a_{k\lambda} + \xi a^+_{k\lambda}\right), \left(\xi a_{k'\lambda'} - \xi a^+_{k'\lambda'}\right)\right] = i\hbar \delta_{kk'} \delta_{\lambda\lambda'} \quad (61)$$

The fundamental properties of the photon, energy E_k, momentum $\vec{p_k}$, and wave vector $\vec{k}$, are complemented by the vector potential amplitude α_{0k} expressing its electromagnetic nature:

$$E_k/\hbar = \left|\vec{p_k}\right| c/\hbar = \left|\vec{k}\right| c = \alpha_{0k}/|\xi| = \omega_k \quad (62)$$

Considering Heisenberg’s *energy-time* uncertainty principle:

$$\delta E_k\, \delta t \geq \hbar \quad (63)$$

we directly deduce from Eq. (62) the *vector potential-time* uncertainty:

$$\delta\alpha_{0k} \delta t \geq |\xi| \quad (64)$$

The energy and vector potential uncertainties with respect to time are intrinsic physical properties of the wave-particle nature of the photon.

4.3 Photon wave-particle equation and wave function

Obviously, the photon vector potential function $\vec{\alpha_{k\lambda}}\left(\vec{r},t\right)$ expressed in Eq. (49) satisfies the wave propagation equation in vacuum issued from Maxwell's equations:

$$\vec{\nabla}^2\vec{\alpha_{k\lambda}}\left(\vec{r},t\right)-\frac{1}{c^2}\frac{\partial^2}{\partial t^2}\vec{\alpha_{k\lambda}}\left(\vec{r},t\right)=0 \tag{65}$$

as well as the *vector potential energy* (*wave-particle*) equation for the photon [2, 54]:

$$i\begin{pmatrix}\xi\\ \hbar\end{pmatrix}\frac{\partial}{\partial t}\vec{\alpha_{k\lambda}}\left(\vec{r},t\right)=\begin{pmatrix}\tilde{\alpha}_{0k}\\ \tilde{H}\end{pmatrix}\vec{\alpha_{k\lambda}}\left(\vec{r},t\right) \tag{66}$$

where the vector potential operator $\tilde{\alpha}_{0k}=-i\xi c\,\vec{\nabla}$ and the relativistic Hamiltonian for a massless particle $\tilde{H}=-i\hbar c\,\vec{\nabla}$ have the eigenvalues $\xi\omega_k$ and $\hbar\omega_k$, respectively [2, 53].

It is worth remarking the symmetry between the pairs $\{E_k,\hbar\}$ and $\{\alpha_{0k},\xi\}$ for a single photon characterising, respectively, the particle (energy) and electromagnetic wave (vector potential) natures, having in mind that the energy corresponds to the integration of the single-mode electromagnetic field energy density over the volume V_k.

Now, when considering the propagation of a k-mode photon with wavelength λ_k, the difficulties for defining a position operator are widely commented in the literature [27, 29, 30, 39–41, 56]. At the same time, the efforts for defining a wave function for the photon based on the electric and magnetic fields were rather fruitless [58–62]. It has been emphasized several times [19, 26, 27, 30, 56] that a photon cannot be localised along the propagation axis in a length shorter than the wavelength λ_k and within a volume smaller than roughly λ_k^3.

In fact, from a theoretical point of view, for a photon propagating in the z direction, Heisenberg's uncertainty for the position z and momentum $P_z=\hbar k_z=h/\lambda_k$ writes:

$$\delta z\ \delta P_z\geq h \quad\rightarrow\quad \delta z\ \delta(1/\lambda_k)\geq 1 \tag{67}$$

Notice that the momentum uncertainty along the propagation axis is expressed through the uncertainty over the inverse of the wavelength.

Considering now the vector potential function with the quantized amplitude $\alpha_{0k}=|\xi|\,\omega_k$ as a real wave function for the photon, then when a k-mode photon is emitted at a coordinate z_e at an instant t_e and propagates in vacuum along the z axis, the probability $\Pi_k(z)$ to be localised at time t and at the coordinate $z = z_e + c\ (t\text{-}t_e)$ corresponds to the square of the modulus of the vector potential and is consequently proportional to the square of the angular frequency [54, 55]:

$$\Pi_k(z)\propto\left|\vec{\alpha_{k\lambda}}\ (z,t)\right|^2=\xi^2\omega_k^2\propto\lambda_k^{-2} \tag{68}$$

Obviously, the shorter the wavelength of the photon, the higher the localization probability in agreement with Heisenberg's uncertainty and the experimental evidence.

4.4 Electromagnetic field ground state, photons, and electrons-positrons

The photon vector potential is composed of a fundamental function $\Xi_{k\lambda}$ times the angular frequency ω_k and writes in the classical (wave) and quantum (particle) formalisms:

$$\vec{\alpha}_{k\lambda} = |\xi|\,\omega_k\left[\hat{\varepsilon}_{k\lambda}e^{i\left(\vec{k}\cdot\vec{r}-\omega_k t+\phi\right)}+\hat{\varepsilon}^{*}_{k\lambda}e^{-i\left(\vec{k}\cdot\vec{r}-\omega_k t+\phi\right)}\right]=\omega_k\vec{\Xi}_{k\lambda}\left(\omega_k,\vec{r},t\right) \tag{69}$$

$$\tilde{\alpha}_{k\lambda} = |\xi|\,\omega_k\left[a_{k\lambda}\hat{\varepsilon}_{k\lambda}e^{i\left(\vec{k}\cdot\vec{r}-\omega_k t+\phi\right)}+a^{+}_{k\lambda}\hat{\varepsilon}^{*}_{k\lambda}e^{-i\left(\vec{k}\cdot\vec{r}-\omega_k t+\phi\right)}\right]=\omega_k\tilde{\Xi}_{k\lambda}\left(a_{k\lambda},a^{+}_{k\lambda}\right) \tag{70}$$

In this way, the general equation for the vector potential of the electromagnetic wave considered as a superposition of plane wave modes writes:

$$\vec{A}\left(\vec{r},t\right)=\sum_{k,\,\lambda}|\xi|\,\omega_k\left[\hat{\varepsilon}_{k\lambda}e^{i\left(\vec{k}\cdot\vec{r}-\omega_k t+\phi\right)}+\hat{\varepsilon}^{*}_{k\lambda}e^{-i\left(\vec{k}\cdot\vec{r}-\omega_k t+\phi\right)}\right]=\sum_{k,\,\lambda}\omega_k\vec{\Xi}_{k\lambda}\left(\omega_k,\vec{r},t\right) \tag{71}$$

and that of a large number of cavity-free photons in quantum electrodynamics is:

$$\tilde{A}=\sum_{k,\,\lambda}|\xi|\,\omega_k\left[a_{k\lambda}\hat{\varepsilon}_{k\lambda}e^{i\left(\vec{k}\cdot\vec{r}-\omega_k t+\phi\right)}+a^{+}_{k\lambda}\hat{\varepsilon}^{*}_{k\lambda}e^{-i\left(\vec{k}\cdot\vec{r}-\omega_k t+\phi\right)}\right]=\sum_{k,\,\lambda}\omega_k\tilde{\Xi}_{k\lambda}\left(a_{k\lambda},a^{+}_{k\lambda}\right) \tag{72}$$

According to Eqs. (55) and (62), for $\omega_k \to 0$ all the physical properties of the photon vanish entailing that the photon exists only for a non-zero frequency of the vector potential oscillation. However, the zero-frequency level does not correspond to perfect inexistence because the fundamental field $\Xi_{k\lambda}$ does not vanish for $\omega_k = 0$ but reduces to $\Xi^0_{k\lambda}$ involving the amplitude ξ and the general expression of the polarisation vectors $\hat{\varepsilon}_{k\lambda}$ [63, 64] and writes in the classical and quantum representations:

$$\vec{\Xi}^{0}_{k\lambda}=|\xi|\left[\hat{\varepsilon}_{k\lambda}e^{i\phi}+\hat{\varepsilon}^{*}_{k\lambda}e^{-i\phi}\right]\quad ;\quad \tilde{\Xi}^{0}_{k\lambda}=|\xi|\left[a_{k\lambda}\hat{\varepsilon}_{k\lambda}e^{i\phi}+a^{+}_{k\lambda}\hat{\varepsilon}^{*}_{k\lambda}e^{-i\phi}\right] \tag{73}$$

The field $\Xi^0_{k\lambda}$ is the *electromagnetic field ground state* (EFGS) permeating all the space ($\lambda_k \to \infty$) and having zero energy and zero vector potential as well as zero electric and magnetic fields. This physical state lies beyond the Bohm-Aharonov situation in which the energy and the electric and magnetic fields are zero but a vector potential is present in space [43]. Thus, in complete absence of energy and vector potential, the field $\Xi^0_{k\lambda}$ can be assimilated to a quantum vacuum component constituting the main "skeleton" of any photon which now clearly appears to be a vacuum oscillation [2, 63, 64].

Combination of the expression $|\xi| = \hbar/4\pi|e|c$ to the fine structure constant definition $\alpha = e^2/4\pi\varepsilon_0\hbar c$ permits to draw directly the electron-positron elementary charge $e = \pm 1.602 \quad 10^{-19} C$, a fundamental physical constant, which now is expressed exactly through the EFGS amplitude ξ [64, 65]:

$$e = \pm(4\pi)^2 \alpha \frac{|\xi|}{\mu_0} \tag{74}$$

Using again Eq. (51) and recalling that the electron mass may be written as $m_e = e\hbar/2\mu_B$, where μ_B is the Bohr magneton, we deduce that the electron mass is also expressed as a function of the EFGS amplitude ξ [64]:

$$m_e = 2\pi c\, e^2 \frac{|\xi|}{\mu_B} \tag{75}$$

entailing that the mass derives also from the EFGS and is proportional to the charge square.

Equations (50), (74), and (75) show the strong physical relationship between photons and electrons-positrons which are all related directly to the EFGS through the amplitude ξ. Obviously, photons and electrons-positrons, also probably leptons-antileptons, are issued from the same quantum vacuum field. This may be at the origin of the physical mechanism governing the photon generation during the electron-positron (and probably lepton-antilepton) annihilation and that of the electron-positron (lepton-antilepton) pair creation during the annihilation of high-energy gamma photons in the vicinity of very heavy nucleus.

5. Conclusion

In this chapter we have presented recent theoretical developments complementing the standard formalism with the purpose of describing a single photon state in conformity with the experiments. We resume below the principal features.

The quantization of the vector potential amplitude α_{0k}, a real physical entity, for a single free of cavity k-mode photon with angular frequency ω_k is expressed by $\alpha_{0k} = |\xi|\,\omega_k$, where $|\xi| = \hbar/4\pi|e|c$, and leads to the establishment of a *vector potential - energy* (electromagnetic wave-particle) formalism (Eq. (66)) expressing the simultaneous wave-particle nature of the photon. A single photon state is a local indivisible entity of the electromagnetic field extending over a wavelength λ_k and consisting of the quantized vector potential oscillating at the angular frequency ω_k, with circular polarisation, giving birth to orthogonally oscillating electric and magnetic fields whose amplitudes are proportional to the square of the angular frequency $|\xi|\,\omega_k^2$ (Eq. (55)). Its lateral expansion, confirmed experimentally, yields a minimum photon volume V_k which is proportional to λ_k^3. The quantum properties of the photon, energy, momentum, and spin are obtained directly from the classical electromagnetic expressions integrated over the volume V_k (Eqs. (56)–(58)). It is also shown (Eq. (61)) that the Heisenberg uncertainty can be readily obtained through the use of the volume V_k.

A single photon, as a local three-dimensional entity of the electromagnetic field, is absorbed and emitted as a whole and propagates guided by the non-local vector potential function (Eq. (49)), which appears to be a natural wave function for the photon satisfying both the propagation equation (Eq. (65)) and the *vector potential - energy* equation (Eq. (66)). The probability for detecting a photon around a given point on the propagation axis is obtained by the square modulus of the vector potential and is proportional to the square of the angular frequency $\xi^2\omega_k^2$ (Eq. (68)) which signifies that the higher the frequency, the better the localization, in agreement with the experiments.

Finally, the electromagnetic field ground state (EFGS) at zero frequency, a real quantum vacuum component, issues naturally from the vector potential wave function putting in evidence that photons are oscillations of the vacuum field. Furthermore, the electron-positron charge and mass are directly proportional to the vector potential amplitude quantization constant showing the strong physical relationship with the photons. Obviously, the origin of the mechanisms governing the transformations of photons to electrons-positrons and inversely lies in the nature of the electromagnetic field ground state.

Author details

Constantin Meis[1,2]

1 National Institute for Nuclear Science and Technology, CEA - Saclay, France

2 Department of Physics, University of Versailles, UVSQ, France

*Address all correspondence to: constantin.meis@cea.fr

References

[1] Ronchi V. The Nature of Light: An Historical Survey. Cambridge (MA) USA: Harvard University Press; 1970

[2] Meis C. Light and Vacuum. 2nd ed. Singapore: World Scientific; 2017

[3] Newton I. Opticks. New York: Dover; 1952

[4] Saleh BEA, Teich MC. Fundamentals of Photonics. New York: John Wiley & Sons; 2007

[5] Read FH. Electromagnetic Radiation. New York: John Wiley & Sons; 1980

[6] Born M, Wolf E. Principles of Optics. Cambridge (MA) USA: Harvard University Press; 1999

[7] Jackson JD. Classical Electrodynamics. New York: John Wiley & Sons; 1998

[8] Planck M. The Theory of Heat Radiation. New York: Dover; 1959

[9] Bransden BH, Joachain CJ. Physics of Atoms and Molecules. 2nd ed. London: Longman; 2003

[10] Mickelson AA et al. Conference on Michelson-Morley Experiment. Astrophysical Journal. 1928;**68**:341

[11] Hertz H. Ueber sehr schnelle electrische Schwingungen. Annalen der Physik. 1887;**33**:983

[12] Einstein A. In: Stachel J, Cassidy DC, Renn J, Schulmann R, editors. The collected papers of Albert Einstein. New Jersey: Princeton University Press; 1987

[13] Bohr N, Kramers HA, Slater JC. The quantum theory of radiation. Philosophical Magazine. 1924;**47**:785

[14] Taylor GI. Interference fringes with feeble light. Proceedings of the Cambridge Philosophical Society. 1909; **15**:114

[15] Compton AH. A Quantum Theory of the Scattering of X-rays by Light Elements. Physical Review. 1923;**21**:483

[16] Wentzel G. Zur Theorie des photoelektrischen Effekts. Zeitschrift für Physik. 1926;**40**:574

[17] Beck G. Zur Theorie des photoeffekts. Zeitschrift für Physik. 1927;**41**:443

[18] Lamb WE Jr, Scully MO. Polarization, Matière et Rayonnement, Volume Jubilaire en L'honneur d'Alfred Kastler. Paris: French Physical Society, Press Universitaires de France; 1969

[19] Garrison JC, Chiao RY. Quantum Optics. New York: Oxford University Press; 2008

[20] Klein O, Nishina Y. über die Streuung von Strahlung durch freie Elektronen nach der neuen relativistischen. Zeitschrift für Physik. 1929;**52**:853

[21] Jin F, Yuan S, De Raedt H, Michielsen K, Mayiashita S. Corpuscular Model of Two-Beam Interference and Double-Slit Experiments with Single Photons. Journal of the Physical Society of Japan. 2010;**79**(7):074401

[22] Schawlow A, Townes C. Infrared and optical masers. Physical Review. 1958;**112**(6):1940-1949

[23] Klyshko DN, Penin AN, Polkovnikov BF. Parametric luminescence and light scattering by polaritons. JETP Letters. 1970;**11**:05

[24] Burnham DC, Weinberg DL. Observation of simultaneity in parametric production of optical photon

pairs. Physical Review Letters. 1970; **25**(2):84

[25] Ghose P, Home D. The two-prism experiment and wave-particle duality of light. Foundations of Physics. 1996;**26** (7):943

[26] Akhiezer AI, Berestetskii BV. Quantum Electrodynamics. New York: Interscience; 1965

[27] Mandel L. Configuration-Space Photon Number Operators in Quantum Optics. Physical Review. 1966;**144**:1071

[28] Pfleegor RL, Mandel L. Interference of Independent Photon Beams. Physical Review. 1967;**159**(5):1084

[29] Grynberg G, Aspect A, Fabre C. Quantum Optics. New York: Cambridge University Press; 2010

[30] Auletta G. Foundations and Interpretation of Quantum Mechanics. Singapore: World Scientific; 2001

[31] Grangier P, Roger G, Aspect A. Experimental evidence for a photon anticorrelation effect on a beam splitter: A new light on single-photon interferences. Europhysics Letters. 1986;**1**(4):173

[32] Robinson HL. Diffraction patterns in circular apertures less than one wavelength. Journal of Applied Physics. 1953;**24**(1):35

[33] Hadlock RK. Diffraction Patterns at the Plane of a Slit in a Reflecting Screen. Journal of Applied Physics. 1958;**29**:918

[34] Hunter G, Wadlinger RLP. Photons and Neutrinos as Electromagnetic Solitons. Physics Essays. 1989;**2**:158

[35] Hunter G. Quantum uncertainties. NATO ASI Series B. In: Proceedings of NATO Advanced Research Workshop; June 23–27, 1986. p. 331

[36] Feynman R. The Strange Theory of Light and Matter. New Jersey: Princeton University Press; 1988

[37] Heitler W. The Quantum Theory of Radiation. Oxford: Clarendon Press; 1954

[38] Ryder LH. Quantum field theory. Cambridge: Cambridge University Press; 1987

[39] Milonni PW. The Quantum Vacuum. London: Academic Press Inc.; 1994

[40] Mittleman MH. Introduction to the Theory of Laser-Atom Interactions. New York: Plenum Press; 1982

[41] Weissbluth M. Photon-Atom Interactions. London: Academic Press Inc.; 1988

[42] Ehrenberg W, Siday RE. The refractive index in electron optics. Proceedings of the Physical Society. Section B. 1949;**62**:8-2

[43] Aharonov Y, Bohm D. Significance of electromagnetic potentials in the quantum theory. Physics Review. 1959; **115**:485-491

[44] Chambers RG. Shift of an electron interference pattern by enclosed magnetic flux. Physical Review Letters. 1960;**5**:3-5

[45] Tonomura A et al. Evidence for aharonov-bohm effect with magnetic field completely shielded from electron wave. Physical Review Letters. 1986;**56**: 792

[46] Osakabe N et al. Experimental confirmation of Aharonov-Bohm effect using a toroidal magnetic field confined by a superconductor. Physical Review A. 1986;**34**:815

[47] Welton TA. Physics Review. 1948; **74**:1157

[48] Milonni PW. Physical Review A. 1982;**25**:1315

[49] Schwinger J, DeRaad LL Jr, Milton KA. Annals of Physics. 1978;**115**:1

[50] Ezawa H, Nakamura K, Watanabe K. The Casimir force from Lorentz's. Frontiers in Quantum Physics. In: Lim SC, Abd-Shukor R, Kwek KH, editors. Proceedings of the 2nd International Conference; Kuala Lumpur, Malaysia; July 9–11, 1997. Springer; 1998. pp. 160-169

[51] Tannoudji CC, Diu B, Laloë F. Mécanique Quantique. Vol. III. Paris: EDP Sciences; 2017

[52] Walther H, Varcoe BTH, Englert B-G, Becker T. Reports on Progress in Physics. 2006;**69**(5):1325

[53] Meis C. Photon wave-particle duality and virtual electromagnetic waves. Foundations of Physics. 1997;**27**: 865

[54] Meis C, Dahoo PR. Vector potential quantization and the photon intrinsic electromagnetic properties: Towards nondestructive photon detection. International Journal of Quantum Information. 2017;**15**(8):1740003

[55] Meis C, Dahoo PR. Vector potential quantization and the photon wave function. Journal of Physics: Conference Series. 2017;**936**:012004

[56] Jeffers S, Roy S, Vigier JP, Hunter G. The Present Status of the Quantum Theory of Light. Boston: Kluwer Academic Publishers; 1997

[57] Rybakov YP, Saha B. Soliton model of atom. Foundations of Physics. 1995; **25**(12):1723-1731

[58] Bialynicki-Birula I. Photon wave function. In: Wolf E, editor. Progress in Optics XXXVI. Amsterdam: Elsevier; 1996

[59] Chandrasekar N. Quantum mechanics of photons. Advanced Studies in Theoretical Physics. 2012;**6** (8):391-397

[60] Sipe JE. Photon wave functions. Physical Review A. 1995;**52**:1875

[61] Smith BJ, Raymer MG. Photon wave functions, wave packet quantization of light and coherence theory. New Journal of Physics. 2007;**9**:414

[62] Khokhlov DL. Spatial and temporal wave functions of photons. Applied Physics Research. 2010;**2**(2):50-54

[63] Meis C. Vector potential quantization and the quantum vacuum. Physics Research International. 2014; **2014**:187432

[64] Meis C. The electromagnetic field ground state and the cosmological evolution. Journal of Physics: Conference Series. 2018;**1141**:012072

[65] Meis C, Dahoo PR. The single photon state, the quantum vacuum and the elementary electron-positron charge. American Institute of Physics: Conference Proceedings. 2018;**2040**: 020011

Section 2

Generation

Chapter 3

Generation and Manipulation of Nonclassical Photon Sources in Nonlinear Processes

Zhi-Yuan Zhou and Bao-Sen Shi

Abstract

Nonclassical photon sources are key components in quantum information science and technology. Here, the basic principles and progresses for single photon generation and their further manipulation based on second- or third-order nonlinear processes in various degrees of freedom are briefly reviewed and discussed. Based on spontaneous parametric down-conversion and spontaneous four-wave mixing, various nonlinear materials such as quasi-phase-matching crystals, dispersion-shifted fibers, and silicon-on-insulator waveguides are used for single photon generation. The kinds of entanglement generated include polarization, time-energy, time-bin, and orbital angular momentum. The key ingredient for photon pair generation in nonlinear processes is described and discussed. Besides, we also introduce quantum frequency conversion for converting a single photon from one wavelength to another wavelength, while keeping its quantum properties unchanged. Finally, we give a comprehensive conclusion and discussion about future perspectives for single photon generation and manipulation in nonlinear processes. This chapter will provide an overview about the status, current challenge, and future perspectives about single photon generation and processing in nonlinear processes.

Keywords: photon pair, spontaneous parametric down-conversion, spontaneous four-wave mixing, polarization, time-bin, time-energy, orbital angular momentum, quantum entanglement, quantum frequency conversion, quasi-phase-matching, dispersion-shifted fiber, silicon-on-insulator waveguide

1. Introduction

Nonclassical photon sources are fundamental resources for researches in quantum information science and technology (QIST), which are widely used for applications like quantum communications, computations, sensing, and studying fundamental physics of quantum mechanics [1–3]. Therefore the ability to generate and manipulate single photon determines how far we can go in QIST. Generally, there are two distinct methods for generating single photons: one is based on excitation-reemission of photon in a semiconductor quantum dot [4], a single defect in NV center [5], or a single atom [6]; another convenient method is based on spontaneous emission based on a second- [7] or a third-order nonlinear process [8]. In this chapter, we will focus on single photon generation by using nonlinear processes. Usually, there are two nonlinear processes for generating nonclassical photon pairs:

(1) spontaneous parametric down-conversion (SPDC), which is a second-order nonlinear process; (2) spontaneous four-wave mixing (SFWM), which is a third-order nonlinear process. In both SPDC and SFWM, energy, linear momentum, and angular momentum conservations should be fulfilled. Due to these conservation laws and the technology of quantum interference used, two photons in each pair generated in SPDC and SFWM can be correlated in various degrees of freedoms, for example, polarization, energy-time, orbital angular momentum, position-linear momentum, angular momentum, and photon number and path [1]; we can utilize these freedoms in a specific application scenario in QIST.

In the subsequent section, we will first introduce the basic principle of SPDC and SFWM for generating photon pairs and then the various materials used for SPDC and SFWM. In the key part of this chapter, we will review the developments of various entangled photon pair sources and methods for charactering these sources. After that we will introduce a nonlinear method for transducing the wavelength of the photon from one to another while keeping its quantum properties unchanged, which is suitable for building up a quantum interface to connect different quantum systems. Finally, we will give a brief summary in which some future perspectives for nonclassical photon pair generation and potential applications are discussed.

2. Photon pair generation using SPDC or SFWM

SPDC is realized in a second-order nonlinear process (see **Figure 1** left image), in which a pump photon at higher frequency (ω_p) is split into two daughter photons at lower frequencies with certain probability in a nonlinear crystal; these two daughter photons are usually called signal (ω_s) and idler (ω_i) photons. The conservation laws of energy, linear momentum, and angular momentum require that the frequency, linear momentum (k), and angular momentum (l) of the pump, signal, and idler photon fulfill the following conditions: $\omega_p = \omega_s + \omega_i$; $k_p = k_s + k_i$; $l_p = l_s + l_i$. These conservation laws are responsible for the generation of various entangled sources.

In correspondence to SPDC, SFWM is a third-order nonlinear process; a big difference is that there are two pump beams in SFWM (see **Figure 1** right image), in comparison to SPDC in which only one pump beam is used. The conservation laws in SFWM require that the corresponding parameters of the pump, signal, and idler photons have the following relationships: $\omega p_1 + \omega p_2 = \omega_s + \omega_i$; $kp_1 + kp_2 = k_s + k_i$; $lp_1 + lp_2 = l_s + l_i$.

For quantum optical description of SPDC and SFWM, the Hamiltonian of the two processes can be expressed as [9]:

$$\hat{H} = \hbar\xi\left(\hat{a}_s^\dagger \hat{a}_i^\dagger + H.C.\right) \tag{1}$$

where ξ depends on the pump intensity, the nonlinear coefficient of the crystal, crystal length, and focusing parameters. Therefore the photon states generated in SPDC and SFWM can be expressed in Fock state basis as [9]:

$$|\Phi\rangle = Exp\left[-\frac{i\hat{H}t}{\hbar}\right]|0,0\rangle = |0,0\rangle + \kappa|1,1\rangle + \kappa^2/2|2,2\rangle + \dots \tag{2}$$

It can be seen from Eq. (2) that we obtain a vacuum state with a high probability if the pump is weak. The second term is the photon pair state we need, and the other terms are multiphoton states which should be avoided. It is clear from Eq. (2) that the pump beam should be at a moderate intensity level in order to eliminate the effects of higher photon number states. The photon pair generated in SPDC and SFWM is of probability and is undetermined, which is a disadvantage for photon

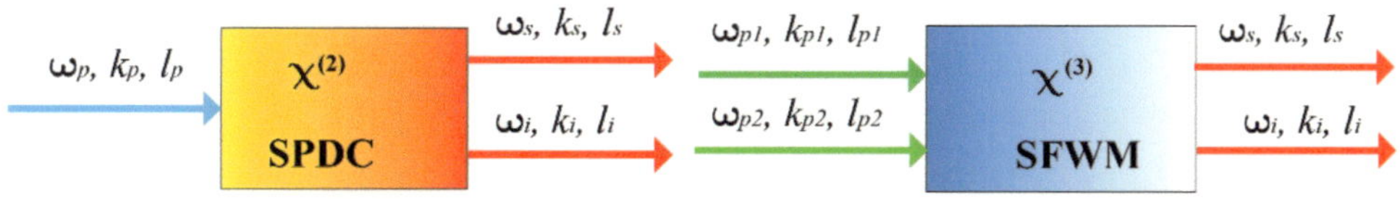

Figure 1.
A simple diagram for SPDC and SFWM. The conservation of energy, linear momentum, and angular momentum holds in both nonlinear processes.

sources generated from nonlinear processes. For this reason, one needs to choose a proper pump intensity level in order to balance between different experimental parameters.

All materials have third-order nonlinearity, but only those materials that are central asymmetric have second-order nonlinearity. The commonly used materials for SPDC can be divided into two kinds according to different phase matching: one is birefringent angle phase-matching materials, such as LBO, BBO, KTP, and LN [10]; another is quasi-phase-matching (QPM) crystals such as PPKTP and PPLN [11]. QPM crystals have the advantages of high generation rate and narrow bandwidth, which are frequently used in photon pair generation in modern quantum optics experiments [12–19]. For SFWM, the commonly used materials are hot or cold atomic ensembles [20–24] and guided-wave materials such as dispersion-shifted fibers (DSF) [25–29], photonic crystal fibers (PCF), [30–32], and silicon-on-insulator (SOI) waveguide [33–41]. To look for new kinds of nonlinear materials for generating high-quality photon sources is still a very hot topic in QIST.

3. Various kinds of photon sources generated in SPDC and SFWM

Because of the conservation of energy, linear momentum, and angular momentum in SPDC and SFWM, various kinds of nonclassical sources can be generated; in this section we will review the recent development and key points in generating various kinds of nonclassical photon sources.

3.1 Polarization-entangled photon source

A polarization-entangled photon source (PEPS) is one of the most important entangled photon sources that have been studied for decades of years. In the literatures, people generate PEPS using different materials with different experimental configurations [12–19, 42, 43]. For SPDC, in the early times, PEPSs are created using birefringence phase-matching (BPM) crystals, for example, a type-II phase-matched BBO crystal is used to create a PEPS in the first practical and effective experiment, in which orthogonal polarized photons are emitted at the intersection cones [42]. Later on, a beam-like design is used for high-brightness photon pair generation, which is widely used in multiphoton quantum experiments [44]. The significant progress in nonlinear crystal fabrication makes a QPM crystal a better choice for researchers in many nonlinear optics applications [11]. The most important merit of using QPM crystals in generation photon pairs is its high spectral brightness in contrast to BPM crystals, due to its large effective nonlinear coefficient and long allowable interaction length.

Recently, to generate PEPS by placing a QPM crystal inside a Sagnac interferometer configuration has been demonstrated to be superior to other configurations (see **Figure 2**). The basic idea for a Sagnac loop-based PEPS is as the following: a pump beam is split into two beams by a double polarized beam splitter (DPBS) and

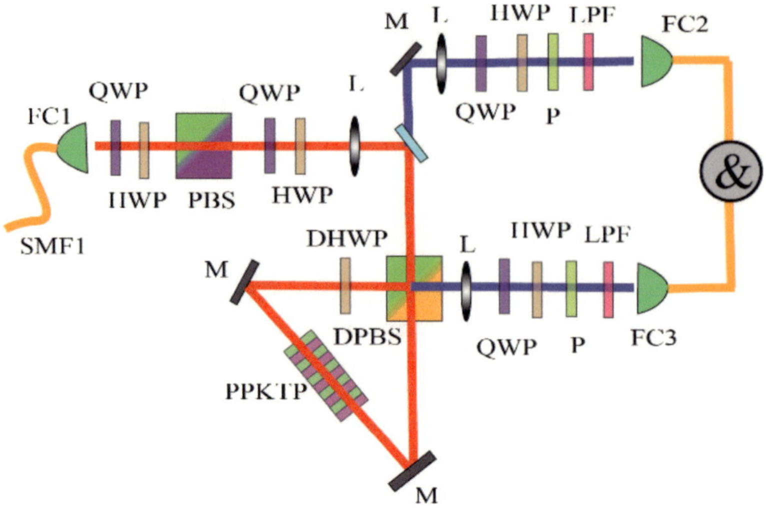

Figure 2.
The experimental setup for a typical polarization-entangled source based on Sagnac interferometer (figure cited from [13]).

counter-propagates in the Sagnac loop; each beam generates a pair of photon with orthogonal polarization, in one circulation direction; the photon pair is rotated by a double half wave plate; then two pairs of photons are recombined in the DPBS; and a PEPS with a form of $|\Phi\rangle = 1/\sqrt{2}(|HV\rangle + e^{i\theta}|VH\rangle)$ is generated; the relative phase θ can be tuned by a pair of wave plates placed in the input port of the Sagnac loop. The merits to use the Sagnac interferometer configuration are its compactness, high stability, and high brightness. The original idea of Sagnac loop-based PEPS is from [43] where a BPM crystal is used, and then this idea is generalized to a QPM crystal by Kim in 2006 [45] for a CW pumped photon source. After that, a pulsed PEPS at 780 nm based on this configuration was developed by Kuzucu and Wong in 2008 [46]. In the early experiments, the wavelengths of the photons generated are in visible range; therefore these photons are not suitable for long-distance quantum communications in fiber. Only recently, telecom band PEPS is developed [13, 16]. A pulsed PEPS at 1584 nm based on a type-II PPKTP was demonstrated by Jin et al. in 2014 [16], and Li et al. reported a tunable CW PEPS in 2015 [13]. Now, PEPS based on QPM crystals in a Sagnac configuration has become a basic tool for many experiments [47–49].

In SFWM, PEPS is generated using an atomic ensemble with different configurations. The PEPS generated with the atomic ensemble has narrow bandwidth; the wavelength is fixed to specific atomic transition lines [50, 51]. Many works report PEPS generation based on guided-wave materials such as DSF [8, 25, 27, 28], PCF [30], and SOI waveguide [37, 52], the advantages of using guided-wave materials are free of free-space coupling, low loss, low cost, and easy to integrate. The guided-wave platform is very promising in large-scale applications which require hundreds of optical components. It is also convenient for building up a compact, versatile photonic source platform for various kinds of applications in QIST.

3.2 Time-energy and time-bin-entangled photon source

Because of conservation of energy in nonlinear processes, the two photons in each pair generated are correlated in frequency and are also generated simultaneously. Although the uncertainty in time and frequency domain for individual particle should meet the requirement of uncertainty principle, the sum of the frequency of signal and idler multiplies the difference between arrive times of the two photon should have a very small value, and violates an inequality for two photons existed classical correlations [53]. A two-photon Franson-type interference is used to characterize the correlations between the two photons; the phases between the two unbalanced Michelson interferometers (UMI) are correlated [54, 55]. To generate a time-energy entangled photon pair, a laser with long coherent time is needed (see **Figure 3(a)**); the time difference between two paths in UMI should be much larger than the coherence time of the single photon but much shorter than the coherent time of the pump laser [53]. A similar kind of entangled photon source is a time-bin entangled photon source [56], in which a pulse pump is split into two pulses in an UMI, and then these two pulses have a certain probability to generate a pair of photon separately; the photon pairs generated by these two pulses are indistinguishable after passing through two UMIs (the time difference of the UMI in measurement part is the same as the UMI in pump part, see **Figure 3(b)**). The quantum states for a time-energy or a time-bin entangled photon source can be expressed as $|\Phi\rangle = 1/\sqrt{2}(|SS\rangle + e^{i\theta}|LL\rangle)$, where S and L represent the short and long arm of the UMIs, respectively. A time-bin entangled photon pair is robust for long-distance transmission, which is widely used in demonstrating various quantum communication protocols [57]. A time-energy entangled photon source has been realized in various material systems such as atomic vapor [21], nonlinear crystals [56, 57], and guided-wave platform [26, 28, 34, 35, 39–41]. The differences between various materials are the photon emission bandwidth and spectral ranges. Furthermore, researchers have realized three photon genuine time-energy entangled photon sources, and their nonclassical correlations are verified [58].

3.3 Orbital angular momentum entangled photon source

Another important degree of freedom of photon is orbital angular momentum (OAM), which has been widely investigated since 1992 [59]. OAM has unbounded dimensions, which is very promising for high-capacity communication task in both classical and quantum optical communications [60–62]. OAM entangled photon pairs can be generated in SPDC and SFWM based on crystals [48, 63–69] and atomic vapors [70, 71]. The quantum state for an OAM entangled photon pair generated directly by pumping a nonlinear crystal (**Figure 4**, left image) can be

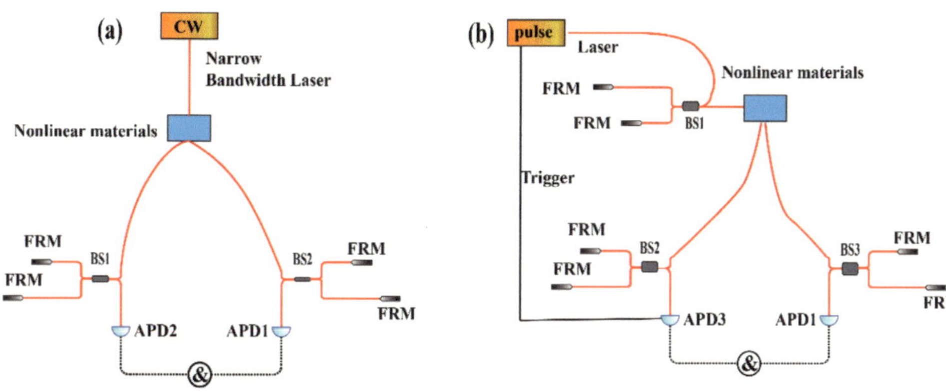

Figure 3.
Simplified diagrams for (a) time-energy; (b) time-bin entangled photon generation. A narrow bandwidth CW laser is used for generating of time-energy entangled photon pair, while a pulse laser is used for generating time-bin entangled photon pair.

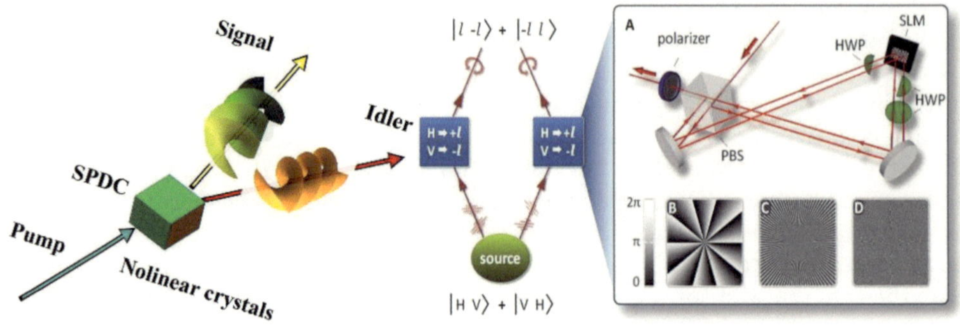

Figure 4.
Generate HD OAM entangled state directly from SPDC (left image); 2D OAM entangled state generation by converting a polarized entangled state into 2D subspace of OAM entangled state (right image, cited from [48]).

expressed as $|\Phi\rangle = \sum C_l|l,-l\rangle$, where C_l is the weight for different OAM modes. One can investigate OAM entanglement in a two-dimensional (2D) subspace [48, 63, 67–70] or in high-dimensional (HD) space [65, 66, 71]. The properties and the methods of characterizing a 2D entangled source in different degrees of freedom are similar and can be converted from one kind to another [48, 68] (please see **Figure 4** (right images)). The post-selected OAM entangled states in a 2D subspace can be expressed as $|\Phi\rangle = 1/\sqrt{2}(|l,-l\rangle + |-l,l\rangle)$. While for a HD entangled source, the properties and the methods of characterization are rather different. [65] reported on the realization of a 11D entangled source, demonstrating the violation of the Bell inequality. Zeilinger's group has demonstrated a 100*100 HD entanglement by measuring the entanglement witness of the generated state [66]. For a 2D OAM entangled photon source, Zeilinger's group converted a polarized entangled photon source into an OAM entangled source with OAM momenta of 300 h in 2D subspace via a spatial light modulator [48]. Later on, a higher OAM momentum of about 10,000 h for a 2D OAM entangled source is realized by using a vortex reflection mirror [68]. A HD OAM entangled photon source is preferred for studying the basic principle of quantum mechanics and for HD quantum communication applications.

4. Methods for characterizing the properties of a nonclassical photon source

Nonclassical photon sources can be characterized from different aspects. For characterizing the properties of a heralded single photon, the heralded efficiency [72], the coincidence to accidental coincidence ratio (CAR) [73], and the single photon Glauber function [74, 75] are important parameters. The heralded efficiency is the probability of detecting the second photon when the first photon is detected. It is a measurement of the photon collection efficiency, filter and transmission losses, and the single photon detector efficiency. The heralded efficiency is the ratio of the coincidence count to the single count rate of the first detected photon. CAR is a measurement of the signal to background noise ratio for a two-photon experiment; high CAR can ensure the quantum nature existed between the two photons. CAR depends on pump power and detector performance. Usually, CAR will increase when the pump power is increased in the low pump power regime. After reaching the maximum value, CAR will decrease with the increase of the pump power [76]. The single photon Glauber function can be measured as shown in [74]. The measured photon is firstly split by a beam splitter, and then by measuring the three party coincidence, single count and two-photon coincidence, we can

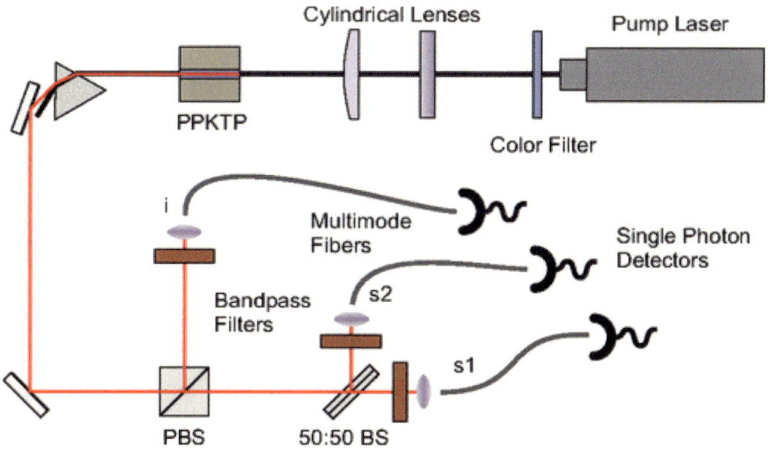

Figure 5.
Experimental setup for measuring heralded single photon autocorrelation function for single photon generated from SPDC (image cited from [74]).

calculate the single photon $g^{(2)}$ function (see **Figure 5**). A near zero $g^{(2)}(0)$ indicates the high quality of single photon nature. For a pulse pumped photon source, the single photon purity is also an important parameter [17, 77]. The purity of photon is a measurement of spectral correlations between two photons; the purity is determined by the Schmitt number in the Schmitt decomposition. The unity single photon purity indicates that the two-photon spectral can be factorized into product of two separate functions of the signal and idler photons. The high single photon purity is very important for realizing high visibility HOM interference between two independent single photon sources, which is the key technique for realizing high photon number entangled states.

There are various available and faithful methods to characterize the quality of entanglement of an entangled two-photon source, including two-photon interference fringes [65, 78], Bell CHSH inequality [79, 80], and quantum state tomography (QST) [81]. Two-photon interference fringe is much easier to measure; through calculating the interference visibility from the measured data, we can evaluate the quality of an entangled source. A high visibility indicates a high quality of the generated state by comparing the ideal maximum Bell states. When the visibility is greater than a threshold value, the two photons have Bell nonlocality; the threshold value is different for two-photon states in different dimension. For two photons existing in classical correlation, the Bell CHSH parameter S is not greater than a certain value. The violation of this value indicates a nonclassical correlation between the two-photon states. Bell CHSH parameter S is an indicator of whether the two-photon state has Bell nonlocality and how strong this kind of nonlocal correlation is. The violation of Bell inequality has been widely studied in literatures for a 2D and a HD entangled state. To fully know the content of a generated quantum state, QST can be used to reconstruct the density matrix of a certain quantum state. By the density matrix of a quantum state, all the properties of the quantum state can be predicted.

5. Quantum frequency conversion for nonclassical quantum state

There are many quantum systems for QIST based on different materials, including atomic ensembles, trapped ions, solid-state materials, and fibers for transmission [82–86]. Each quantum system has some advantages in QST, and these

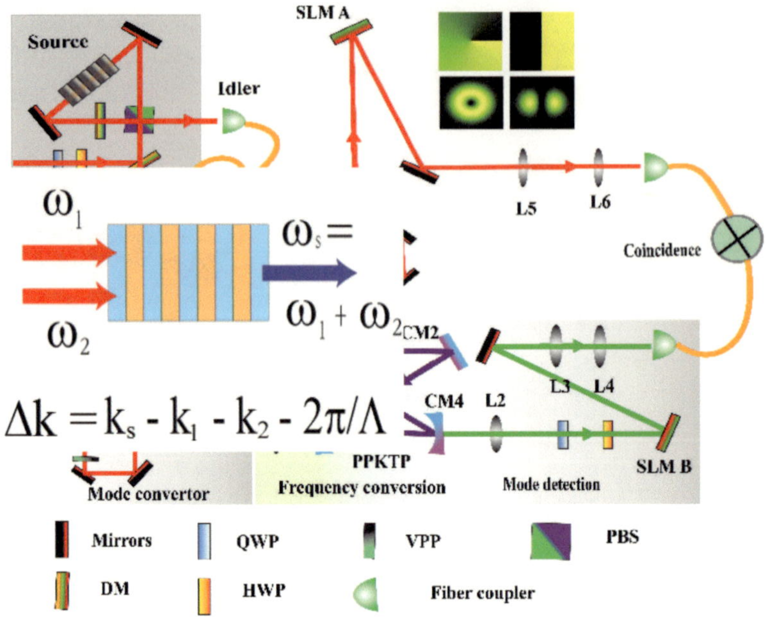

Figure 6.
Left image: simple diagram for sum frequency generation in QPM crystal. Right image: experimental setup of QFC for an OAM qubit, an OAM-polarization hybrid entangled state, and an OAM-OAM entangled state (cited from [99]).

systems usually work at different frequencies, which may have a big frequency mismatching. To build up a quantum network consisting of various quantum systems for information encoding, storage, transmission, and processing, a quantum frequency converter (QFC) to link different quantum systems is indispensable. Such a frequency transducer can be realized by utilizing nonlinear processes such as sum frequency generation (SFG) and Bragg reflection in four-wave mixing. The theory of quantum frequency conversion for SFG was first proposed by P. Kumar in 1990 [87]. In SFG, a strong pump laser can convert a weak signal beam with high quantum efficiency; the unity quantum efficiency can be reached when the pump beam is strong enough (see **Figure 6** left image), and the quantum correlations are unchanged after frequency conversion. Since it has been proposed, some significant progresses have been made in this field; researchers have realized that frequency up-conversion and down-conversion for a single photon generated from quantum dot, and various qubit states or entangled states such as polarization, time-energy, and OAM entangled state [39, 88–101] have been up- or down-converted. A typical setup for QFC of an OAM qubit, an OAM-polarization hybrid entangled state, and an OAM-OAM entangled state is shown in **Figure 6** (right image). For frequency down-conversion, the visible single photons generated from atomic ensemble, trapped irons, or NV centers have been converted to telecom band successfully [102–105]. In all these demonstrations, the single photon properties and entanglement are preserved in the conversion processes, which ensures that quantum information can be coupled to different quantum systems by using a quantum frequency interface.

In QFC, there are four parameters to evaluate the quality of a converter: quantum conversion efficiency, noise level, spectral bandwidth, and spatial bandwidth. These parameters are not independent; therefore in practical applications, one needs to balance between different parameters [98]. A longer nonlinear crystal is preferred to reach maximum conversion efficiency when the pump power is limited, but a longer nonlinear crystal would lead to a smaller spectral bandwidth and spatial bandwidth; a proper crystal length should be chosen to balance conversion efficiency and spectral bandwidth. The noise in QFC comes from SPDC and SRS of the intense pump beam; therefore a longer pump wavelength is preferred to reduce the noise photon in QFC [106]. The noise photon can also be dramatically reduced by using a narrow bandwidth filters to filter out the converted photon.

6. Discussions and conclusion

Nonclassical photon sources are used in almost all fields of QIST; the ability to generate and control its properties is at the heart for applications in QIST. Though many progresses have been made in single photon generation and manipulation in nonlinear processes, lots of further techniques should be developed to harness the quality of single photon generated in SPDC or SFWM. The detailed techniques for optimizing the parameter of the photon source depend on the specific applications. For a pulsed heralded single photon source, the heralded efficiency and total photon count are important parameters, but the probability of single photon generation per pulse is very low, which limits the flux of photon pair generation. These defects can be overcome by using time, frequency, and OAM multiplexing to enhance the photon generation probability per pulse and total count rate [41, 107–112]. When the optical elements for multiplexing have low losses, the heralded efficiency and rate can be increased substantially [112]. For applications taking advantages of the sharp time correlations in SPDC, a broadband spectrum of the photon pair is needed. Such a broadband photon pair can be realized with an ultrathin nonlinear crystal or using a chirp quasi-phase-matching crystal; the bandwidth of the photon pair generated can be greater than 100 nm, which has a time correlation of sub-femtosecond [113]. For quantum information applications, a multiplexed time-energy and polarized entangled photon pair is preferred for high-capacity quantum communication by using dense-wave division multiplexing technique. The multiplexed entangled sources are easier to be realized using a waveguide platform such as a PPLN waveguide, a DSF, or SOI waveguide. A SOI ring cavity is also preferred in generating frequency comb entangled states [114]. For generating HD entangled states, by shaping the profile of a pump beam, a much greater Hilbert space can be reached [115, 116]. For QFC of OAM entangled states, the mode-dependent conversion efficiency has not been solved yet. We recently proposed and demonstrated that if we use a flat-top beam to pump the SFG crystal, then we can solve the problem of mode-dependent conversion efficiency by using a Gaussian pump beam [117].

For a compact application, integrated optics will offer a great advantage over free-space implementation; the trends of modern optics are to convert a free-space module to an equivalent integrated optical device, which will be of high compact, robust to environment fluctuations and much easier for larger amounts of fabrication [118, 119].

In conclusion, most of the advances and progresses for generation and manipulation of single photon sources in nonlinear processes are briefly reviewed in this chapter; this review will provide a glance at the current status, and challenges remain to be solved in this field. The general properties for single photon generation in nonlinear processes are introduced firstly; then we introduce the development of various entangled states and the methods to characterize nonclassical photonic states. Next, we review the progresses for frequency conversion of a photonic state in nonlinear processes. Finally, we give comprehensive discussions about the remaining challenges in generating high-quality and HD entangled states, the unsolved problems for QFC of HD OAM photonic states, and the development of integrated optics for small footprint optical devices and large-scale quantum information processing on chip. This book chapter should be helpful for new researchers working in this field.

Author details

Zhi-Yuan Zhou* and Bao-Sen Shi
Key Laboratory of Quantum Information, CAS, University of Science and Technology of China, Hefei, Anhui, China

*Address all correspondence to: zyzhouphy@ustc.edu.cn

References

[1] Flamini F, Spagnolo N, SciarrinoF.Photonicquantuminformation processing: A review. Reports on Progress in Physics. 2019;**82**:016001. DOI: 10.1088/1361-6633/aad5b2

[2] Pan JW, Chen ZB, Lu CY, Weinfurter H, Zeilinger A, Zukowski M. Multiphoton entanglement and interferometry. Reviews of Modern Physics. 2012;**84**:777-838. DOI: 10.1103/RevModPhys.84.777

[3] Kimble J. The quantum internet. Nature. 2008;**453**:1023-1030. DOI: 10.1038/nature07127

[4] Lodahl P. Quantum-dot based photonic quantum networks. Quantum Science and Technology. 2018;**3**:013001. DOI: 10.1088/2058-9565/aa91bb

[5] Kurtsiefer C, Mayer S, Zarda P, Weinfurter H. Stable solid-state source of single photons. Physical Review Letters. 2000;**85**:290. DOI: 10.1103/PhysRevLett.85.290

[6] Kuhn A, Hennrich M, Rempe G. Deterministic single-photon source for distributed quantum networking. Physical Review Letters. 2002;**89**:067901. DOI: 10.1103/PhysRevLett.89.067901

[7] Burnham DC, Weinberg DL. Observationofsimultaneityinparametric production of optical photon pairs. Physical Review Letters. 1970;**25**:84. DOI: 10.1103/PhysRevLett.25.84

[8] Takesue H, Inoue K. Generation of polarization-entangled photon pairs and violation of Bell's inequality using spontaneous four-wave mixing in a fiber loop. Physical Review A. 2004;**70**:031802. DOI: 10.1103/PhysRevA.70.031802

[9] Hiesmayr BC, de Dood MJA, Löffler W. Observation of four-photon orbital angular momentum entanglement. Physical Review Letters. 2016;**116**:073601. DOI: 10.1103/PhysRevLett.116.073601

[10] Boyd RW. Nonlinear Optics. 3rd ed. Chichester: Academic Press; 2008. 640 p

[11] Armstrong JA, Bloembergen N, Ducuing J, Perhsan PS. Interactions between light waves in a nonlinear dielectric. Physics Review. 1962;**127**:1918. DOI: 10.1103/PhysRev.127.1918

[12] Jin RB, Shimizu R, Kaneda F, Mitsumori Y, Kosaka H, Edamatsu K. Entangled-state generation with an intrinsically pure single-photon source and a weak coherent source. Physical Review A. 2013;**88**:012324. DOI: 10.1103/PhysRevA.88.012324

[13] Li Y, Zhou ZY, Ding DS, Shi BS. CW-pumped telecom band polarization entangled photon pair generation in a Sagnac interferometer. Optics Express. 2015;**23**:28792-28800. DOI: 10.1364/OE.23.028792

[14] Zhou ZY, Jiang YK, Ding DS, Shi BS, Guo GC. Actively switchable nondegenerate polarization-entangled photon-pair distribution in dense wave-division multiplexing. Physical Review A. 2013;**87**:045806. DOI: 10.1103/PhysRevA.87.045806

[15] Zhou ZY, Jiang YK, Ding DS, Shi BS. An ultra-broadband continuously-tunable polarization-entangled photon-pair source covering the C+L telecom bands based on a single type-II PPKTP crystal. Journal of Modern Optics. 2013;**60**:720-725. DOI: 10.1080/09500340.2013.807363

[16] Jin RB, Shimizu R, Wakui K, Fujiwara M, Yamashita T, Miki S, et al. Pulsed Sagnac polarization-entangled photon source with a PPKTP crystal at

telecom wavelength. Optics Express. 2014;**22**:11498-11507. DOI: 10.1364/OE.22.011498

[17] Jin RB, Shimizu R, Wakui K, Benichi H, Sasaki M. Widely tunable single photon source with high purity at telecom wavelength. Optics Express. 2013;**21**:10659-10666. DOI: 10.1364/OE.21.010659

[18] Hentschel M, Hubel H, Poppe A, Zeilinger A. Three-color Sagnac source of polarization-entangled photon pairs. Optics Express. 2009;**17**:23153-23159. DOI: 10.1364/OE.17.023153

[19] Steinlechner F, Ramelow S, Jofre M, Gilaberte M, Jennewein T, Torres JP, et al. Phase-stable source of polarization-entangled photons in a linear double-pass configuration. Optics Express. 2013;**21**:11943-11951. DOI: 10.1364/OE.21.011943

[20] Ding DS, Zhou ZY, Shi BS, Zou XB, Guo GC. Generation of non-classical correlated photon pairs via a ladder-type atomic configuration: Theory and experiment. Optics Express. 2012;**20**:11433-11444. DOI: 10.1364/OE.20.011433

[21] Park J, Jeong T, Kim H, Moon HS. Time-energy entangled photon pairs from Doppler-broadened atomic ensemble via collective two-photon coherence. Physical Review Letters. 2018;**121**:263601. DOI: 10.1103/PhysRevLett.121.263601

[22] Shu C, Chen P, Chow TKA, Zhu L, Xiao Y, Loy MMT, et al. Subnatural-linewidth biphotons from a Doppler-broadened hot atomic vapour cell. Nature Communications. 2016;7:12783. DOI: 10.1038/ncomms12783

[23] Qian P, Gu Z, Cao R, Wen R, Ou ZY, Chen JF, et al. Temporal purity and quantum interference of single photons from two independent cold atomic ensembles. Physical Review Letters. 2016;**117**:013602. DOI: 10.1103/PhysRevLett.117.013602

[24] Lee JC, Park KK, Zhao TM, Kim YH. Einstein-Podolsky-Rosen entanglement of narrow-band photons from cold atoms. Physical Review Letters. 2016;**117**:250501. DOI: 10.1103/PhysRevLett.117.250501

[25] Li X, Voss PL, Sharping JE, Kumar P. Optical-fiber source of polarization-entangled photons in the 1550 nm telecom band. Physical Review Letters. 2005;**94**:053601. DOI: 10.1103/PhysRevLett.94.053601

[26] Takesue H, Inoue K. Generation of 1.5μm band time-bin entanglement using spontaneous fiber four-wave mixing and planar light-wave circuit interferometers. Physical Review A. 2005;**72**:041804. DOI: 10.1103/PhysRevA.72.041804

[27] Zhou Q, Zhang W, Wang P, Huang Y, Peng J. Polarization entanglement generation at 1.5 μm based on walk-off effect due to fiber birefringence. Optics Letters. 2012;**37**:1679-1681. DOI: 10.1364/OL.37.001679

[28] Li YH, Zhou ZY, Xu ZH, Xu LX, Shi BS, Guo GC. Multiplexed entangled photon-pair sources for all-fiber quantum networks. Physical Review A. 2016;**94**:043810. DOI: 10.1103/PhysRevA.94.043810

[29] Li YH, Xu ZH, Wang S, Xu LX, Zhou ZY, Shi BS. Hong-Ou-Mandel interference between two independent all-fiber multiplexed photon sources. Acta Physica Sinica. 2017;**66**:120302. DOI: 10.7498/aps.66.120302

[30] Fulconis J, Alibart O, O'Brien JL, Wadsworth WJ, Rarity JG. Nonclassical interference and entanglement generation using a photonic crystal fiber pair photon source. Physical Review

Letters. 2007;**99**:120501. DOI: 10.1103/PhysRevLett.99.120501

[31] Cohen O, Lundeen JS, Smith BJ, Puentes G, Mosley PJ, Walmsley IA. Tailored photon-pair generation in optical fibers. Physical Review Letters. 2009;**102**:123603. DOI: 10.1103/PhysRevLett.102.123603

[32] Cui L, Li X, Zhao N. Spectral properties of photon pairs generated by spontaneous four-wave mixing in inhomogeneous photonic crystal fibers. Physical Review A. 2012;**85**:023825. DOI: 10.1103/PhysRevA.85.023825

[33] Silverstone JW, Bonneau D, Ohira K, Suzuki N, Yoshida H, Iizuka N, et al. On-chip quantum interference between silicon photon-pair sources. Nature Photonics. 2014;**8**:104-108. DOI: 10.1038/nphoton.2013.339

[34] Reimer C, Kues M, Roztocki P, Wetzel B, Grazioso F, Little BE, et al. Generation of multiphoton entangled quantum states by means of integrated frequency combs. Science. 2016;**351**:1176-1180. DOI: 10.1126/science.aad8532

[35] Mazeas F, Traetta M, Bentivegna M, Kaiser F, Aktas D, Zhang W, et al. High quality entanglement on a chip-based frequency comb. Optics Express. 2016;**24**:28731-28738. DOI: 10.1364/OE.24.028731

[36] He J, Bell BA, Casas-bedoya A, Zhang Y, Clark AS, Xiong C, et al. Ultracompact quantum splitter of degenerate photon pairs. Optica. 2015;**2**:779-782. DOI: 10.1364/OPTICA.2.000779

[37] Li YH, Zhou ZY, Feng LT, Fang WT, Liu SL, Liu SK, et al. On-chip multiplexed multiple entanglement sources in a single silicon nanowire. Physical Review Applied. 2017;**7**:064005. DOI: 10.1103/PhysRevApplied.7.064005

[38] Preble SF, Fanto ML, Steidle JA, Tison CC, Howland GA, Wang Z, et al. On-chip quantum interference from a single silicon ring-resonator source. Physical Review Applied. 2015;**4**:021001. DOI: 10.1103/PhysRevApplied.4.021001

[39] Li YH, Fang WT, Zhou ZY, Liu SL, Liu SK, Xu ZH, et al. Quantum frequency conversion for multiplexed entangled states generated from micro-ring silicon chip. Optics Express. 2018;**26**:28429-28440. DOI: 10.1364/OE.26.028429

[40] Grassani D, Azzini S, Liscidini M, Galli M, Strain MJ, Sorel M, et al. Micrometer-scale integrated silicon source of time-energy entangled photon. Optica. 2015;**2**:88-94. DOI: 10.1364/OPTICA.2.000088

[41] Fang WT, Li YH, Zhou ZY, Xu LX, Guo GC, Shi BS. On-chip generation of time-and wavelength-division multiplexed multiple time-bin entanglement. Optics Express. 2018;**26**:12912-12921. DOI: 10.1364/OE.26.012912

[42] Kwiat PG, Mattle K, Weinfurter H, Zeilinger A, Sergienko AV, Shih Y. New high-intensity source of polarization-entangled photon pairs. Physical Review Letters. 1995;**75**:4337-4341. DOI: 10.1103/PhysRevLett.75.4337

[43] Shi BS, Tomita A. Generation of a pulsed polarization entangled photon pair using a Sagnac interferometer. Physical Review A. 2004;**69**:013803. DOI: 10.1103/PhysRevA.69.013803

[44] Zhang C, Huang YF, Wang Z, Liu BH, Li CF, Guo GC. Experimental Greenberger-Horne-Zeilinger-type six-photon quantum nonlocality. Physical Review Letters. 2015;**115**:260402. DOI: 10.1103/PhysRevLett.115.260402

[45] Kim T, Fiorentino M, FNC W. Phase-stable source of polarization

entangled photons using a polarization Sagnac interferometer. Physical Review A. 2006;**73**:012316. DOI: 10.1103/PhysRevA.73.012316

[46] Kuzucu O, FNC W. Pulsed Sagnac source of narrow-band polarization-entangled photons. Physical Review A. 2008;**77**:032314. DOI: 10.1103/PhysRevA.77.032314

[47] Giustina M, Mech A, Ramelow S, Wittmann B, Kofler J, Beyer J, et al. Bell violation using entangled photons without the fair-sampling assumption. Nature. 2013;**497**:227-230. DOI: 10.1038/nature12012

[48] Fickler R, Lapkiewicz R, Plick WN, Krenn M, Schaeff C, Ramelow S, et al. Quantum entanglement of high angular momenta. Science. 2012;**338**:640-643. DOI: 10.1126/science.1227193

[49] Hu MJ, Zhou ZY, Hu XM, Li CF, Guo GC, Zhang YS. Observation of non-locality sharing among three observers with one entangled pair via optimal weak measurement. npj Quantum Information. 2018;**4**:63. DOI: 10.1038/s41534-018-0115-x

[50] Park J, Kim H, Moon HS. Polarization-entangled photons from a warm atomic ensemble using a Sagnac interferometer. Physical Review Letters. 2019;**122**:143601. DOI: 10.1103/PhysRevLett.122.143601

[51] Yu YC, Ding DS, Dong MX, Shi S, Zhang W, Shi BS. Self-stabilized narrow-bandwidth and high-fidelity entangled photons generated from cold atoms. Physical Review A. 2018;**97**:043809. DOI: 10.1103/PhysRevA.97.043809

[52] Takesue H, Fukuda H, Tsuchizawa T, Watanabe T, Yamada K, Tokura Y, et al. Generation of polarization entangled photon pairs using silicon wire waveguide. Optics Express. 2008;**16**:5721-5727. DOI: 10.1364/OE.16.005721

[53] Franson JD. Bell inequality for position and time. Physical Review Letters. 1989;**62**:2205. DOI: 10.1103/PhysRevLett.62.2205

[54] Franson JD. Two-photon interferometry over large distances. Physical Review A. 1991;**44**:4552. DOI: 10.1103/PhysRevA.44.4552

[55] Ou ZY, Zou XY, Wang LJ, Mandel L. Observation of nonlocal interference in separated photon channels. Physical Review Letters. 1990;**65**:321. DOI: 10.1103/PhysRevLett.65.321

[56] Brendel J, Gisin N, Tittel W, Zbinden H. Pulsed energy-time entangled twin-photon source for quantum communication. Physical Review Letters. 1999;**82**:2594. DOI: 10.1103/PhysRevLett.82.2594

[57] Tittel W, Brendel J, Zbinden H, Gisin N. Quantum cryptography using entangled photons in energy-time bell states. Physical Review Letters. 2000;**84**:4737. DOI: 10.1103/PhysRevLett.84.4737

[58] Shalm LK, Hamel DR, Yan Z, Simon C, Resch KJ, Jennewein T. Three-photon energy-time entanglement. Nature Physics. 2013;**9**:19-22. DOI: 10.1038/nphys2492

[59] Allen L, Beijersbergen MW, Spreeuw RJC, Woerdman JP. Orbital angular momentum of light and the transformation of Laguerre-Gaussian laser modes. Physical Review A. 1992;**45**:8185-8189. DOI: 10.1103/PhysRevA.45.8185

[60] Yao AM, Padgett MJ. Orbital angular momentum: Origins, behavior and applications. Advances in Optics and Photonics. 2011;**3**:161-244. DOI: 10.1364/AOP.3.000161

[61] Wang J, Yang JY, Fazal IM, Ahmed N, Yan Y, Huang H, et al.

Terabit free-space data transmission employing orbital angular momentum multiplexing. Nature Photonics. 2012;**6**:488-496. DOI: 10.1038/nphoton.2012.138

[62] Barreiro JT, Wei TC, Kwiat PG. Beating the channel capacity limit for linear photonic superdense coding. Nature Physics. 2008;**4**:282-286. DOI: 10.1038/nphys919

[63] Mair A, Vaziri A, Weihs G, Zeilinger A. Entanglement of the orbital angular momentum states of photons. Nature. 2001;**412**:313-316. DOI: 10.1038/35085529

[64] Leach J, Jack B, Romero J, Jha AK, Yao AM, Franke-Arnold S, et al. Quantum correlations in optical angle-orbital angular momentum variables. Science. 2010;**329**:662-665. DOI: 10.1126/science.1190523

[65] Dada AC, Leach J, Buller GS, Padgett MJ, Andersson E. Experimental high-dimensional two-photon entanglement and violations of generalized Bell inequalities. Nature Physics. 2011;**7**:677-680. DOI: 10.1038/nphys1996

[66] Krenn M, Huber M, Fickler R, Lapkiewicz R, Ramelow S, Zeilinger A. Generation and confirmation of a (100 × 100)-dimensional entangled quantum system. PNAS. 2014;**111**:6243-6247. DOI: 10.1073/pnas.1402365111

[67] Leach J, Jack B, Romero J, Ritsch-Marte M, Boyd RW, Jha AK, et al. Violation of a Bell inequality in two-dimensional orbital angular momentum state-spaces. Optics Express. 2009;**17**:8287-8293. DOI: 10.1364/OE.17.008287

[68] Fickler R, Campbell G, Buchler B, Lam PK, Zeilinger A. Quantum entanglement of angular momentum states with quantum numbers up to 10,010. PNAS. 2016;**113**:13642-13647. DOI: 10.1073/pnas.1616889113

[69] Zhou ZY, Li Y, Ding DS, Zhang W, Shi S, Shi BS. Classical to quantum optical network link for orbital angular momentum-carrying light. Optics Express. 2015;**23**:18435-18444. DOI: 10.1364/OE.23.018435

[70] Ding DS, Zhang W, Zhou ZY, Shi S, Xiang GY, Wang XS, et al. Quantum storage of orbital angular momentum entanglement in an atomic ensemble. Physical Review Letters. 2015;**114**:050502. DOI: 10.1103/PhysRevLett.114.050502

[71] Ding DS, Zhang W, Shi S, Zhou ZY, Li Y, Shi BS, et al. High-dimensional entanglement between distant atomic-ensemble memories. Light: Science and Applications. 2016;**5**:e16157. DOI: 10.1038/lsa.2016.157

[72] Fasel S, Alibart O, Tanzilli S, Baldi P, Beveratos A, Gisin N, et al. High-quality asynchronous heralded single-photon source at telecom wavelength. New Journal of Physics. 2014;**6**:163. DOI: 10.1088/1367-2630/6/1/163

[73] Chen J, Lee KF, Liang C, Kumar P. Fiber-based telecom-band degenerate-frequency source of entangled photon pairs. Optics Letters. 2006;**31**:2798-2800. DOI: 10.1364/OL.31.002798

[74] Bocquillon E, Couteau C, Razavi M, Laflamme R, Weihs G. Coherence measures for heralded single-photon sources. Physical Review A. 2009;**79**:035801. DOI: 10.1103/PhysRevA.79.035801

[75] Fortsch M, Furst JU, Wittmann C, Strekalov D, Aiello A, Chekhova MV, et al. A versatile source of single photons for quantum information processing. Nature Communications. 2013;**4**:1818. DOI: 10.1038/ncomms2838

[76] Clark AS, Collins MJ, Judge AC, Mägi EC, Xiong C, Eggleton BJ. Raman scattering effects on correlated photon pair generation in chalcogenide. Optics Express. 2012;**20**:16807-16814. DOI: 10.1364/OE.20.016807

[77] Mosley PJ, Lundeen JS, Smith BJ, Wasylczyk P, U'Ren AB, Silberhorn C, et al. Heralded generation of ultrafast single photons in pure quantum states. Physical Review Letters. 2008;**100**:133601. DOI: 10.1103/PhysRevLett.100.133601

[78] Rarity JG, Tapster PR, Jakeman E, Larchuk T, Campos RA, Teich MC, et al. Two-photon interference in a Mach-Zehnder interferometer. Physical Review Letters. 1990;**65**:1348. DOI: 10.1103/PhysRevLett.65.1348

[79] Clauser JF, Horne MA, Shimony A, Holt RA. Proposed experiment to test local hidden-variable theories. Physical Review Letters. 1969;**23**:880-884. DOI: 10.1103/PhysRevLett.23.880

[80] Collins D, Gisin N, Linden N, Massar S, Popescu S. Bell inequalities for arbitrarily high dimensional systems. Physical Review Letters. 2002;**88**:040404. DOI: 10.1103/PhysRevLett.88.040404

[81] James DFV, Kwiat PG, Munro WJ, White AG. Measurement of qubits. Physical Review A. 2001;**64**:052312. DOI: 10.1103/PhysRevA.64.052312

[82] Blinov BB, Moehring DL, Duan LM, Monroe C. Observation of entanglement between a single trapped atom and a single photon. Nature. 2004;**428**:153-157. DOI: 10.1038/nature02377

[83] Matsukevich DN, KA. Quantum state transfer between matter and light. Science. 2004;**306**:663-666. DOI: 10.1126/science.1103346

[84] Togan E, Chu Y, Trifonov AS, Jiang L, Maze J, Childress L, et al. Quantum entanglement between an optical photon and a solid-state spin qubit. Nature. 2010;**466**:730-734. DOI: 10.1038/nature09256

[85] Piro N, Rohde F, Schuck C, Almendros M, Huwer J, Ghosh J, et al. Heralded single-photon absorption by a single atom. Nature Physics. 2011;7:17-20. DOI: 10.1038/nphys1805

[86] Clausen C, Usmani I, Bussieres F, Singouard N, Afzelius M, de Riedmatten H, et al. Quantum storage of photonic entanglement in a crystal. Nature. 2011;**469**:508-511. DOI: 10.1038/nature09662

[87] Kumar P. Quantum frequency conversion. Optics Letters. 1990;**15**:1476-1478. DOI: 10.1364/OL.15.001476

[88] Tanzilli S, Tittel W, Halder M, Alibart O, Baldi P, Gisin N, et al. A photonic quantum information interface. Nature. 2005;**437**:116-120. DOI: 10.1038/nature04009

[89] Takesue H. Single-photon frequency down-conversion experiment. Physical Review A. 2010;**82**:013833. DOI: 10.1103/PhysRevA.82.013833

[90] Curtz N, Thew R, Simon C, Gisin N, Zbinden H. Coherent frequency down-conversion interface for quantum repeaters. Optics Express. 2010;**18**:22099-22104. DOI: 10.1364/OE.18.022099

[91] Zaske S, Lenhard A, Kebler CA, Kettler J, Hepp C, Arend C, et al. Visible-to-telecom quantum frequency conversion of light from a single quantum emitter. Physical Review Letters. 2012;**109**:147404. DOI: 10.1103/PhysRevLett.109.147404

[92] Takesue H. Erasing distinguishability using quantum frequency up-conversion. Physical Review Letters. 2008;**101**:173901. DOI: 10.1103/PhysRevLett.101.173901

[93] Rakher MT, Ma L, Slattery O, Tang X, Srinivasan K. Quantum transduction of telecommunications-band single photons from a quantum dot by frequency upconversion. Nature Photonics. 2010;**4**:786-791. DOI: 10.1038/nphoton.2010.221

[94] Guinness HJ, Raymer MG, McKinstrie CJ, Radic S. Quantum frequency translation of single-photon states in a photonic crystal fiber. Physical Review Letters. 2010;**105**:093604. DOI: 10.1103/PhysRevLett.105.093604

[95] Ates S, Agha I, Gulinatti A, Reach I, Rakher MT, Badolato A, et al. Two-photon interference using background-free quantum frequency conversion of single photons emitted by an InAs quantum dot. Physical Review Letters. 2012;**109**:147405. DOI: 10.1103/PhysRevLett.109.147405

[96] Ikuta R, Kusaka Y, Kitano T, Kato H, Yamamoto T, Koashi M, et al. Wide-band quantum interface for visible-to-telecommunication wavelength conversion. Nature Communications. 2011;**2**:537. DOI: 10.1038/ncomms1544

[97] Guerrerio T, Martin A, Sanguinetti B, pelc JS, Langrock C, Fejer MM, et al. Nonlinear interaction between single photons. Physical Review Letters. 2014;**113**:173601. DOI: 10.1103/PhysRevLett.113.173601

[98] Zhou ZY, Li Y, Ding DS, Zhang W, Shi S, Shi BS, et al. Orbital angular momentum photonic quantum interface. Light: Science and Applications. 2016;**5**:e16019. DOI: 10.1038/lsa.2016.19

[99] Zhou ZY, Liu SL, Li Y, Ding DS, Zhang W, Shi S, et al. Orbital angular momentum-entanglement frequency transducer. Physical Review Letters. 2016;**117**:103601. DOI: 10.1103/PhysRevLett.117.103601

[100] Zhou ZY, Liu SL, Liu SK, Li YH, Ding DS, Guo GC, et al. Superresolving phase measurement with short-wavelength NOON states by quantum frequency up-conversion. Physical Review Applied. 2017;**7**:064025. DOI: 10.1103/PhysRevApplied.7.064025

[101] Liu SL, Liu SK, Li YH, Shi S, Zhou ZY, Shi BS. Coherent frequency bridge between visible and telecommunications band for vortex light. Optics Express. 2017;**25**:24290-24298. DOI: 10.1364/OE.25.024290

[102] Walker T, Miyanishi K, Ikuta R, Takahashi H, Kashanian SV, Tsujimoto Y, et al. Long-distance dingle photon transmission from a trapped ion via quantum frequency conversion. Physical Review Letters. 2018;**120**:203601. DOI: 10.1103/PhysRevLett.120.203601

[103] Ikuta R, Kobayashi T, Kawakami T, Miki S, Yabuno M, Yamashita T, et al. Polarization insensitive frequency conversion for an atom-photon entanglement distribution via a telecom network. Nature Communications. 2018;**9**:1997. DOI: 10.1038/s41467-018-04338-x

[104] Bock M, Eich P, Kucera S, Kreis M, Lenhard A, Becher C, et al. High-fidelity entanglement between a trapped ion and a telecom photon via quantum frequency conversion. Nature Communications. 2018;**9**:1998. DOI: 10.1038/s41467-018-04341-2

[105] Dréau A, Tchebotareva A, Mahdaoui AE, Bonato C, Hanson R. Quantum frequency conversion of single photons from a nitrogen-vacancy center in diamond to telecommunication wavelengths. Physical Review Applied. 2018;**9**:064031. DOI: 10.1103/PhysRevApplied.9.064031

[106] Shentu GL, Pelc JS, Wang XD, Sun QC, Zheng MY, Fejer MM, et al. Ultralow noise up-conversion detector

and spectrometer for the telecom band. Optics Express. 2013;**21**:13986-13991. DOI: 10.1364/OE.21.013986

[107] Liu SL, Zhou Q, Zhou ZY, Liu SK, Li Y, Li YH, et al. Multiplexing heralded single photons in orbital angular momentum space. Physical Review A. 2019;**100**:013833. DOI: 10.1103/PhysRevA.100.013833

[108] Migdall AL, Branning D, Castelletto S. Tailoring single-photon and multiphoton probabilities of a single-photon on-demand source. Physical Review A. 2002;**66**:053805. DOI: 10.1103/PhysRevA.66.053805

[109] Collins MJ, Xiong C, Rey IH, Vo TD, He J, Shahnia S, et al. Integrated spatial multiplexing of heralded single-photon sources. Nature Communications. 2013;**4**:2582. DOI: 10.1038/ncomms3582

[110] Kaneda F, Christensen BG, Wong JJ, Park HS, McCusker KT, Kwiat PG. Time-multiplexed heralded single-photon source. Optica. 2015;**2**:1010-1013. DOI: 10.1364/OPTICA.2.001010

[111] Puigibert MG, Aguilar GH, Zhou Q, Marsili F, Shaw MD, Verma VB, et al. Heralded single photons based on spectral multiplexing and feed-forward control. Physical Review Letters. 2017;**119**:083601. DOI: 10.1103/PhysRevLett.119.083601

[112] Joshi C, Farsi A, Clemmen S, Ramelow S, Gaeta AL. Frequency multiplexing for quasi-deterministic heralded single-photon sources. Nature Communications. 2018;**9**:847. DOI: 10.1038/s41467-018-03254-4

[113] Nasr MB, Carrasco S, Saleh BEA, Sergienko AV, Teich MC, Torres JP, et al. Ultrabroadband biphotons generated via chirped quasi-phase-matched optical parametric down-conversion. Physical Review Letters. 2008;**100**:183601. DOI: 10.1103/PhysRevLett.100.183601

[114] Kues M, Reimer C, Roztocki P, Cortés LR, Sciara S, Wetzel B, et al. On-chip generation of high-dimensional entangled quantum states and their coherent control. Nature. 2017;**546**:622. DOI: 10.1038/nature22986

[115] Liu SL, Zhou ZY, Liu SK, Li YH, Li Y, Yang C, et al. Coherent manipulation of a three-dimensional maximally entangled state. Physical Review A. 2018;**98**:062316. DOI: 10.1103/PhysRevA.98.062316

[116] Kovlakov EV, Straupe SS, Kulik SP. Quantum state engineering with twisted photons via adaptive shaping of the pump beam. Physical Review A. 2018;**98**:060301. DOI: 10.1103/PhysRevA.98.060301

[117] Liu SL, Yang C, Xu ZH, Liu SK, Li Y, Li YH, et al. A high-dimensional quantum frequency converter. arXiv:1908.10569 [quant-ph]

[118] Wang JW, Paesani S, Dong YH, Santagati R, Skrzypczyk P, Salavrakos A, et al. Multidimensional quantum entanglement with large-scale integrated optics. Science. 2018;**360**:285-291. DOI: 10.1126/science.aar7053

[119] Qiang X, Zhou X, Wang J, Wilkes CM, Loke T, O'Gara S, et al. Large-scale silicon quantum photonics implementing arbitrary two-qubit processing. Nature Photonics. 2018;**12**:534-539. DOI: 10.1038/s41566-018-0236-y

Chapter 4

Single-Photon Frequency Conversion for Quantum Interface

Yuanhua Li and Xianfeng Chen

Abstract

Single-photon frequency conversion for quantum interface plays an important role in quantum communications and networks, which is crucial for the realization of quantum memory, faithful entanglement swapping and quantum teleportation. In this chapter, we will present our recent experiments about single-photon frequency conversion based on quadratic nonlinear processes. Firstly, we demonstrated spectrum compression of broadband single photons at the telecom wavelength to the near-visible window, marking a critical step towards coherent photonic interface. Secondly, we demonstrated the nonlinear interaction between two chirped broadband single-photon-level coherent states, which may be utilized to achieve heralding entanglement at a distance. Finally, we theoretically introduced and experimentally demonstrated single-photon frequency conversion in the telecom band, enabling switching of single photons between dense wavelength-division multiplexing channels. Moreover, quantum entanglement between the photon pair is maintained after the frequency conversion. Our researches have realized three significant quantum interfaces via single-photon frequency conversion, which hold great promise for the development of quantum communications and networks.

Keywords: quantum interface, quantum network, single-photon frequency conversion, periodically poled lithium niobate waveguide, sum frequency generation, cascaded nonlinear process, spectrum compression, spontaneous down-conversion

1. Introduction

In recent years, nonlinear quantum optics has developed rapidly, such as quantum communication [1], quantum computation [2], quantum memory [3], quantum network [4], and so on. In order to realize these quantum applications, coherent quantum interface is a significant quantum device as it is capable of frequency and bandwidth in the telecom band is converted simultaneously. Quantum network is an important platform to study quantum communication, quantum computation, and quantum memory. Quantum network consists of many nodes and the quantum communication channels of the connected nodes, and the quantum communication channels of different connected nodes need to be connected by a quantum interface. Any node in a quantum network has the capability of quantum communication, quantum memory, quantum entanglement swapping, and generation of single photon sources. When the quantum channel of different nodes performs the conversion of quantum communication and quantum memory, a quantum interface is needed, which can simultaneously realize spectral compression and frequency conversion because the bandwidth and the center frequency of the single photon used in quantum communication and quantum memory are different. When two broadband photons of different nodes' quantum channels are connected by quantum entanglement swapping, the connected quantum interface can efficiently couple the two broadband photons and simultaneously realize the nonlinear frequency conversion of the two broadband photons. The nonlinear up-conversion of two broadband photons in nonlinear crystals can be converted into a high frequency narrowband photon, which provides a basis for implementing different types of quantum interfaces.

Periodically polarized lithium niobate (PPLN) waveguides have higher second-order nonlinear coefficients than other nonlinear crystals. PPLN waveguide not only transmits a wide spectrum but is also easily integrated and processed into PPLN waveguide chips. It also can preserve the quantum properties of photons. The nonlinear effect of PPLN waveguide chip can realize the up-conversion and down-conversion of nonlinear frequencies of different wavelength photons. Therefore, PPLN waveguide chip is ideal for implementing different types of quantum interfaces.

In our work, we utilized PPLN waveguide chip to realize several kinds of different functions of single-photon frequency conversion for coherent quantum interface. First, we have demonstrated the generated coherent quantum interface suitable for quantum communication at 1550 nm and quantum memory in the near-visible window. We exploit a positively chirped single-photon-level laser pulse and a negatively chirped classical laser pulse by sum frequency generation (SFG) process to compress the bandwidth of the positively chirped single-photon-level laser pulse in a PPLN waveguide chip—from 800 to 13.7 GHz—which is approaching the bandwidth regime of some quantum memories. In the same time, one can flexibly convert the 1550-nm telecom-band photons into the near-infrared window [5]. Second, we have experimentally demonstrated the SFG between two broadband single-photon-level coherent states by using a high-efficiency PPLN waveguide chip. The SFG efficiency of 1.06×10^{-7} is realized, which provides potentially feasible quantum applications, such as faithful entanglement swapping without post-selection and nonlinear interaction between single photons with an integrated device at room temperature. What's more, long-distance quantum communication can be achieved by broadband single photons generated in a spontaneous parametric down conversion (SPDC) source [6]. Finally, we have realized the core quantum interface for fiber quantum networks. We report single-photon frequency conversion in a telecommunication band based on cascaded quadratic nonlinearity, i.e., SFG and difference frequency generation (DFG), in a PPLN waveguide. It shows that the frequency of single photons can be precisely converted to a DFG with continuous adjustability in a wide telecommunication band and their quantum characteristics are protected after the single-photon frequency conversion [7].

2. Methodology and result

2.1 Spectral compression of single-photon-level laser pulse

Photons at 1550 nm are critical to all quantum information tasks via an optical-fiber network. Nevertheless, the narrowband photons in the near-visible wavelength regime possess the most efficient quantum memories and an ability of being easily detected by a silicon avalanche photodiode (APD). Many theoretical schemes have been proposed to achieve the pulse compression or the frequency conversion. For instance, the 1550-nm photons can be converted into the near-infrared window through the nonlinear processes, such as the SFG. As theoretical schemes are diverse, they can be characterized by one common shortage, namely realizing only one operation. Therefore, it is highly expected that an optical technology is capable of simultaneously performing spectrum compression and frequency conversion in the telecom band.

In our experiment, spectral compression of single-photon-level laser pulse is generated by SFG between a positively chirped single-photon-level laser pulse and a negatively chirped classical laser pulse. As known, a laser pulse can be expressed as the frequency-dependent electric field $E(\nu) = U(\nu)e^{i\phi(\nu)}$, where $U(\nu)$ and $\phi(\nu)$ represent the amplitude information and phase information of the laser pulse, respectively. Obviously, we can obtain a chirp result when a transform-limited laser pulse is subject to a quadratic phase $\phi(\nu) \approx A(\nu - \nu_0)^2$, where A is a constant and ν_0 is the center frequency. In terms of $d\phi(\nu)/d\nu = 2\pi t$, one can obtain $d\phi(\nu)/d\nu = 2\pi t = 2A(\nu - \nu_0)$; thus, $\nu = \nu_0 + \pi t/A$ is realized.

The negatively chirped classical laser pulse of frequency with $\nu_{0,P}$ increases linearly in time t_1, i.e., $\nu_{0,P}(t_1) = \nu_{0,P} + \pi t_1/A$, and the positively chirped single-photon-level pulse frequency with $\nu_{0,Q}$ decreases linearly in time t_2, $\nu_{0,Q}(t_2) = \nu_{0,Q} - \pi t_2/A$. Here, A is the chirp rate, $\nu_{0,P}$ and $\nu_{0,Q}$ are the center frequency of these two laser pulse sources, and $\Delta t = t_1 - t_2$ is a relative time delay between the negatively chirped classical laser pulse and positively chirped single-photon-level laser pulse. In our work, $\nu_{0,P}$ and $\nu_{0,Q}$ are equal as chirped laser pulse and negatively laser pulse are two replicas of the laser source. When the positively chirped single-photon-level laser pulse and negatively classical laser pulse simultaneously reach the PPLN waveguide chip, a blue-shifted frequency component of negatively classical laser pulse $(\nu_{0,P} + \pi t_1/A)$ would match a red-shifted frequency component of positively chirped single-photon-level laser pulse $(\nu_{0,Q} - \pi t_2/A)$ with the relative time delay Δt, and all frequency components of these two laser pulses would sum to a new narrow frequency with $\nu_{0,SFG}(\Delta t) = \nu_{0,P} + \nu_{0,Q} + \pi \Delta t/A$. The expected (TH) intensity bandwidth (FWHM) of the SFG photon is given by the following equation [8]:

$$\Delta\nu_{SFG}^{TH} \approx \frac{\ln 4}{A}\sqrt{\frac{1}{\Delta\nu_P^2} + \frac{1}{\Delta\nu_Q^2}}, \tag{1}$$

where $\Delta\nu_P$ and $\Delta\nu_Q$ are the bandwidths (FWHM). The FWHM bandwidth $\Delta\nu$ is limited by group velocity dispersion, and decreases linearly with the length of the PPLN waveguide, i.e., $\Delta\nu = \Delta\hat{\nu}/L$, where $\Delta\hat{\nu} = 4200\,\text{GHz}\cdot\text{cm}$ is the spectral acceptance of the waveguide. When the full FWHM bandwidths of positively chirped single-photon-level laser pulse and negatively chirped classical laser pulse are used in the waveguide, the maximum SFG efficiency is guaranteed.

A schematic of our experimental setup is shown in **Figure 1**. In our experiment, the mode-locked optical-fiber laser pulse source generates 500-fs pulses at 1551.54 nm center wavelength, about 6.4 nm spectral bandwidth (6.4 nm is the FWHM of the spectral intensity distribution), 59.98 MHz repetition rate, and 45.2 MW average power. We split the laser pulse source into two replicas using a 50:50 beam splitter (BS), and then one of the two replicas of laser pulse is sent to a broadband fiber Bragg grating 1 (FBG1); at the same time, the other laser pulse is coupled into the FBG2. The parameters of FBG1 and FBG2 are exactly the same (1547 nm center wavelength, 39 nm FWHM bandwidth, and 5 nm/cm chirp rate).

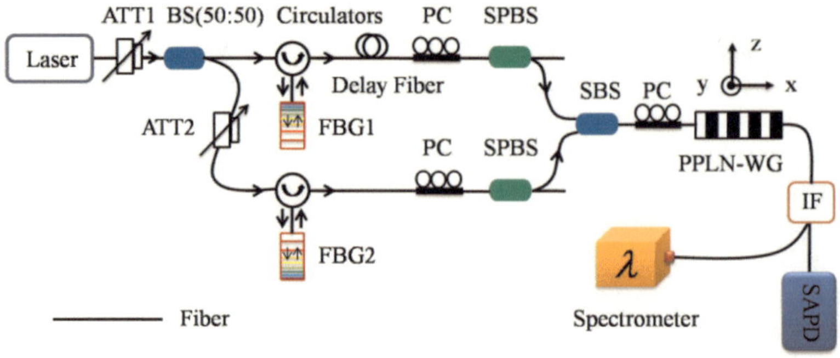

Figure 1.
Experimental set-up. ATT, variable optical attenuator; BS, beam splitter (50:50); Circulators, optical fiber circulators; PC, polarization controller; FBG, fiber Bragg grating; Delay Fiber, optical adjustable delay fiber; SPBS, single mode polarization beam splitter (single mode to polarization maintaining); SBS, single mode beam splitter (single mode to polarization maintaining); PPLN-WG, PPLN waveguide chip; IF, interference filter; SAPD, silicon APD [5].

It is known that FBG can be used for up-chirping and down-chirping, depending on the choice of the side from which the laser pulse is reflected. Thus, the two different chirp laser pulses after FBG1 and FBG2 are the same but with the opposite sign. It means that the positively chirped and negatively laser pulses have an equal and opposite chirp, $\pm A$. A positively chirped laser pulse is generated through FBG1 to introduce a linear chirp by group velocity dispersion. The other laser pulse is negative after a broadband FBG2. A variable optical attenuator (ATT1) is used to create a positively chirped single-photon-level laser pulse, and the other variable optical attenuator (ATT2) is used to control the energy of negatively chirped classical laser pulse for this experiment.

Then, the positively chirped single-photon-level laser pulse and the negatively chirped classical laser pulse are combined by a 1550/1550 nm 50:50 single-mode beam splitter (SBS) and couple into the z-cut PPLN waveguide chip through the optical-fiber pigtail. Two single-mode polarization beam splitters (SPBS (200:1)) and two polarization controllers (PCs) are used for controlling the positively chirped single-photon-level laser pulse and the negatively chirped classical laser pulse to the TM mode; it is known that the PPLN waveguide chip only supports Type-0 ($ee \rightarrow e$) phase matching in our work. A temperature controller (TC) is used for adjusting the PPLN waveguide chip's temperature to keep the QPM of the SFG process. The spectrally narrowed SFG photon pulse can be obtained in the PPLN waveguide chip, after interference filter (IF) with a nominal bandwidth of 20 nm (FWHM) centered around 780 nm (loss is about 1.2 dB), and then coupled into an optical-fiber-coupled spectrometer. Finally, the SFG photons are detected by a SAPD, whose detection efficiency is up to 60% at 775 nm and dark count rate is 26 Hz. In our experiment, a superconducting single photon detector (SSPD) is used to calibrate and monitor the counts of photons of positively chirped single-photon-level laser pulse, whose detection efficiency is up to 10% at 1551 nm and dark count rate is 600 Hz. Using the IF, any residue of the positively or negatively chirped photons have to be filtered out from the SFG photons by a factor of 10^{-18}.

The reverse-proton-exchange PPLN waveguide chip is 52-mm long and QPM to perform the SFG process 1551 nm + 1551 nm $\rightarrow$ 775.5 nm. It is poled through the quasi-phase-matching period of 19.6 μm. Moreover, one has a total fiber-to-output-facet throughput of approximately −1.5 dB for the telecom band. The PPLN waveguide chip is antireflection coated to prevent interference fringes and enhance the system efficiency.

We first obtain the spectrum of the positively chirped laser pulse by using an optical-fiber-coupled spectrometer and find a width 800 ± 20 GHz FWHM centered at 1551.54 nm (shown in red). The positively chirped laser pulse is then coupled through an optical fiber and superposed with the negatively chirped classical laser pulse (790 ± 20 GHz, centered at 1551.54 nm) in the PPLN waveguide chip for SFG. The SFG photons, after IF, are sent to a single-mode optical fiber and coupled into the optical-fiber-coupled spectrometer. Here, the FWHM bandwidths of both negatively and positively chirped laser pulses are smaller than the spectral acceptance of the PPLN waveguide chip ($\Delta\nu = \Delta\hat{\nu}/L = 807\,\text{GHz}$). Thus, the full FWHM bandwidths of positively and negatively chirped laser pulses are used in the PPLN waveguide chip, as expected. As shown in **Figure 2(a)**, we measure significant spectral compression of the positively chirped laser pulse. The initial bandwidth of the positively chirped laser pulse is 800 GHz centered at 1551.54 nm (shown in red). When the quadratic phase is applied and the two laser pulses are up-converted, the bandwidth of laser pulse generated reduces to 33 ± 1 GHz (FWHM) centered at 775.77 nm (shown in black), where the relative time delay $\Delta t = 0$.

Taking the resolution of our spectrometer into account, $\Delta\nu_R = 30 \pm 1$ GHz (FWHM), the actual bandwidth of the SFG photons after deconvolution is $\Delta\nu_{SFG}^{EXP} = \sqrt{\Delta\nu_M^2 - \Delta\nu_R^2} = 13.7 \pm 4.2$ GHz (FWHM). The spectra are given by normalized intensities and, for the up-converted case, correspond to the average of 10 consecutive scans of 15 min acquisition time. This result agrees closely with theory, $\Delta\nu_{SFG}^{TH} = 9.8 \pm 0.7$ GHz (FWHM) from Eq. (1), using the expected chirp parameter $A = (-2.52 \pm 0.01) * 10^8 fs^2$ given by the geometry of our FBG. Therefore, a bandwidth compression ratio of 58:1 is achieved in the positively chirped laser pulse (**Figure 2(b)**).

The center wavelength of the SFG photons can be controlled by adjusting the relative delay Δt between the input pulses at the PPLN waveguide chip. The SFG spectrum of the created laser pulse could be given by a function of the delay time, with the fitted center wavelengths shown in **Figure 3**. The experimental results show that the wavelength depends linearly on the delay time, as expected. The linear fit gives a slope of -0.0247 ± 0.001 nm/ps. In terms of the slope data, we measure the negatively chirp parameter of $A = (-2.55 \pm 0.01) * 10^8 fs^2$, in good agreement with the chirp parameter $A = (-2.52 \pm 0.01) * 10^8 fs^2$ of the FBG1. It is also shown that the bandwidth compression ratio independent of the optical relative delay Δt, which agrees closely with the theoretical result from the above Eq. (1).

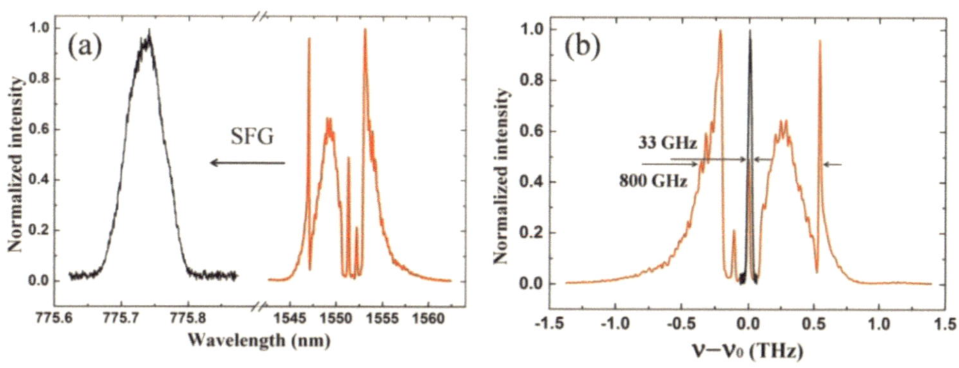

Figure 2.
The positively chirped pulse spectrum and up-converted laser pulse spectrum (a) and relative frequency (b) [5].

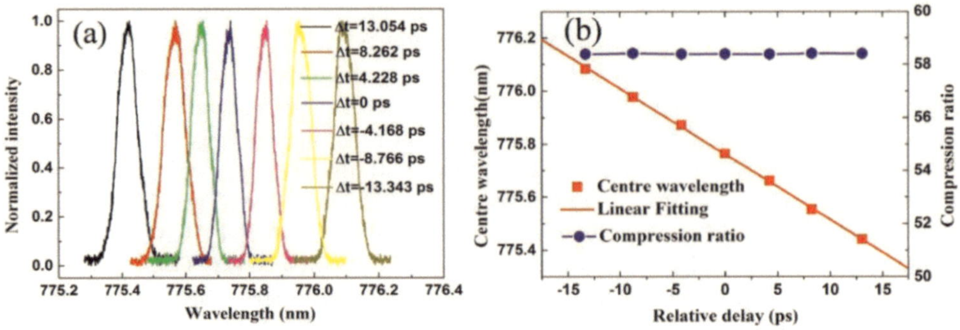

Figure 3.
The SFG spectrum of the created laser pulse (a), central wavelength and compression ratio of the output pulses versus the optical relative delay (b). Error bars are smaller than the data points [5].

In our experiment, it is verified that any SFG photons detected by the SAPD is the result of the SFG process, and not a SHG of the positively or negatively chirped photons. Moreover, any residue of photons the positively or negatively chirped laser pulse has to be filtered out from SFG photons by a factor of 10^{-18}. Once the number of positively chirped laser pulse is controlled to single-photon level, the detected SHG counts from the positively chirped laser pulse drop to its dark counts (3.5 Hz). When the input power of the negatively chirped laser pulse is less than 0.6 nW, the SHG photons are also equal to the dark counts. The efficiency of SFG is then given by $\eta_{SFG} = P_{SFG}/\beta N$, where P_{SFG} is the number of SFG photons per second, β is the repetition rate of seed laser, and N is average of photons per second of positively chirped laser pulse.

As shown in **Figure 4**, the power of the negatively chirped laser pulse is keeping at 0.6 nW. The SFG photons and SFG efficiencies are measured. The average of photons per second ($N_1 = 0.933$ and $N_2 = 0.302$) of positively chirped laser pulse can be obtained with the ATT2. By adjusting the relative delay Δt, SFG photons and SFG efficiencies of different situations are measured (like **Figure 3(b)**). At the same time, it is found that the overall conversion efficiency of SFG varies with the relative delay Δt. When the relative time delay $\Delta t = 0$, the maximum SFG efficiency is 7.82×10^{-6} with the average of photons of positively chirped laser pulse (0.933), where the dark counts (3.5 Hz) are subtracted. Here, the total losses have

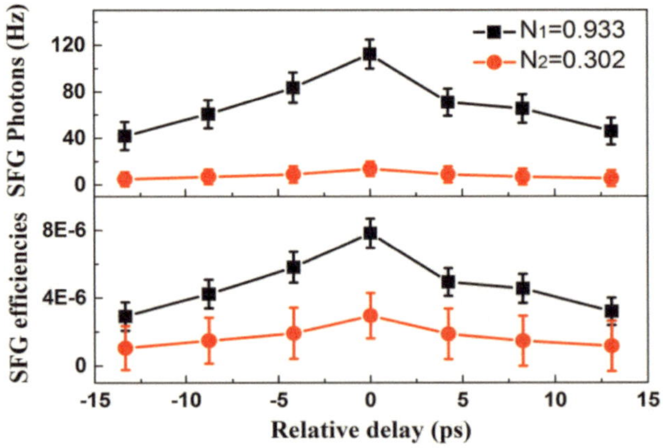

Figure 4.
SFG photons (top) and SFG efficiencies (bottom). The abscissa is a variable optical relative delay between the negatively and positively chirped laser pulses at the PPLN waveguide chip [5].

been considered, such as the coupling loss of 0.7 dB, reflection loss of 1.2 dB, total fiber-to-output-facet loss of 1.5 dB, and detection efficiency of 60% (see **Figure 4**).

The lower SFG signal for single photons required longer times than for the intense photons states. Thus, all the data are measured within a day to reduce the effects of drift. The results show that the SFG efficiency increases with increasing the average of photons of the positively chirped pulse (see **Figure 4**).

It is found that the SFG efficiency decreases with reducing the photons of negatively chirped laser pulse, and the efficiency of SFG also increases with increasing input power of the positively and negatively chirped laser pulse. Next, we obtain the efficiency of SFG in two ways: one, by controlling the photons of the negatively chirped laser pulse with the ATT1 and ATT2; the other by increasing the power of positively and negatively chirped laser pulse with the ATT1 and ATT2. **Figure 5** depicts the results of these two measurements. The SFG efficiencies, SFG photons, the power of produced harmonics, and error bars of them are accounted, where the dark counts (3.5 Hz) are subtracted.

As shown in **Figure 5(a)**, when the negatively chirped laser pulse (10 photons per pulse) and the positively chirped single-photon-level laser pulse (0.933 photons per pulse) are simultaneously sent to the PPLN waveguide chip, the maximum SFG efficiency of 4.58×10^{-7} is obtained, where the relative time delay $\Delta t = 0$. In **Figure 5(b)**, we use the ATT1 and ATT2 to keep the input power of positively and negatively chirped laser pulse at 203.1 and 202.8 μW, respectively. The power of produced harmonics $E_i (i = 0, 1, 2)$ can be measured, where E_0 is the total power of SFG and SHG of the positively and negatively chirped laser pulse, E_1 is the power of SHG of the positively chirped laser pulse, and E_2 is the power of SHG of the negatively chirped laser pulse. When the relative time delay $\Delta t = 0$, the power of SHG generated is $E_0 = 21.62\,\mu W$, which is obtained from SHG of the positively chirped laser pulse ($E_1 = 0.28\,\mu W$), SHG of the negatively chirped laser pulse ($E_2 = 0.01\,\mu W$), and SFG photons ($E_{SFG} = E_0 - E_1 - E_2 = 21.33\,\mu W$). In the case, the maximum SFG efficiency of 20% is obtained, where the relative time delay $\Delta t = 0$. Here, the total losses have been taken into account. We also find that the rate of SFG photons generated is 73 times of the rate of SHG photons generated of these two independent laser pulses.

In our scheme, although both the negatively and positively chirped laser pulses are at the same center wavelength, the power of SHG from each is kept below the power of SFG (see **Figure 5(b)**). At the same time, the SHG photons from the two independent laser pulses are also lower than the SFG photons when the bandwidth of positively chirped single-photon-level laser pulse is compressed

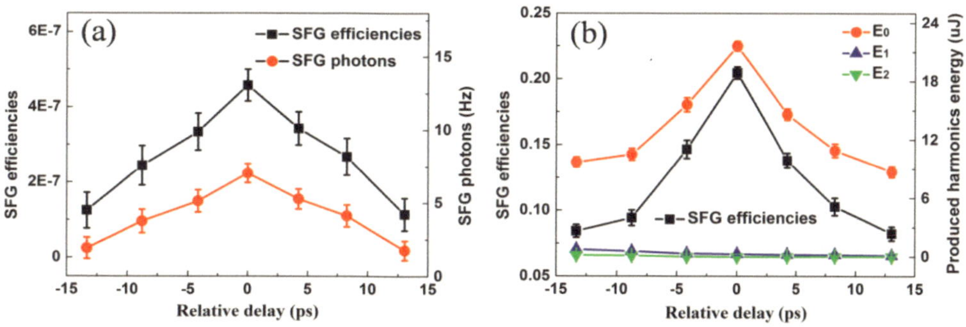

Figure 5.
SFG photons and SFG efficiencies (a), SFG efficiencies and the energy of generated SHG photons (b). The abscissa is a variable optical relative time delay between the negatively and positively chirped laser pulses at the PPLN waveguide chip [5].

(see **Figures 4** and **5(a)**). We can also confirm that by controlling the power of the negatively chirped laser pulse, considering a positively chirped single-photon-level laser pulse (0.933 photons per pulse). **Figure 6** depicts the results of experimental and theoretical SFG and SHG.

Once the input power of the negatively chirped laser pulse is more than 0.6 nW, the up-converted photons generated consists of SHG photons of the negatively chirped laser pulse, and SFG photons of the negatively chirped laser pulse and the positively chirped single-photon-level laser pulse. In our experiment, up-converted photons cannot be filtered out separately; thus, the SFG photons P_{SFG} cannot be measured. Here, we first send the negatively chirped laser pulse to the PPLN waveguide chip alone, and the SHG photons P_1 of the negatively chirped laser pulse can be measured. If we simultaneously couple the negatively chirped laser pulse and positively chirped single-photon-level laser pulse together into the PPLN waveguide chip, the photons P_0 of SFG and SHG can be obtained. The SFG photons generated are obtained with the equation $P_{SFG} = P_0 - P_1$. When the relative time delay $\Delta t = 0$, the SHG and SFG photons of different situations are obtained by controlling the power of the negatively chirped laser pulse (see **Figure 6(a)**). When the power of negatively chirped laser pulse is less than 4.8 nW, we find that SHG photons generated are lower than the SFG photons generated. When $P_{SFG} = P_1$, the SFG efficiency of 3.12×10^{-5} is obtained. The measured results show that the number of SHG photons will be more than the number of SFG photons when the power of negatively chirped laser pulse is more than 4.8 nW.

Next, we carry out the theoretical analysis for SHG and SFG photons. As shown in **Figure 6(b)**, the spectrum of the negatively chirped laser pulse is measured. It is found that the intensity of the negatively chirped laser pulse at 1551.54 nm is very close to zero. When the negatively chirped laser pulse is sent to the PPLN waveguide alone, the number of SHG photons generated is very low. Here, we assume that the power of the negatively chirped laser pulse which can be converted into SHG photons is E_{N_2} (black area), thus, the SHG photons $P_1 \propto |E_{N_2}|^2$. However, when the negatively and positively chirped laser pulses are simultaneously couple together into the PPLN waveguide chip, photons in all spectrum of the negatively chirped laser pulse can be used to produce the SFG photons. The full power of the negatively chirped laser pulse is E_{N_1}, as shown in **Figure 6(b)**. Thus, the SFG photons $P_{SFG} \propto E_{N_1} E_S$, where E_S is the power of the positively chirped single-photon-level laser pulse. When $P_{SFG}/P_1 \geq 1$, the number of SFG photons generated is more than the number of SHG photons. In the case, we obtain

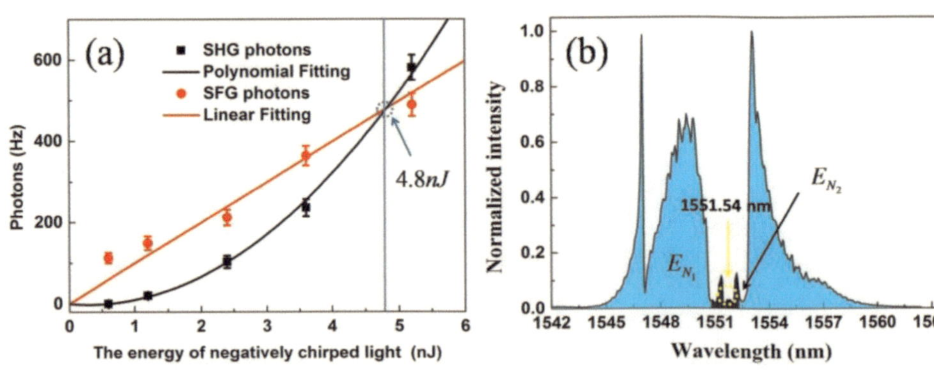

Figure 6.
SHG photons and SFG photons (a), the negatively chirped laser pulse spectrum (b). The dark counts (3.5 Hz) are subtracted, and the error bars are accounted [5].

$$\frac{E_{N_1}E_S}{|E_{N_2}|^2} \geq 1. \quad (2)$$

In terms of $E_{N_1} = qE_{N_2}$, one can obtain $E_{N_1} \leq q^2 E_S$, where q is proportional coefficient. In our experiment, one has $E_S = 7.3 \times 10^{-3}$nJ and $q = 26.8$; thus, $E_{N_1} \leq 5.2$ nJ is realized. This result agrees closely with experiment, as shown in **Figure 6(a)**.

In order to reduce the number of SHG photons to the dark counts (3.5 Hz), the power of the negatively chirped laser pulse must be very low. Thus, the SFG efficiency is limited. The way to improve SFG efficiency is to filter out the photons of wavelengths centered at 1551.54 nm of the negatively chirped laser pulse.

Furthermore, our results may provide potential application in standard decoy-state quantum key distribution. By considering a fiber attenuation of 0.2 dB/km, the coupling loss of 0.7 dB, the dark counts of 3.5 Hz, total fiber-to-output-facet loss of 1.5 dB, reflection loss of 1.2 dB, detection efficiency of 60%, and laser pulse with a 59.98 MHz repetition rate, the SFG efficiency of 7.82×10^{-6} will achieve a rate of about 8 bits/h on a distance of 20 km.

2.2 Nonlinear interaction between broadband single-photon-level coherent states

It has been demonstrated that parametric interactions hold numerous advanced applications in quantum communication, but strong optical fields are usually used to preserve quantum property [9]. Nonlinear interactions between single photons have been experimentally measured, such as spontaneous down-conversion [10] and cross-phase modulation [11]. Here, we take the next step and report, a SFG between two broadband single-photon-level coherent states. In our experiment, the SFG efficiency of 1.06×10^{-7} is realized, which provides potentially feasible quantum applications, such as faithful entanglement swapping without post-selection and nonlinear interaction between single photons with an integrated device at room temperature. What's more, long-distance quantum communication can be achieved by broadband single photons generated in a spontaneous parametric down conversion (SPDC) source.

In our experiment, a mode-locked optical fiber laser generates 500-fs pulses at 1551 nm with a repetition of 59.98 MHz and is used to generate the two chirped broadband single-photon-level coherent states after FBG1 and FBG2. These two chirped broadband coherent states are combined via a 50:50 SBS and sent to a PPLN waveguide chip. The PPLN waveguide chip length is 52 mm, and its total losses are 2.2 dB including a coupling loss of 0.7 dB and a total fiber-to-output-facet loss of 1.5 dB. The unconverted photons are deterministically separated from the SFG photons after IF, and the SFG photons are coupled into a silicon APD.

A schematic of the experimental setup is shown in **Figure 7**. The mode-locked optical fiber laser can generate two copies of the pulses with equal energy with a 50:50 BS. These two copies of the pulses are used to produce two broadband single-photon-level coherent states with ATT1 and ATT2. One of the two copies of the laser pulses is couple into the FBG1, and the other laser pulse is coupled into the FBG2. Thus, the spectrums of two copies of the photons after FBG1 and FBG2 are the same but with the opposite sign. In our experiment, the positively chirped single-photon-level coherent state is generated with the FBG2, and the other single-photon-level coherent state is the negatively chirped coherent state after the FBG1.

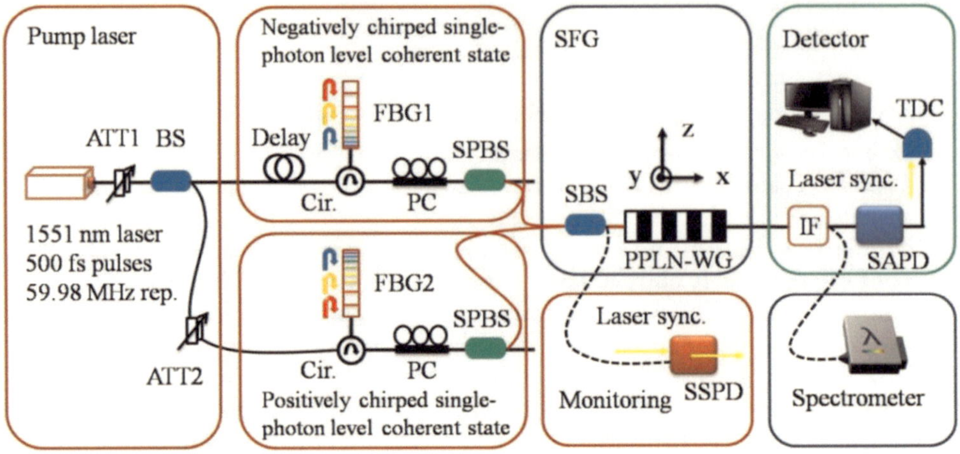

Figure 7.
Experimental set-up. ATT, variable optical attenuator; BS, beam splitter (50:50); Circulators, optical fiber circulators; PC, polarization controller; FBG, fiber Bragg grating; Delay Fiber, optical adjustable delay fiber; SPBS, single mode polarization beam splitter (single mode to polarization maintaining); SBS, single mode beam splitter (single mode to polarization maintaining); PPLN-WG, PPLN waveguide chip; IF, interference filter; SAPD, silicon APD [6].

The FBG can be used to produce the up-chirping and down-chirping, depending on the choice of the side from which the laser pulse is reflected. As the two copies of the laser pulses are from the same seed laser, they have the same initially center frequency ω_0. When two copies of the laser pulses with instantaneous frequencies described as $\omega_1(t) = \omega_0 + At$ and $\omega_2(t) = \omega_0 - At$ (where A is the linear chirp parameter) undergo SFG, the frequency of the laser pulse generated is constant $(\omega_1(t) + \omega_2(t) = 2\omega_0)$; thus, the high frequency long narrowband laser pulse can be realized.

Subsequently, the positively and negatively chirped coherent states are sent to the PPLN waveguide chip by the fiber pigtail. The PPLN waveguide chip is a reverse-proton-exchange waveguide that is QPM to perform the SFG process 1551 nm + 1551 nm → 775.5 nm. The PPLN waveguide chip has a QPM period of 19.6 μm. Two SPBS (200:1) and two PCs are used for controlling the positively and negatively chirped single-photon-level coherent states to the TM mode. A SSPD is used to calibrate and monitor the counts of the positively and negatively chirped single-photon-level photons, whose detection efficiency is up to 10% at 1551 nm and dark count rate of 600 Hz. A stable TC is used to keep at 27° to maintain the QPM condition of the SFG process. The long narrowed SFG photons of higher frequency are generated after the IF, with 20 nm FWHM bandwidth and 780 nm center wavelength (about 1.2 dB loss). Finally, the SFG photons are detected with a SAPD. The SFG photons and the laser clock signal are recorded using a TDC.

We first measure the spectrums of the negatively chirped laser pulse (800 ± 20 GHz spectral FWHM bandwidth, and 1551.56 nm center wavelength) and the positively chirped laser pulse (790 ± 20 GHz FWHM, and 1551.56 nm center wavelength) by using a spectrometer, which are shown in **Figure 8(a)**. The pump light (the negatively chirped laser pulse) and the signal light (the positively chirped laser pulse) are simultaneously sent to the PPLN waveguide chip. By using an IF, the generated SFG photons are sent into the spectrometer.

In our experiment, when the classical pump and signal laser pulses are coupled into the PPLN waveguide chip, the up-converted photons consist of SHG of pump light, SHG of signal light, and SFG of pump light and signal light. In our experiment, up-converted photons cannot be filtered out separately; thus, the SFG

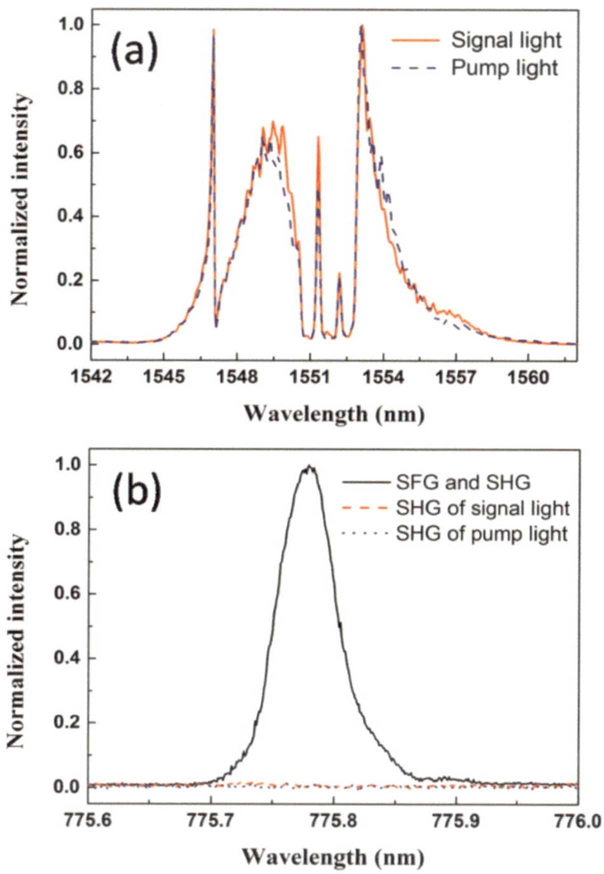

Figure 8.
Pump and signal light spectrums (a), and the spectrums of up-converted light (SFG and SHG), SHG of signal light, SHG of pump light (b) [6].

photons N_{SFG} cannot be measured. First, the pump light is sent to the PPLN waveguide chip alone, and the number of SHG photons N_1 can be obtained. Similarly, the number of SHG photons N_2 of signal light is obtained when only the signal light is sent to the PPLN waveguide chip alone. When we simultaneously couple the pump and signal laser pulses together into the PPLN waveguide chip, we can obtain the number of photons N_0 of SFG and SHG. Therefore, the number of SFG photons is obtained with the equation $N_{SFG} = N_0 - N_1 - N_2$. For the SFG photons to be measured distinctly, any residue of pump and signal light has to be filtered out from up-conversion photons in this work. Here, the efficiency of SFG is given by $\eta_{SFG} = N_{SFG}/N_A$, where N_A is the number of photons per second of the signal light.

For instance, the input power of the signal and pump light is keeping at 200.2 and 200.4 μW, respectively. When they are simultaneously sent to the PPLN waveguide chip, the FWHM bandwidth and power of the created up-conversion light can be measured. If pump light (or signal light) is sent to the PPLN waveguide chip alone, the bandwidth and power of SHG of pump light (or signal light) can be obtained. When the PPLN waveguide chip's temperature is kept at 27°, as shown in **Figure 8(b)**, the FWHM bandwidth of the created up-conversion light is about 0.07 nm, centered at 775.78 nm. In this case, the power of up-conversion light is 20.9 μW (involving the SFG and SHG), which is obtained from SHG of signal light (0.25 μW), SHG of pump light (0.01 μJ), and SFG of pump light and signal light (20.54 μW). The maximum SFG efficiency of 5% is obtained, which is used for estimating the efficiency of SFG between two single-photon-level states in our work. As shown in **Figure 9**, the efficiency of SFG depends on the PPLN waveguide chip's temperature. Correcting for all of these losses, the intrinsic device maximum SFG efficiency of 20% is obtained, as expected.

When the number of photons per pulse of pump light and signal light is attenuated to 5.13 and 5.64, respectively, the detected count of SHG of signal light (or pump light) drop to 3.8 Hz (dark count). It can be shown that any photons detected by the SPAD are the SFG photons when the signal and pump light are attenuated to single-photon-per-pulse simultaneously. Therefore, photons of SHG of pump light and signal light are not considered in our scheme.

In our experiment, the number of photons per pulse (equal for pump and signal) are obtained with ATT1 and ATT2, as they can be detected and calibrated by the SSPD. According to our experimental results, the SFG efficiency and SFG photons are shown in **Figure 10**. Here, dark counts of 3.8 Hz and the total losses of about 5.6 dB have been taken into account.

The overall conversion efficiency of SFG is given by $\eta'_{SFG} = \xi(\lambda)hc\Delta\nu L^2/\lambda tbp$, where $\xi(\lambda)$ is the measured up-conversion efficiency of the PPLN waveguide chip, λ is the center wavelength of pump light, tbp is the time-bandwidth product, $\Delta\nu$ is the bandwidth of pump light, and L is the length of the PPLN waveguide chip. Consider that $\xi(\lambda) = 5\%/(W \cdot cm^2)$ and $tbp = 0.4$ in our experiment, thus the expected SFG efficiency is $\eta'_{SFG} \approx 1 \times 10^{-7}$. We measure the efficiency of $\eta_{SFG} = (1.06 \pm 0.23) \times 10^{-7}$. It is shown that the SFG efficiency is high enough to provide efficient, yet simpler solutions to linear optics based protocols for the heralded creation of maximally entangled pairs or for the implementation of device-independent quantum key distribution.

For SFG between two single photons, our efficiency of SFG is about eight times of the efficiency of SFG given by Sangouard et al. [12]. When the single-photon-level pump and signal light are not chirped in our experiment, the SFG photons are zero. This is because the intensity of pump light (or signal light) at 1551.56 nm is very low (see **Figure 8(a)**). However, when the negatively and positively chirped pulses are simultaneously coupled into the PPLN waveguide chip, photons in all spectrums of the negatively and positively chirped light are used to create the SFG photons. Therefore, we can improve the efficiency of SFG between single photons by using the chirped technology.

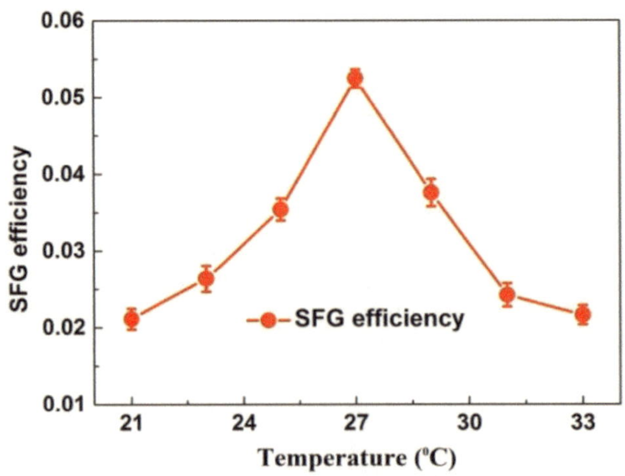

Figure 9.
SFG efficiency. The efficiency of SFG can be controlled by keeping the PPLN-WG chip's temperature [6].

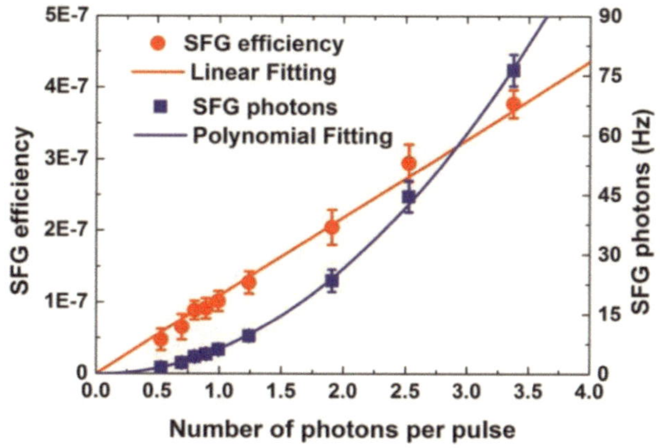

Figure 10.
SFG efficiency and SFG photons [6].

2.3 Single-photon frequency conversion via cascaded quadratic nonlinear processes

In quantum networks, many nodes are needed, which are used to perform quantum information memory/processing tasks. Each node has the ability to generate quantum states and perform quantum Bell-state measurements. All nodes are connected by using optical fibers. Frequency conversion has important applications in fiber quantum networks, and frequency converters are set to light. At the intermediate node of the fiber quantum network, the information transmission mode of the corresponding wavelength is obtained, and the specific wavelength signal carrying the information is transferred to the other wavelength. The development of this technology has greatly improved the transmission capacity of the optical network and the flexibility of the entire network.

In addition to the frequency conversion between the communication band and the visible band, single-photon frequency conversion between communication bands, like classical fiber networks, has important applications in large-scale quantum networks, as well as between independent sources of different users. Quantum cryptic transmission or quantum key distribution also requires different wavelengths to be converted to coincidence before interference. Therefore, the single photon frequency conversion interface between communication bands is critical in quantum communication.

However, there are not many experiments to achieve single-photon frequency conversion in the communication band. There are only two known solutions and each of these experimental solutions has imperfections. The first solution is to achieve high-precision frequency conversion by optical single sideband modulator (OSSB). This method can eliminate the frequency distinguishability between different single photons, but the frequency conversion range that this scheme can achieve covers only dozens. Gigahertz does not meet the requirements of communication networks. The second scheme is consistent with the four-wave mixing principle of the classical light in the previous section. The third-order nonlinearity of the optical fiber is used to realize the frequency conversion of the communication band, but we know that the third-order nonlinear coefficient is much smaller than 2. The order nonlinear coefficient, thus one must use 750 m long fiber, which is very unfavorable for device integration.

In order to make up for the shortcomings of the above two schemes, we use the high second-order nonlinear coefficients of the PPLN waveguide and the wide-band type-0 quasi-phase matching to realize the single-photon frequency conversion based on the cascaded second-order nonlinear process. In the experiment, we realized the precise frequency conversion between DWDM channels through the cascading process of SFG + DFG. At the same time, we also proved that the quantum characteristics of single photons remain in this process. Our experiment is very suitable for the construction of quantum networks.

The nonlinear process of frequency conversion of a single photon can be described by the following effective Hamiltonian [13]:

$$\hat{H} = i\hbar\left(\chi_1 E_{P1}\hat{\alpha}_s\hat{\alpha}_m^\dagger + \chi_2 E_{P2}\hat{\alpha}_m\hat{\alpha}_t^\dagger - \mathrm{H}.c.\right), \tag{3}$$

where $\hat{\alpha}_i$ a is the annihilation operator for the wave at frequency ω_i, ($i = s; m; t$ is signal, mediate, and target photons, respectively). $\chi_{1,2}$ are coupling constants that are proportional to the second-order susceptibility $\chi^{(2)}$ of the PPLN waveguide chip, E_{P1} and E_{P2} are the electric field amplitudes of pump lasers, and H.c. is a Hermitian conjugate. The conversion efficiency η_c can be obtained by using the Heisenberg equation of motion, which is given by the following equation:

$$\eta_c(L) = \frac{\eta_1\eta_2 P_{P1}P_{P2}|\cos\left[2(\varphi_1 - \varphi_2)\right]|}{(\eta_1 P_{P1} + \eta_2 P_{P2})} \times \left\{1 - \cos\left[\eta_1 P_{P1} + \eta_2 P_{P2}\right]^{(1/2)} L\right\}^2, \tag{4}$$

where φ_1 and φ_2 are the phases of the two pumps, respectively. η_1 and η_2 are the efficiencies of the normalized power, and $\eta_1 \approx \eta_2 = 1.1/\mathrm{W\ cm}^2$. The efficiency of single-photon frequency conversion is 100% if $P_{P1} = P_{P2} = \pi^2/\left(2\eta_1 L^2\right)$.

It is very challenging for realizing simultaneous phase matching in our work. However, this problem can be easily solved using QPM. In the experiment, we realized the broadband single photon frequency conversion of the communication band by the type-0 cascading SFG/DFG process. A 5-cm-long PPLN waveguide chip is used, and its poling period is 19.0 μm. In addition, the cascaded $\chi^{(2)} : \chi^{(2)}$ processes give rise to a large effective third nonlinearity typically $10^4 - 10^5$ times larger than a pure $\chi^{(3)}$ process, which manifests an advantage over its counterpart of FWM, e.g., in fibers.

The experimental setup of the single-photon frequency conversion is shown in **Figure 11(a)**. The center wavelengths of the two auxiliary pumps P1 and P2 are 1547.72 nm (CH37) and 1544.53 nm (CH41), respectively. Both narrow-band continuous lasers increase power through an erbium-doped fiber amplifier (EDFA). A set of DWDMs placed behind the EDFA, using 150 dB of isolation to filter out the noise generated during the EDFA amplification process. Then, we use another set of DWDMs to combine the three signals of signal single photon, P1 and P2 into one beam and couple into the waveguide. The combined light undergoes a cascaded nonlinear process SFG + DFG in the PPLN waveguide, converting the signal photons into target photons. At the output of the waveguide, we use a third set of DWDMs to pick out the target photons, while using 180 dB of isolation to filter out the noise generated during P1, P2, and conversion. In our experimental scheme, frequency-adjustable single-photon frequency conversion can be achieved by adjusting the wavelength of the auxiliary pump light.

For the performance of the converter, we tested the photon pair prepared by SPDC instead of the weak coherent pulse. The photon pair preparation process is shown in **Figure 11(b)**. After a continuous laser with a center wavelength of 1555.8 nm is amplified by EDFA power, a continuous light of 777.9 nm is generated by a frequency doubling process in a PPLN waveguide. The SPDC photon pair is prepared by pumping the second waveguide with the frequency-doubled

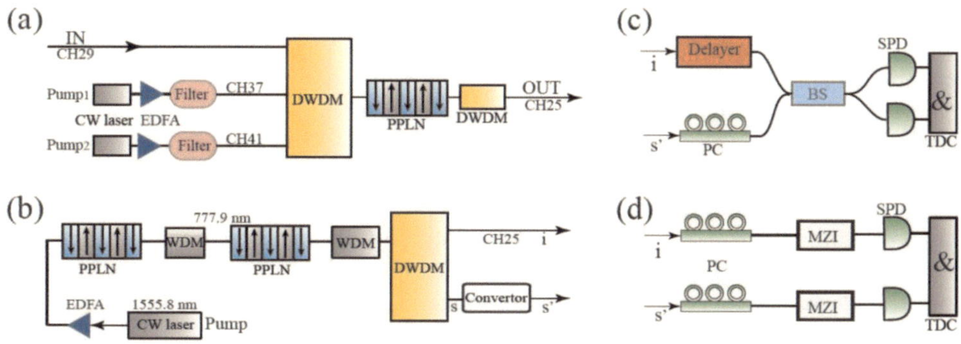

Figure 11.
Experimental setup of (a) the single-photon frequency convertor, (b) photon-pairs preparation, (c) Hong-Ou-Mandel interference, and (d) measurement of time-energy entanglement. DWDM, 100-GHz dense wavelength-division multiplexing; CH25 and CH37 and CH41, DWDM channels with 100-GHz spacing defined by ITU-TG.694.1; Filter, combination of DWDM and band pass filter (200–1540 and 1560–1800 nm); PC, polarization controller; SPD, single-photon detector (quantum efficiencies, $\eta_d = 10.0 \pm 0.2\%$; repetition frequency of gate, f = 50 MHz; width of gate, 1 ns; dark count probability per nanosecond, $D = 1 \times 10^{-6}$); EDFA, erbium-doped fiber amplifier; WDM, 780–1550-nm wavelength-division multiplexing; TDC, time-to-digital convertor (coincidence time window, t = 1 ns); Delayer, fiber path-length delayer; BS, 50:50 fiber beam splitter; MZI, 1-GHz unbalanced planar lightwave circuit Mach-Zehnder interferometers [7].

continuous light. WDM with an isolation of 180 dB is used to filter out noise. Finally, the corresponding two channels in signal (1554.13 nm, CH29) and idler (1557.36 nm, CH25) DWDM are separated.

First, we use classical light to test the conversion efficiency of tunable frequency conversion. By changing the center wavelength of the auxiliary pump P2, we achieved frequency conversion of the signal photon ±12 DWDM channels. In the classic light test, we set the signal power to 1 mW, and both P1 and P2 have a power of 10 mW (because the PPLN waveguide is limited by thermal effects, the maximum total input power of the waveguide we use for conversion is around 20 mW). We can get that the theoretical value is in good agreement with the experimental value, and the conversion efficiency of ±12CH is about 0.8%. In theory, the tunable frequency conversion has a full width at half maximum of about 76 nm, which covers the entire communication C-band.

In our experiment, the photon-pair generation rate is set to 0.002 per detection gate. The maximum single-photon conversion efficiency in the experiment is that when $P_{P1} = P_{P2} = 10$ mW, the maximum number of converted photons is 5.5×10^4/s, and the conversion efficiency is calculated to be 0.55%. At the same time, we measured that the noise generated by the frequency conversion process is 10^{-7}/gate. When the incident power of both auxiliary pumps is 179.5 mW, 100% conversion efficiency can be obtained. However, there are three main reasons for the reduction in conversion efficiency in actual experiments. The first reason is that the thermal effect of the PPLN waveguide limits the power of the incident light. This limitation is also the most important cause of the drop in conversion efficiency. We know that if a PPLN waveguide doped with MgO is used, the damage threshold can be greatly improved without changing the scattering properties of its refractive index, and it can withstand the total incident power of 360 mW. Another reason is the phase difference between the two auxiliary pumps P1 and P2, and we get the conversion efficiency proportional to $|\varphi_1 - \varphi_2|$. Since there is no synchronous lock between the phase differences between P1 and P2 in our experiments, $|\varphi_1 - \varphi_2|$ is equal to 0.5 after averaging over time. This reason will directly lead to a 50% reduction in conversion efficiency. The last reason is also the problem that other frequency conversion methods will encounter, namely, the loss of fiber coupling and the loss caused by the filter. In our experiment, the total propagation and coupling loss in the PPLN waveguide and the filters is only 4.9 dB.

After measuring the maximum conversion efficiency experimentally, we measured the conversion accuracy of our single-photon frequency converter by HOM interference. The experimental setup for HOM interference is shown in **Figure 11(c)** [14], where i′ is the idler photon in the photon pair and s′ represents the converted signal photon. We placed a fiber optic delay in the i-photon beam path (Delayer, Delayer has an adjustment accuracy of 0.02 mm.), Delayer is used to change the optical path difference δx between i and s′; placing polarization control in the s′ photon path (PC), PC is used to change the polarization of the s′ photon to match the polarization of the i-photon, because the HOM interference visibility of the identical particles is best. In our experiments, the ratio of BS transmittance to reflectance used in our experiments was measured as T:R = 49.9:50.1. The single-photon detector used in this experiment is still a pulse gate detection method, but the performance is upgraded. The dark counts of both detectors are $D = 1 \times 10^{-6}$ per gate.

In HOM, we set the photon pair generation rate μ = 0.002 per gate; the single photon conversion efficiency is set to the maximum conversion efficiency under the constraint condition, i.e., 0.55%; and the measurement time of each data point is 1000 s. Under these conditions, the HOM interference curve we measured is shown in **Figure 12**. The calculated HOM interference visibility of the converted photon pair is $(80.5 \pm 3.5)\%$, and this contrast is much larger than the classical and nonclassical limit of 50%, which proves that our single photon converter does. We further analyzed the HOM interference gram and found that the full width at half maximum of the interference gram is 0.56 mm, and the corresponding time is 0.28 ps. Our theoretical full width at half maximum is about 0.50 mm; thus, the theoretical and experimental results are more consistent.

In addition to the true conversion of this feature, another important feature of single-photon frequency conversion is the preservation of quantum properties. As with some previous quantum frequency converters, we demonstrate that the quantum properties are not corrupted during the conversion process by measuring the quantum state visibility of the photon pairs before and after the conversion. In our experiments, the signal and idler photon pairs were prepared as time-energy entangled photon pairs. The time-energy entanglement pair is generated by a

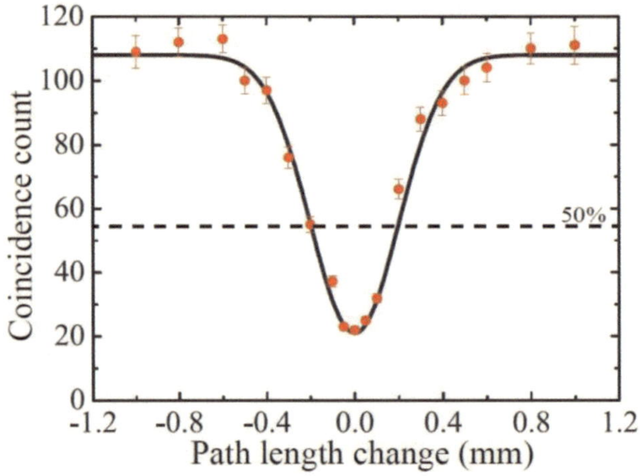

Figure 12.
Coincidence count as a function of the path-length change of one photon. The standard deviation is calculated by assuming a Poisson distribution of photon counts. The dashed horizontal line at 50% is the dividing line between the classical and nonclassical interference [7].

continuous laser (cw-laser) pumping the PPLN waveguide through the SPDC process [15]. Because the coherence time τ_1 of cw-laser is extremely long, and the bandwidth of the down-converted photon pair is much larger than the bandwidth of the pump photon, that is, the coherence time τ_2 between photon pairs is very short.

To measure the characteristics of time-energy entanglement and to exploit this entanglement, we use two unbalanced Mach-Zehnder interferometers (MZI) as shown in **Figure 11(d)**, connecting a single photon detector at the output of the MZI, measuring two coincidence count at the output. We define the optical path difference of the two paths of the MZI interferometer as τ_3. It is assumed that when $\tau_1 \geq \tau_3 > \tau_2$, the exit end of MZI does not have a single photon interference image, and the image of two-photon interference can be observed by the coincidence measurement.

The MZI used in our experiments is to change the phase difference between the long and short arms by adjusting the temperature. The phase change of 2π corresponds to a temperature change of 0.7°. The entangled interference image before single-photon frequency conversion is shown in **Figure 13**. Because it is necessary to observe the interference image under the two non-collinear base vectors, we can prove that the two-photon is entangled, so we set the MZI temperature of the signal

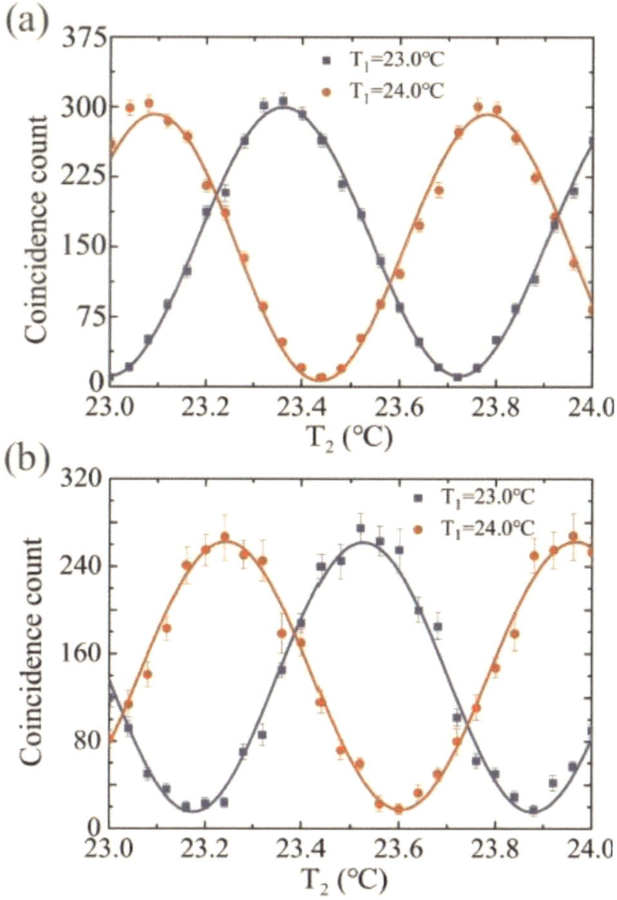

Figure 13.
Two-photon interference pattern (a) before and (b) after the frequency conversion. T_1 is the temperature of the MZI in the signal channel, and T_2 is the temperature in the idler channel. The integration time for each dot is (a) 15 s and (b) 3000 s [7].

channel to 23.0 and 24.0°, respectively. The collinear base vector is measured. From **Figure 13(a)**, we calculated the average pre-conversion entanglement visibility as $V = (93.8 \pm 1.6)\%$.

After the single photon frequency conversion, we again measure the entanglement visibility of the converted photon pair, as shown in **Figure 13(b)**. It is calculated that the converted entanglement visibility is $V = (88.2 \pm 5.1)\%$, and this visibility can still break the 71% visibility of Bell's inequality. Therefore, the 88.2% visibility after conversion proves that our single-photon frequency converter maintains the quantum properties of photons with a theoretical visibility of 91%. Since the converted count efficiency is low, the measurement time is extended from 15 s before conversion to 1000 s. The result convincingly shows that quantum entanglement is well preserved during the frequency conversion. Thus, the photon pairs can still be used for quantum communication tasks. We expect that our scheme may have applications in quantum systems, such as quantum communication on multiuser fiber quantum networks and quantum cryptography with independent single photon sources.

3. Conclusion

We have demonstrated three kinds of quantum interfaces with different functions. First, we have experimentally demonstrated that the spectrum of single-photon-level laser pulse was compressed by a factor of 58 in a PPLN waveguide chip, where a chirped single-photon-level laser pulse and an antichirped laser pulse by fiber Bragg gratings are used to achieve a pulse with new frequency through SFG. Our results have demonstrated the potentially application for PPLN waveguide chip as an integrated platform for spectrum compressing and frequency conversing in the telecom band, such as coherent photonic interfaces between quantum communication at 1550 nm and quantum memory in the near-visible window. Second, we have realized high efficiency SFG between two broadband single-photon-level coherent states by using a high-efficiency PPLN waveguide chip. The result is already competitive with methods based on linear optics, and offers new possibilities such as heralding entanglement at a distance. This technique in our proposal marks a critical step toward the implementation of DI-QKD. Final, we have demonstrated single-photon frequency conversion using a cascaded quadratic nonlinearity in PPLN waveguides chip. The clear HOM dip observed in our experiment shows that the frequency has been precisely switched between DWDM channels. Moreover, the time-energy entanglement is well preserved during the frequency conversion. All works above are of great significance to the development of quantum optics.

Conflict of interest

The authors declare no conflict of interest.

Author details

Yuanhua Li[1*] and Xianfeng Chen[2]

1 Department of Physics, Jiangxi Normal University, Nanchang, China

2 State Key Laboratory of Advanced Optical Communication Systems and Networks, Department of Physics and Astronomy, Shanghai Jiao Tong University, Shanghai, China

*Address all correspondence to: lyhua1984@163.com

References

[1] Sun QC, Mao YL, Chen SJ, Zhang W, Jiang YF, Zhang YB, et al. Quantum teleportation with independent sources and prior entanglement distribution over a network. Nature Photonics. 2016; **10**(10):671-675. DOI: 10.1038/nphoton.2016.179

[2] Miller J, Miyake A. Resource quality of a symmetry-protected topologically ordered phase for quantum computation. Physical Review Letters. 2015;**114**(12):120506. DOI: 10.1103/PhysRevLett.114.120506

[3] Specht HP, Nölleke C, Reiserer A, Uphoff M, Figueroa E, Ritter S, et al. A single-atom quantum memory. Nature. 2011;**473**(7346):190-193. DOI: 10.1038/nature09997

[4] Yurke B, Denker JS. Quantum network theory. Physical Review A. 1984;**29**(3):1419. DOI: 10.1103/PhysRevA.29.1419

[5] Li YH, Xiang T, Nie YY, Sang MH, Chen XF. Spectral compression of single-photon-level laser pulse. Scientific Reports. 2017;7:43494. DOI: 10.1038/srep43494

[6] Li YH, Xiang T, Nie YY, Sang MH, Chen XF. Nonlinear interaction between broadband single-photon-level coherent states. Photonics Research. 2017;**5**(4): 324-328. DOI: 10.1364/PRJ.5.000324

[7] Xiang T, Sun QC, Li YH, Zheng YL, Chen XF. Single-photon frequency conversion via cascaded quadratic nonlinear processes. Physical Review A. 2018;**97**(6):063810. DOI: 10.1103/PhysRevA.97.063810

[8] Lavoie J, Donohue JM, Wright LG, Fedrizzi A, Resch KJ. Spectral compression of single photons. Nature Photonics. 2013;7(5):363-366. DOI: 10.1038/nphoton.2013.47

[9] Thew RT, Zbinden H, Gisin N. Tunable upconversion photon detector. Applied Physics Letters. 2008;**93**(7): 071104. DOI: 10.1063/1.2969067

[10] Shalm LK, Hamel DR, Yan Z, Simon C, Resch KJ, Jennewein T. Three-photon energy–time entanglement. Nature Physics. 2013;**9**(1):19-22. DOI: 10.1038/nphys2492

[11] Matsuda N, Shimizu R, Mitsumori Y, Kosaka H, Edamatsu K. Observation of optical-fibre Kerr nonlinearity at the single-photon level. Nature Photonics. 2009;**3**(2):95-98. DOI: 10.1038/nphoton.2008.292

[12] Sangouard N, Sanguinetti B, Curtz N, Gisin N, Thew R, Zbinden H. Faithful entanglement swapping based on sum-frequency generation. Physical Review Letters. 2011;**106**(12):120403. DOI: 10.1103/PhysRevLett.106.120403

[13] Kumar P. Quantum frequency conversion. Optics Letters. 1990;**15**(24): 1476-1478. DOI: 10.1364/OL.15.001476

[14] Hong CK, Ou ZY, Mandel L. Measurement of subpicosecond time intervals between two photons by interference. Physical Review Letters. 1987;**59**(18):2044-2046. DOI: 10.1103/PhysRevLett.59.2044

[15] Franson JD. Bell inequality for position and time. Physical Review Letters. 1989;**62**(19):2205-2208. DOI: 10.1103/PhysRevLett.62.2205

Section 3

Nonreciprocal Control

Chapter 5

Optical Chirality and Single-Photon Isolation

Lei Tang and Keyu Xia

Abstract

Optical isolation is important for protecting a laser from damage due to the detrimental back reflection of light. It typically relies on breaking Lorentz reciprocity and normally is achieved via the Faraday magneto-optical effect, requiring a strong external magnetic field. Single-photon isolation, the quantum counterpart of optical isolation, is the key functional component in quantum information processing, but its realization is challenging. In this chapter, we present all-optical schemes for isolating the backscattering from single photons. In the first scheme, we show the single-photon isolation can be realized by using a chiral quantum optical system, in which a quantum emitter asymmetrically couples to nanowaveguide modes or whispering-gallery modes with high optical chirality. Secondly, we propose a chiral optical Kerr nonlinearity to bypass the so-called dynamical reciprocity in nonlinear optics and then achieve room-temperature photon isolation with low insertion loss. The concepts we present may pave the way for quantum information processing in an unconventional way.

Keywords: single-photon isolation, optical chirality, chiral light-matter interaction, optical isolator, optical circulator, chiral Kerr nonlinearity

1. Introduction

Controlling the flow of light is extremely essential for quantum information processing in integrated optical circuits. Nonreciprocal propagation of light at the single-photon level is in great demand for applications in quantum networks [1, 2], quantum computing [3], quantum entanglement [4], and quantum measurement [5]. For this purpose, nonreciprocal photonic elements, such as optical isolators and circulators, processing and routing of photonic signals at ultralow light level, or single-photon level in integrated optical circuits has been attracting a lot of interest.

The conventional implementations of nonreciprocal optical devices are achieved by using the Faraday magneto-optical effect. However, such Faraday-effect-based devices suffer large optical losses and conflict with miniaturization and integration. To date, integrated nonreciprocal photonic elements have been demonstrated via magneto-optical effect [6, 7], optical nonlinearity [8–10], and opto-mechanical system [11–13]. Very recently, Dong et al. proposed and experimentally realized a scheme to achieve a true single-photon non-reciprocity in a cold atomic ensemble [14]. However, most of these devices cannot achieve high isolations, low losses, and compatibility with single-photon level at the same time.

Nanophotonic devices control and confine the flow of light at a subwavelength scale. The strong confinement in these structures yields optical chirality, which is an inherent link between local polarization and the propagating direction of light [15]. If quantum emitters are embedded in these structures, chiral light-matter interaction is obtained, leading to propagation-direction-dependent emission, absorption, and scattering of photons. As a result, chiral light-matter interaction can be used to break time symmetry and achieve on-chip single-photon isolation. Some feasible schemes based on chiral quantum optics have been proposed to realize non-reciprocity at the single-photon level [16, 17], and optical isolators and circulators have been experimentally demonstrated in full quantum regime [18, 19].

Besides strong confinement of light, atoms can induce optical chirality. Here, optical chirality is chiral cross-Kerr (XKerr) nonlinearity induced in atoms. As a result of the chirality of atomic nonlinearity, the phases and transmission amplitudes of the forward- and backward-moving probe fields are sufficiently different after passing through atoms in two opposite directions. Thus, chiral XKerr nonlinear can achieve chip-compatible optical isolation with high isolation and low insert losses [20]. And very recently, XKerr-based optical isolators and circulators for high isolation, low loss, and an ultralow probe field at room temperature have been experimentally demonstrated [21].

2. Optical chirality and chiral light-matter interaction

The strong light confinement in subwavelength structures, e.g., nanofibers, nanowaveguides, or whispering-gallery mode (WGM) microresonators, can lock the local polarization of the light to its propagation direction. In these structures, the light is strongly confined transversely, leading to a longitudinal component of the electric field (e-field), which is parallel with the propagation direction. The longitudinal and transverse components, denoted as $\mathbf{E}_{\parallel}$ and $\mathbf{E}_{\perp}$, respectively, are comparable, and the former oscillates $\pm\pi/2$ radians out of phase with respect to the latter, with the $\pm$ sign depending on the propagation direction of the light (forward or backward) [15]:

$$\boldsymbol{E}_{\text{local}} = \boldsymbol{E}_{\perp} \pm i\boldsymbol{E}_{\parallel} \quad . \tag{1}$$

As a consequence, the local polarization of the light is elliptical, yielding a transverse spin angular momentum component, whose e-field rotates around an axis perpendicular to the propagation direction. The transverse spin components flip sign when the propagation of light reverses. This correlation of the polarization and the propagation direction is named the spin-momentum locking (SML) [15]. For the ideal case, $|\boldsymbol{E}_{\perp}| = |\boldsymbol{E}_{\parallel}|$, the e-field is circularly polarized.

In order to characterize what degree the e-field is locked to the momentum or what percentage of circular polarization of the local light in the nanostructures, the circular polarization unit vectors are defined as

$$\hat{\boldsymbol{\sigma}}^{\pm} = \frac{\hat{\mathbf{x}} \pm i\hat{\mathbf{y}}}{\sqrt{2}} \quad , \tag{2}$$

where $\hat{\boldsymbol{\sigma}}$ is for the right circularly polarized unit vector and $\hat{\boldsymbol{\sigma}}^{-}$ for the left circularly polarized one and $\hat{\mathbf{x}}$ and $\hat{\mathbf{y}}$ are unit vectors along the x and y directions. Thus, the optical chirality (OC) of an e-field is defined as [17, 22]:

$$C = \frac{|E(r)\cdot\hat{\sigma}^{-}|^2 - |E(r)\cdot\hat{\sigma}^{+}|^2}{|E(r)|^2} \quad . \tag{3}$$

Obviously, the OC is limited to a region from -1 to 1. Note that the value $\mathcal{C} = 1(-1)$ implies the e-field is entirely σ^--(σ^+-) polarized, while $\mathcal{C} = 0$ corresponds to a linear polarization. The intensity difference between the right circularly (σ^+) and the left circularly (σ^-) polarized components at the position r is calculated by $\mathcal{D} = |\mathbf{E}(\mathbf{r}) \cdot \hat{\sigma}^-|^2 - |\mathbf{E}(\mathbf{r}) \cdot \hat{\sigma}^+|^2$.

Then we focus on the interaction between the light possessing photonic SML and chiral quantum emitters with polarization-dependent dipole transitions. If a pair of counter-propagating spin-momentum-locked light interacts with quantum emitters, the interaction becomes chiral. In other words, the interaction strength for forward- and backward-propagating light modes is different. In this case, photon emission, absorption, and scattering become unidirectional. As a result, optical nonreciprocal flow of light can be achieved when a quantum emitter with degenerate transitions is populated in a specific spin state or one can shift the transition energy to make it couple (decouple) with one of the two of counter-propagating modes. On the basis of these effects, optical isolation can be realized at the single-photon level, which enables nonreciprocal single-photon devices, e.g., single-photon isolator and circulator. Next, we introduce the realization of single-photon isolators and circulators based on chiral light-matter interaction.

3. Single-photon isolation using chiral light-matter interaction

A single-photon isolator and circulator can be achieved by chirally coupling a quantum emitter to a passive, linear nanophotonic waveguide or a WGM microresonator which possesses optical chirality.

3.1 Single-photon isolator based on a nanophotonic waveguide

The type-I single-photon isolator is based on a line defect photonic crystal waveguide [16]. By carefully engineering the photonic crystal waveguide, it can have an in-plane circular polarization, and counter-propagating modes are counter circulating [22]. A quantum emitter is doped at the position where the waveguide possesses only the right-propagating σ^+-polarized light or left-propagating σ^--polarized light, as shown in **Figure 1a**. The doped emitter strongly interacts with the σ^+-polarized light but weakly couples to the σ^--polarized light. As a result, the time-reverse symmetry of the waveguide-emitter system breaks. The emitter scatters the forward- (right-) propagating single photons into an open environment whereas behaves transparently for the backward- (left-) propagating photons.

The steady-state transmission for the two atomic transitions coupling with waveguide is calculated by using the photon transport method [16, 23, 24]

$$t_{\pm}(\omega) = \frac{\omega - \omega_q - i(\gamma_{\pm} - \Gamma_{\pm})}{\omega - \omega_q + i(\gamma_{\pm} - \Gamma_{\pm})}, \tag{4}$$

where ω is the frequency of the input photon and ω_q is the frequency of the atomic transition. The detuning is defined as $\Delta = \omega_q - \omega$. In $\Gamma_{\pm} = V_{\pm}^2/2v_g$, $V_{\pm}$ is the coupling strength between the atom and the field in the waveguide, which is proportional to the atomic dipole moments $\mu_{\pm}$, and v_g is the group velocity of the photon in the waveguide. A Cs atom is used as the quantum emitter so that $\mu_+ = \sqrt{45}\mu_-$, and $\gamma_{\pm}$, $\Gamma_{\pm} \propto |\mu_{\pm}|^2$. As a consequence, $\gamma_+/\gamma_- = \Gamma_+/\Gamma_- \gg 1$. The transmission is defined as $T_{\pm} = |t_{\pm}|^2$. The isolation contrast is evaluated as $\Upsilon = (T_+ - T_-)/(T_+ + T_-)$ [23].

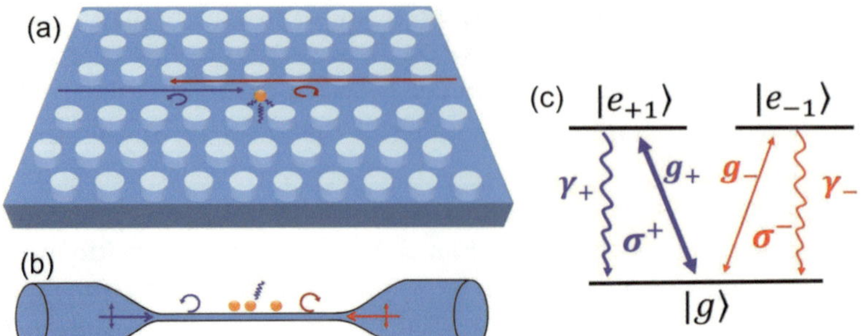

Figure 1.
Schematics of the single-photon isolators. (a) Single-photon isolator based on a photonic crystal waveguide asymmetrically coupling with a quantum emitter. The waveguide possesses local circular polarization, and its rotating direction is dependent on the propagating direction [16]. The quantum emitter is doped in these specific sites. (b) Single-photon isolator based on a photonic nanofiber asymmetrically coupling with quantum emitters. The nanofiber is realized as the waist of a tapered silica fiber, whose evanescent fields exhibit propagation-direction-dependent circular polarization [18]. Quantum emitters are located in the vicinity of the nanofiber. (c) Energy-level diagram for a quantum emitter with unbalanced decay rates $\gamma_+ \gg \gamma_-$ and different coupling strengths with $\sigma^{\pm}$-polarized light $g_+ \gg g_-$. The states $|e_{\pm 1}\rangle$ and $|g\rangle$ correspond to excited states and a ground state, respectively, and the transition $|g\rangle \leftrightarrow |e_{+1}\rangle$ is driven by σ^+-polarized light, while $|g\rangle \leftrightarrow |e_{-1}\rangle$ transition is driven by σ^--polarized light. Here, quantum emitters can be Cs atoms [25], Rb atoms [26], or quantum dots [27].

Due to the coupling of the atom to the waveguide and open environment, the ratio of atomic dissipation rate is set to $\alpha = \Gamma_+/\gamma_+ = \Gamma_-/\gamma_-$. If $\alpha \approx 1$, the single-photon isolation is achieved, as shown in **Figure 2a**. Obviously, T_- is almost equal to unity for a right-hand input, while T_+ is small if $10 \leqslant |\Delta|/\gamma_- \leqslant 30$. Note that the transmissions are the same, ~ 0 at $\Delta = 0$ for both of the right-handed and left-handed inputs. At vanishing detuning, irrespective of the propagating direction, photons cannot be transmitted through the waveguide. However, the linewidths of the dips for the left-handed input (blue solid line) are much broader than those for the right-handed input (red dashed line). Because of this directionality-dependent linewidth, a single-photon wave packet with a duration $\Gamma_+^{-1} \ll \tau \ll \Gamma_-^{-1}$ when incident from the right is mostly transmitted through the waveguide, while when it is incident from the left, it is mostly scattered away to the open environment. Note that the performance of the single-photon isolation is dependent on the ratio α. As seen from **Figure 2b**, a good nonreciprocal behavior occurs only around the critical coupling $\alpha \approx 1$, and if $5\alpha \leqslant |\Delta|/\gamma_- \leqslant 10\alpha$ and $0.53 < \alpha < 1.8$, the isolation contrast Υ can be larger than 0.8.

Low-loss silica nanophotonic waveguides with a strongly nonreciprocal transmission controlled by the internal state of spin-polarized atoms have been

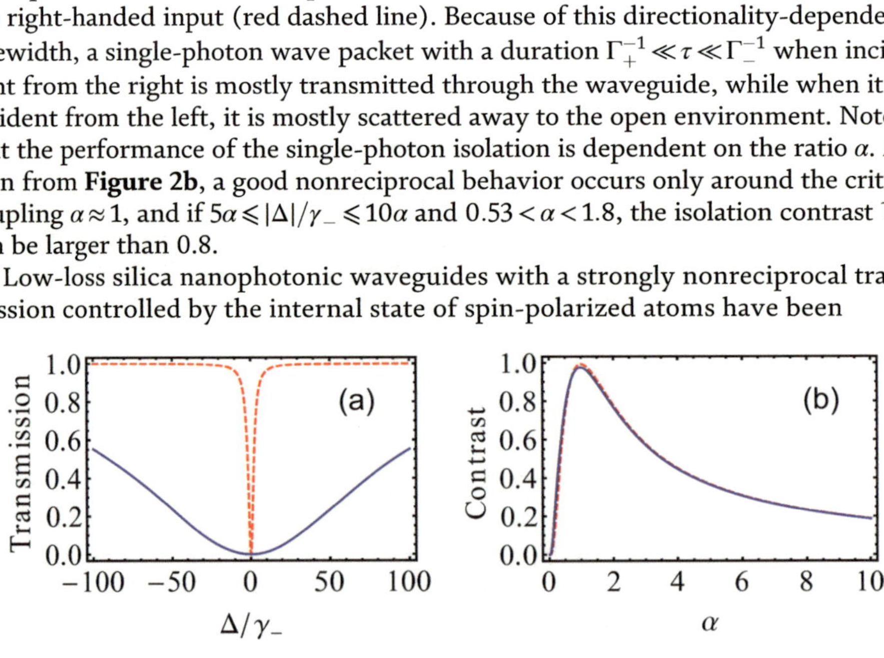

Figure 2.
(a) Steady-state transmission as a function of Δ for $\alpha = 1$. Solid blue curve is for transmission T_+, and dashed red curve is for transmission T_-. (b) Isolation contrast as a function of α. Solid blue curve indicates Υ for $|\Delta|/\gamma_- = 10\alpha$ and dashed red curve for $|\Delta|/\gamma_- = 5\alpha$. The two curves are mostly overlapped. Figures are reproduced with permission from [16].

demonstrated [18]. In the experiment, an ensemble of individual cesium atoms is located in the vicinity of a subwavelength-diameter silica nanofiber (250-nm radius) trapped in a nanofiber-based two-color optical dipole trap [28]. As shown in **Figure 1b**, a quasilinearly polarized light incident to the nanofiber exhibits chiral character at the position of the atoms: when the evanescent field propagates in the forward direction, it is almost fully σ^{+}-polarized, while it is almost fully σ^{-}-polarized if it propagates in the backward direction [18]. The experimental results show that the probe light with a power of 0.8 pW, corresponding to about 0.1 photon per excited-state lifetime, incident into nanofiber from different port obtains nonreciprocal transmissions, $T_{+} = 0.13 \pm 0.01$ and $T_{-} = 0.78 \pm 0.02$, yielding an isolation $\mathcal{F} = 10|\log(T_{-}/T_{+})| = 7.8$ dB [18]. Furthermore, trapping more atoms in the vicinity of the nanofiber can increase the isolation [18].

3.2 Single-photon isolator and circulator based on a WGM microresonator

The type-II single-photon isolator is based on a WGM microresonator. In this setup, when the linear polarized light enters the bus-waveguide from port P_1, it excites a σ^{+}-polarized counterclockwise (CCW) mode, while when it is incident from port P_2, it drives σ^{-}-polarized clockwise (CW) mode [16]. As a result, the two counter-propagating modes in the WGM microresonator couple to a quantum emitter with different dipole moments μ_{+} and μ_{-} corresponding to coupling strength g_{+} and g_{-}.

The transmission into the bus and drop waveguides are calculated by [16].

$$t_{\pm,B}(\omega) = 1 + \frac{2i\kappa_{ex1}}{\omega_c - \omega - i\kappa - \frac{|g_{\pm}|^2}{\omega_q - \omega - i\gamma_{\pm}}}, \tag{5}$$

$$t_{\pm,D}(\omega) = \frac{2i\sqrt{\kappa_{ex1}\kappa_{ex2}}}{\omega_c - \omega - i\kappa - \frac{|g_{\pm}|^2}{\omega_q - \omega - i\gamma_{\pm}}}. \tag{6}$$

where $\kappa_{ex1(2)} = V_{1(2)}^2/2v_g$ is the decay rate of the resonator due to the external coupling $V_{1(2)}$ to the bus (drop) waveguide, and the photons in both of the bus and drop waveguides have the same group velocity v_g assumed. The total decay rate of the resonator is $\kappa = \kappa_i + \kappa_{ex1} + \kappa_{ex2}$ where κ_i is the intrinsic decay rate of the resonator. The detuning is defined as $\Delta = \omega_c - \omega$, and $\omega_c = \omega_q$ is assumed where ω_c is the resonating frequency of the resonator and ω_q is the transition frequency of the quantum emitter.

In the configuration of this device, if the drop waveguide is removed, i.e., $\kappa_{ex2} = 0$, single-photon isolator is achieved (see **Figure 3**). In this case, $T_{\pm,B}$ is substituted with $T_{\pm}$. As shown in **Figure 4**, if $g_{-} = 0$ and $g_{+} \gg \kappa_i$, at $\Delta = 0$, $T_{+} = 1$, while $T_{-} \approx 0$. This can be achieved by using a negatively charged quantum dot as the quantum emitter [27]. If $|g_{-}| > 0$ and $\Delta \approx 0$, the nonreciprocal window disappears. However, when $|\Delta| \approx |g_{-}|$, $\gamma_{+} = 0$, and $g_{+}/\kappa_i \gg 1$, the right-moving photon can pass through the device, corresponding to $T_{+} = 1$ (solid blue curve), while the left-moving photon decays into the environment via the resonator, corresponding to $T_{-} = 0$ (solid red curve). At $|\Delta| \approx |g_{+}|$, the optical nonreciprocity is reversed. The device is transparent for left-moving photon but blocks the right-moving photon. If $\gamma_{+} \gg \kappa_i$, the part of the excitation of the right-moving photon can pass through the device (dotted green curve).

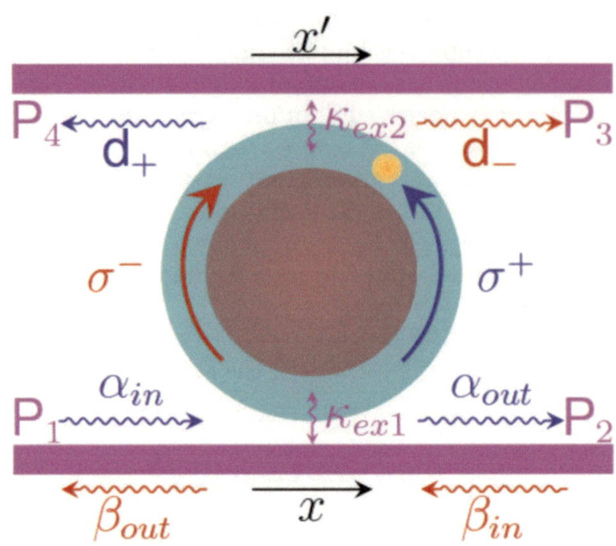

Figure 3.
Schematic of the single-photon isolator or circulator. There is a quantum emitter doped in a WGM microresonator, which possesses a σ^+-polarized CCW mode and a σ^--polarized CW mode. The microresonator couples to a lower bus waveguide with a rate κ_{ex1} and a upper drop waveguide with a rate κ_{ex2}. Reproduced with permission from [16].

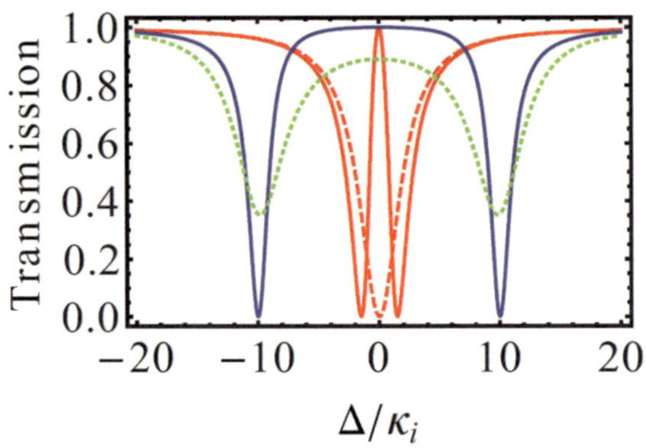

Figure 4.
Steady-state transmissions of the single-photon isolator using a WGM microresonator in the absence of the drop waveguide, i.e., $\kappa_{ex2} = 0$, and under the critical coupling condition $\kappa_{ex1} = \kappa_i$. Dashed and solid curves are for the transmission T_- when $g_- = 0$ and $g_- = g_+/\sqrt{45}$, while solid blue and dotted green curves are for the transmission T_+ when $\gamma_+ = 0$ and $\gamma_+ = 3\kappa_i$, respectively. $g_+ = 10\kappa_i$. Reproduced with permission from [16].

A WGM bottle microresonator coupling to the optical fiber and a single ^{85}Rb atom to realize the type-II optical isolator has been demonstrated [18]. In the experiment, for the bottle microresonator, it sustains WGMs with ultrahigh quality factor and small mode volume [26]. As a result of strong transverse confined, its evanescent fields of WGMs are almost fully circularly polarized, with OC $C > 0.96$ [26]. The single ^{85}Rb atom is prepared in the outermost $m_F = 3$ Zeeman substrate of the $F = 3$ hyperfine ground state. As seen from **Figure 1c**, the states $|e_{+1}\rangle$ and $|e_{-1}\rangle$ correspond to the excited states $|F' = 4, m_{F'} = +4\rangle$ and $|F' = 4, m_{F'} = +2\rangle$, respectively. In the experiment, the transition $|g\rangle \to |e_{+1}\rangle$ is much stronger than the $|g\rangle \to |e_{-1}\rangle$ transition, corresponding to the coupling strength, g_+ and g_-, between the atom and the two counterrotating WGMs, yielding $g_+/g_- = 5.8$ [18]. The experimental results show that when the probe light with power of 3 pW, corresponding to about 0.2 photon per resonator lifetime, obtains nonreciprocal transmissions through the system of $T_+ = 0.72 \pm 0.02$ in the forward direction and $T_- = 0.03 \pm 0.01$ in the backward direction, yielding an isolation $\mathcal{F} = 13$ dB.

The single-photon circulator consists of two waveguides and a WGM microresonator, and both of the bus and drop waveguides overcouple to the resonator, i.e., $\kappa_{ex1} = \kappa_{ex2} = 3\kappa_i$ (see **Figure 3**). As seen from **Figure 5a**, at $\Delta \sim 0$, for port P_1 input α_{in}, most excitation of the photon can transport to the bus-waveguide port P_2, $T_{+,B} = 0.85$ (solid blue curve), while the output to the drop-waveguide port P_4 is vanishingly small (dashed blue curve). As for port P_2 input β_{in}, there is a dip (peak) in the transmission $T_{-,D}$ ($T_{-,B}$), but the linewidth is very small, $\sim 0.16\kappa_i$, as shown in **Figure 5a**. In contrast, the whole transmission spectrum has a linewidth of $11\kappa_i$. As a result, a single-photon pulse bandwidth $0.16\kappa_i \ll \Delta B \ll 11\kappa_i$ can transport to the drop-waveguide port P_3 with a probability of 0.74. The probability of transmitting to the bus-waveguide port P_1 is small, ~ 0.02, yielding a contrast 0.95. The numerical simulations of the propagation of a single-photon pulse are performed in [16], which match the analytic forms well (see gray curves in **Figure 5a**). If $|\Delta| \sim g_-$, $T_{+,B} = 0.835$ to the P_2, $T_{+,D} = 0.032$ to P_4, and $T_{-,B} = 0.021$ to the P_1, $T_{-,D} = 0.733$ to P_3. As a consequence, the device forms a $P_1 \to P_2 \to P_3$ circulator. The single-photon incident from port P_1 transmits to port P_2, but the photon entering port P_2 comes out from port P_3.

If $\Delta \sim 0$, the numerical simulations of the propagation of a single-photon pulse in time as it passed through the circulator are performed in [16]. **Figure 5b** shows Gaussian pulse wave packets, $\phi(x,0)_{\pm,B} = \sqrt[4]{\tau^2/\pi} e^{-(x-x_0)^2/2\tau^2}$, incident from port P_1 and P_2 at the same time t_d. The transmissions are calculated by $T_{\pm,B/D} = \int_{-\infty}^{+\infty} \phi^*_{\pm,B/D}(x,t_d)\phi(x,t_d)dx$ to be $\{T_{+,B}, T_{-,B}, T_{+,D}, T_{-,D}\} = \{0.9, 0.178, 0.02, 0.675\}$ excitations output to port $\{P_2, P_1, P_4, P_3\}$. Obviously, a three-port circulator at the single-photon level is achieved.

Note that if the states are initially populated to $|6^2S_{1/2}, F = 4, m = -4\rangle$ for Cs atoms or $|5^2S_{1/2}, F = 3, m = -3\rangle$ for Rb atoms, $\mu_+ \ll \mu_-$, the optical nonreciprocity can be reversed, and the single-photon circulator forms a $P_2 \to P_1 \to P_4$ circulator.

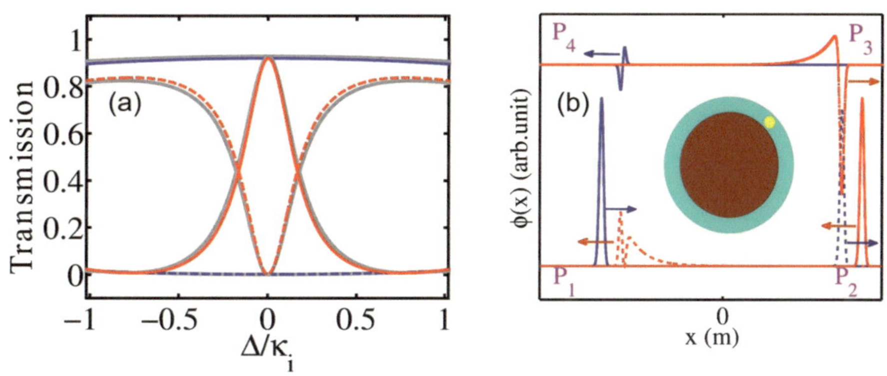

Figure 5.
(a) Steady-state transmissions of the single-photon circulator using a WGM microresonator and both of the bus and drop waveguides overcouple to the resonator, i.e., $\kappa_{ex1} = \kappa_{ex2} = 3\kappa_i$. Solid blue (red) curve is for the transmission $T_{+,B}$ ($T_{-,B}$) in the bus waveguide, while the dashed blue (red) curve is for the transmission $T_{+,D}$ ($T_{-,D}$) in the drop waveguide. The gray curves are the results from numerical simulations, which mostly overlap with other curves. $g_+ = 5\kappa_i$, $g_- = g_+/\sqrt{45}$, $\gamma_+ = 0.3\kappa_i$, and $\gamma_- = \gamma_+/45$. (b) Propagation of single-photon pulses with $\sim 4\kappa_i$ in the resonator for $\Delta = 0$ and $v_g = 1 \times 10^8 m/s$. Blue (red) lines are for the input and transmitted excitations for the left-handed (right-handed) input. The arrows indicate the moving directions of photons. Reproduced with permission from [16].

A quantum optical circulator operated by a single atom has been demonstrated [19]. In the experiment, a single ^{85}Rb atom is coupled to the WGM of a bottle microresonator, which is interfaced by two tapered fiber couplers, realizing a four-port device. The single ^{85}Rb atom is prepared in the outermost Zeeman sublevel $m_F = +3$ of the $5S_{1/2}$, $F = 3$ hyperfine ground state. The light in the CCW mode excites state $|F' = 4, m_{F'} = +4\rangle$ more strongly than CW mode exciting $|F' = 4, m_{F'} = +2\rangle$ state, corresponding to coupling strength of resonator modes and the atom, $g_+ \gg g_-$. The presence of the atom changes the resonator field decay rate from $\kappa_{\text{tot}} = \kappa_i + \kappa_{ex1} + \kappa_{ex2}$ to $\kappa_{\text{tot}} + \Gamma_\pm$, where $\Gamma_\pm = g_\pm^2/\gamma$ is the direction-dependent atom-induced loss rate [19] and $\gamma = 2\pi \times 3$ MHz is the dipole decay rate of Rb. For the CW mode, Γ_- is small, and the resonator field decay rate is not substantially modified by the atom, whereas for the CCW mode, Γ_+ can become comparable with or even exceed κ_{tot}. As a result, when light is incident into the device from ports P_2 and P_4 for which it couples to the CW mode (see **Figure 3**), the add-drop functionality is achieved. However, for the two other input ports P_1 and P_3, the light couples to the CCW mode, and the incident light field remains in its initial fiber in the condition of the resonator-atom system operating in the undercoupled regime, $\kappa_{ex1}, \kappa_{ex2} \ll \Gamma_+$. Overall, the device realizes an optical circulator that routes light from the input port P_i to the adjacent output port P_{i+1} with $i \in \{1, 2, 3, 4\}$ (see **Figure 3**).

In the experiment, the transmissions T_{ij} to all output ports P_j when sending a weak coherent probe field into the four different input ports P_i have been measured [19]. And the performance of the circulator can be quantified with the fidelity $\mathcal{F}$ and the average photon survival probability η. The fidelity is evaluated as the overlap of the renormalized transmission matrix $\tilde{T} = (T_{ij}/\eta_i)$ with the one expected for the ideal circulator, T^{id}. Here, $\eta_i = \sum_k T_{i,k}$ is the survival probability of a photon entering port P_i. Thus, the average operation fidelity of the circulator is [19]

$$\mathcal{F} = \frac{\text{Tr}\left[\tilde{T} T^{\text{id},T}\right]}{\text{Tr}\left[T^{\text{id}} T^{\text{id},T}\right]}, \tag{7}$$

giving the probability of the correct circulator operation average over various inputs. The minimum fidelity is $\mathcal{F} = 0$, whereas $\mathcal{F} = 1$ is reached for ideal operation. The experimental results show an optimum circulator performance for $\kappa_{\text{tot}}/2\kappa_i = 2.2$, where $\mathcal{F} = 0.72 \pm 0.03$ and, at the same time, $\eta = 0.73 \pm 0.04$.

Furthermore, the circulator performance can also be quantified by the isolations [19].

$$I_i = 10 \log \left(T_{i,i+1}/T_{i+1,i}\right). \tag{8}$$

For the optimum working point, it achieves $\{I_i\} = \{10.9 \pm 2.5, 6.8 \pm 1.3, 4.7 \pm 0.7, 5.4 \pm 1.1\}$ dB and an average insertion loss of $-10 \log \eta = 1.4$ dB [19].

Note that when the atom is prepared in the opposite Zeeman ground state, $F = 3, m_F = -3$, the operation direction of the circulator is reversed.

The type-III single-photon isolator is based on a microring resonator coupling to a QD and a nearby waveguide [17]. In the approach, the silicon microring resonator in which light is tightly transversely confined has an exceptionally strong evanescent e-field and a near-unity OC surrounding the whole outside and inside walls of the resonator. By initializing a quantum dot (QD) in a specific spin ground state or using the optical Stark control, a broadband single-photon isolation over several gigahertz is achieved.

The QD-resonator system consists of a silicon waveguide, a silicon microring resonator, and a single negatively charged quantum dot (QD). Numerical

DOI: http://dx.doi.org/10.5772/intechopen.90354

simulations using the finite-difference time-domain (FDTD) method are performed to calculate the properties of the resonator. At the resonant wavelength $\lambda_c \sim 1.556$ μm, the intrinsic quality factor Q_{in} is about 3.9×10^4, and the mode volume V_m is about 1.55 μm^3. The corresponding resonance frequency and the intrinsic decay rate are $\omega_c/2\pi \approx 192.67$ THz and $\kappa_i/2\pi \approx 4.94$ GHz, respectively, yielding a total decay rate of $\kappa = \kappa_{ex} + \kappa_i \approx 2\pi \times 9.88$ GHz, where WGMs decay into the waveguide at the rate κ_{ex} and $\kappa_{ex} = \kappa_i$ at resonance.

When the light enters the waveguide from port $P_1(P_2)$ with transverse electric mode and excites the CCW (CW) WGMs, the evanescent fields of interest circulating around the sidewalls of the resonator are tightly confined in the transverse direction as a transverse magnetic mode. The e-field distribution and the OC of the microring resonator are numerically investigated by FDTD simulation. For a TE mode incident to port $P_1(P_2)$, the intensity difference distribution $\mathcal{D}$ is shown in **Figure 6a–c**. When the light enters the waveguide from port P_1, the outer (inner) evanescent field of the WGM is σ^+-(σ^--) polarized, indicated by $\mathcal{C} \approx -1(1)$, as shown in **Figure 6b**. For the light incident to port P_2, the polarization of the evanescent field is reversed, as shown in **Figure 6d**. Note that in this resonator, $|\mathcal{C}| > 0.99$ from the surface of the outside wall to a position 280 nm away in the radial direction [17]. This large chiral area greatly relaxes the requirement for precisely positioning a QD. Importantly, the intensities of the evanescent fields near the outside wall are almost equal to that in the middle of the resonator, and they are still strong even at a position tens of nanometers away from the surface. These

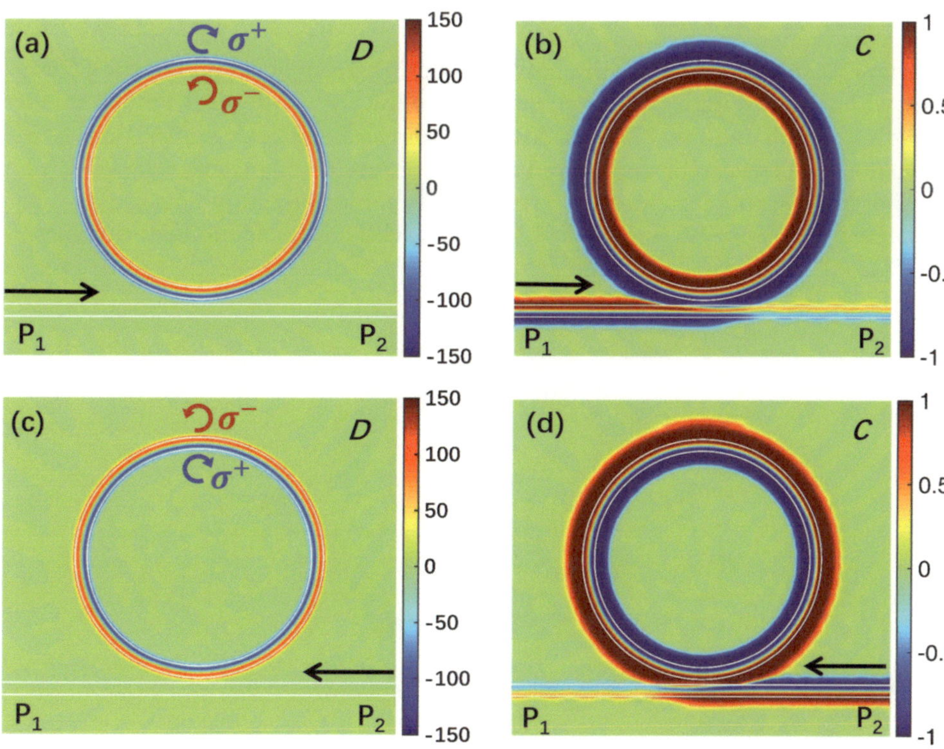

Figure 6.
(a, c) Intensity difference $\mathcal{D}$ and (b, d) optical chirality $\mathcal{C}$ for light with $\lambda = 1.556$ μm. Here, to clearly show the chiral e-fields in the vicinity of the resonator and wipe off the negligibly weak background, we use the definition for $C = \left(|\mathbf{E}(\mathbf{r}) \cdot \hat{\sigma}^-|^2 - |\mathbf{E}(\mathbf{r}) \cdot \hat{\sigma}^+|^2\right) / \left(|\mathbf{E}(\mathbf{r})|^2 + \varrho\right)$, where we introduce a small bias, $\varrho = max\{|\mathbf{E}(\mathbf{r})|^2\} \times 10^{-4}$, in the denominator. Light incident to port P_1 (a, b) and port P_2 (c, d). White lines are for the waveguide boundaries. Reproduced with permission from [17].

features of the resonator allow a strong chiral coupling between a nearby QD and the resonator.

As seen in **Figure** 7, a negatively charged QD is doped near the outside wall of the resonator. It has two energy-degenerate transitions at $\lambda_q \sim 1.556\ \mu$m, driven by a circularly polarized e-field, as seen in **Figure 8a**. It can be an InAs self-assembled QD grown on silicon dioxide/silicon substrates [29], with two electronic spin ground states $|\pm 1/2\rangle$ and two optically excited states $|\pm 3/2\rangle$.

By initializing the QD in a specific spin ground state or shifting the transition energy with the optical Stark effect (OSE), chiral QD-resonator interaction can be achieved. As shown in **Figure 8b**, by applying a magnetic field along the direction perpendicular to the growth direction of the QD, the spin-flip Raman transitions are enabled and can couple to linearly polarized e-fields. In this case, the spin ground state $|1/2\rangle$ or $|-1/2\rangle$ can be selectively prepared with a near-unity possibility [27, 30]. When the spin ground state, e.g., $|1/2\rangle$, is populated and the magnetic field is switched off, the QD can be treated as a two-level system with a dipole moment coupling only with a σ^+-polarized e-field, as shown in **Figure 8c**. The second method involves all-optical control of the QD via the optical Stark control. The polarization-selective transition, $|1/2\rangle \leftrightarrow |3/2\rangle$ or $|-1/2\rangle \leftrightarrow |-3/2\rangle$, can also be tuned to have different energies by inducing a large optical Start shift with a large detuned circularly polarized light [31, 32]. As shown in **Figure 8d**, the σ^+-polarized transition is shifted by σ^+-polarized classical light to be on resonance with the CCW mode, while the σ^--polarized transition of the QD decouples to the resonator due to a large detuning $\Delta_- = \Delta_c + 2\Delta_{OSE}$, where Δ_c is the detuning of resonator's resonance and Δ_{OSE} is the detuning which resulted from the OSE. In this case, the QD can also be treated as a two-level system with a σ^+-polarized transition.

After QD spin ground state preparation, the QD strongly couples to the CCW mode with large strength g_+ but decouples from the CW mode with a much smaller strength g_-. Note that the OSE-based method allows an all-optical operation. In fabrication, the QD can be engineered to have various resonance wavelengths, dipole moments, and decoherence rates. Self-assembled quantum dots can be engineered to possess a transition at 1.556 μm, and their dipole moment can vary

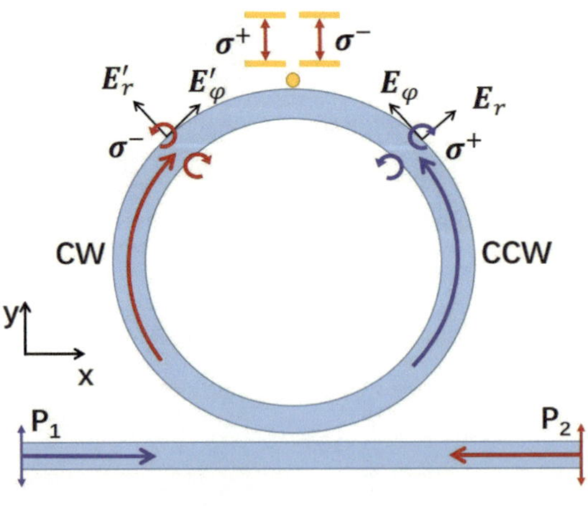

Figure 7.
Schematic of the single-photon isolation based on a microring resonator. The silicon resonator couples to a nearby silicon waveguide with refractive index n = 3.48 and a single negatively charged QD. The resonator and the waveguide are 0.44 μm wide and 0.22 μm thick. The resonator has a 4.22 μm radius. The light incident to port P_1 (P_2) drives the counterclockwise (CCW) [clockwise (CW)] WGM. The polarization of the evanescent field of the CCW mode is σ^+- (σ^--) polarized near the whole outside (inside) wall, while that for the CW mode is σ^-- (σ^+-) polarized. After initialization for the QD, it is treated as a two-level system with σ^+-polarized transition. Reproduced with permission from [17].

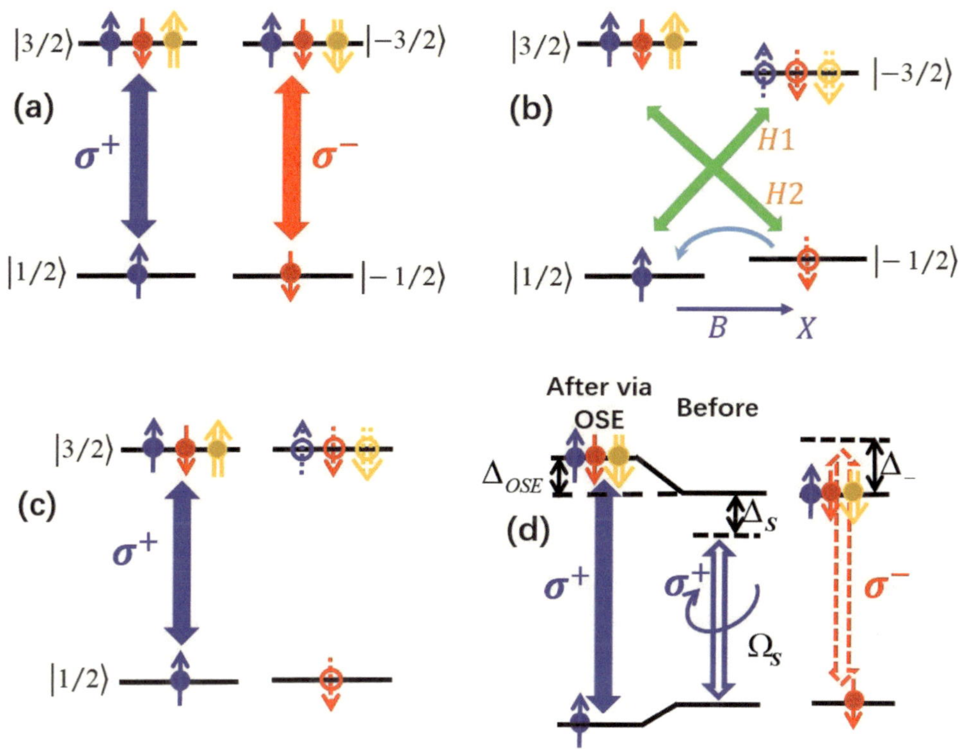

Figure 8.
Initialization of a negatively charged QD including two methods: Coherent population trapping (a–c) and optical Stark effect (d). (a) Four-level configuration of an electron spin in a single negatively charged QD. (b) Four-level configuration with dipole-allowed transitions, enabled by a magnetic field along the X direction. (c) The Trion system which has been pumped with linearly polarized light at the magnetic field can be treated as a two-level system only with σ^+-polarized light excitation at zero magnetic field. (d) A σ^+-polarized classical light Ω_s with a detuning Δ_s from the σ^+-polarized transition $|1/2\rangle \leftrightarrow |3/2\rangle$ is applied to shift the transition energy by $\Delta_{OSE} \propto \Omega_s^2/\Delta_S$. The σ^--polarized CW mode decouples from the QD because it is detuned by Δ_- from the relevant transition $|-1/2\rangle \leftrightarrow |-3/2\rangle$. Figures are reproduced with permission from [17] and are slightly modified.

from a few Debye to 40 Debye [33]. Here, we choose the resonance wavelength $\lambda_q \approx 1.556$ μm, $\omega_q = \omega_c$, and the dipole moment $|\mathbf{d}| = 30$ Debye, yielding a spontaneous emission rate $\gamma_q = |\mathbf{d}|^2\omega_q^2/3\pi\varepsilon_0\hbar c^3 = 2\pi \times 11.88$ MHz. The strength of the zero-point fluctuation of this mode is $|\mathbf{E}_0| = \sqrt{\hbar\omega_c/(2\varepsilon_0 V_m)} \approx 6.82 \times 10^4$ V/m, where ε_0 is the vacuum permittivity and $\hbar$ is the Planck constant. Correspondingly, the QD-resonator coupling strength $g = \mathbf{d} \cdot \mathbf{E}_0/\hbar \approx 2\pi \times 10.29$ GHz. And asymmetry coupling strength $|g_+| = \alpha g$ and $|g_-| = \beta g$, where $\alpha = \sqrt{(1-C)/2}$ and $\beta = \sqrt{(1+C)/2}$ [17]. As a consequence, the QD-resonator system is chiral and subsequently achieves the optical isolator at the single-photon level.

The steady-state forward (backward) transition amplitude t_+ (t_-), corresponding to the left-handed (right-handed) input, is derived by using the single-photon scattering method [17, 24, 34]

$$t_+ = \frac{\tilde{\Delta}_c\left[\tilde{\Delta}_c\tilde{\Delta}_q - G^2\right] + \tilde{\Delta}_q\kappa_{ex}^2 - g_+^* g_- h - g_+ g_-^* h^* - \tilde{\Delta}_q|h|^2 + i\left(|g_-|^2 - |g_+|^2\right)\kappa_{ex}}{\left(\tilde{\Delta}_c + i\kappa_{ex}\right)\left[\tilde{\Delta}_q\left(\tilde{\Delta}_c + i\kappa_{ex}\right) - G^2\right] - g_+^* g_- h - g_+ g_-^* h^* - \tilde{\Delta}_q|h|^2}, \tag{9}$$

$$t_- = \frac{\tilde{\Delta}_c\left[\tilde{\Delta}_c\tilde{\Delta}_q - G^2\right] + \tilde{\Delta}_q\kappa_{ex}^2 - g_-^* g_+ h - g_- g_+^* h^* - \tilde{\Delta}_q|h|^2 + i\left(|g_+|^2 - |g_-|^2\right)\kappa_{ex}}{\left(\tilde{\Delta}_c + i\kappa_{ex}\right)\left[\tilde{\Delta}_q\left(\tilde{\Delta}_c + i\kappa_{ex}\right) - G^2\right] - g_-^* g_+ h - g_- g_+^* h^* - \tilde{\Delta}_q|h|^2}, \tag{10}$$

where $\tilde{\Delta}_c = \omega - \omega_c + i\kappa_i$, $\tilde{\Delta}_q = \omega - \omega_q + i\gamma_q$, and $G^2 = |g_+|^2 + |g_-|^2$. The detuning is defined as $\Delta_c = \omega - \omega_c$ and $\omega_c = \omega_q$ is assumed. In this device, $|\mathcal{C}| = 0.99$ and $|h| \ll \kappa_i$, the transmissions, $T_\pm = |t_\pm|^2$, are shown in **Figure 9**. In the absence of the backscattering, i.e., $h = 0$, at $\Delta_c = 0$, $T_+ \approx 0.99$ and $T_- \approx 0$, yielding the insertion loss of $\mathcal{L} = -10\log(T_+) \approx 0.04$ dB and the isolation contrast $\Upsilon \approx 1$. Consequently, at vanishing detuning, the single-photon isolation is achieved with almost zero insert loss and near-unity isolation contrast. The nonreciprocal bandwidth is about $1.3\kappa \approx 2\pi \times 12.8$ GHz, which is about two to three orders broader than those in [16, 18–20, 35]. It can be seen from **Figure 9a** that the nonreciprocal spectral window becomes narrower and narrower as the backscattering strength increases; for a relatively large backscattering $|h| = \kappa_i$, both the backward and forward transmissions only change very slightly, but for an extremely large backscattering $|h| = 3\kappa_i$, the nonreciprocal performance is much affected. As shown in **Figure 9b**, in the absence of backscattering, the isolation contrast is quite robust, decreasing slowly from 1 to 0.8 as the OC changes from -1 to -0.5 (blue solid curve), while the insertion loss increases almost linearly in this region.

This device can achieve optical isolation when oppositely propagating photons enter the system at the same time, avoiding the dynamic reciprocity problem [36].

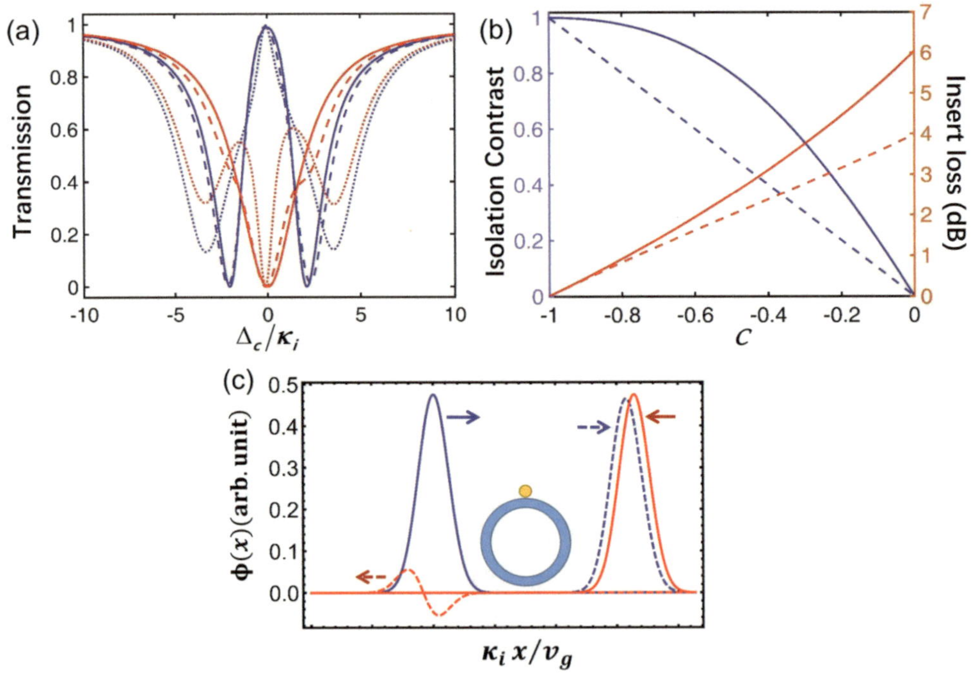

Figure 9.
(a) Steady-state transmissions for $|D| = 0.99$. Blue (red) curves are for transmissions T_+ (T_-), $h = 0$ (solid curves) for $|h| = \kappa_i$ (dashed curves), and $|h| = 3\kappa_i$ (dotted curves). (b) Blue curve is for isolation contrast, and red dashed curve is for insert loss as a function of the optical chirality D for $h = 0$ (solid curves) and $|h| = \kappa_i$ (dashed curves). (c) Propagation of single-photon pulses incident to ports P_1 and P_2 simultaneously. Red thin (blue thick) curves are for the propagation of the right-moving (left-moving) single-photon pulses. Solid curves are for incident single-photon wave function, and dashed curves are for transmitted wave function. $|D| = 1$ for simplicity.

Numerical simulations for the propagation of single-photon wave packets incident to ports P_1 and P_2 simultaneously are performed by using wave-vector-space method [17]. The propagation of single-photon pulses in the system is shown in **Figure 9c**. At resonance, a right-moving single photon can pass through the system with transmission probability 0.98, while that of a left-moving single photon is only 0.02.

4. Optical isolation via chiral cross-Kerr nonlinearity

In a waveguide embedded with N-type atoms (see the upper waveguide in **Figure 10a**), the classical switching and coupling fields are applied to induce the phase shift ϕ and amplitude modulation ξ of the probe field. The forward and backward amplitude transmissions ξ_f and ξ_b are sufficiently different after the probe field passes through the ensemble of atoms. Thus, the type-IV optical isolator is achieved.

Rb atoms are used to create the chiral XKerr nonlinearity. In the $|2\rangle \rightarrow |1\rangle$ transition, the $|2\rangle \rightarrow |3\rangle$ transition, and $|4\rangle \rightarrow |3\rangle$ transition of the Rb atoms with decay rates γ_{21}, γ_{22}, and γ_{43}, respectively, $\gamma_{21} = \gamma_{23} = \gamma_{43} = \gamma_0$ is assumed, and $\gamma_0 \gg \Gamma$, where Γ is the dephasing rates of both ground states $|1\rangle$ and $|3\rangle$ and $\gamma_0 = 2\pi \times 6$ MHz. The XKerr nonlinearity can be efficiently induced between the probe and switching fields in the configuration and can be modified by the coupling laser. As shown in **Figure 10b**, the switching (coupling, probe) field drives the transition $|1\rangle \leftrightarrow |2\rangle$ ($|3\rangle \leftrightarrow |2\rangle$, $|3\rangle \leftrightarrow |4\rangle$) with a detuning Δ_s (Δ_c, Δ_p) in the absence of

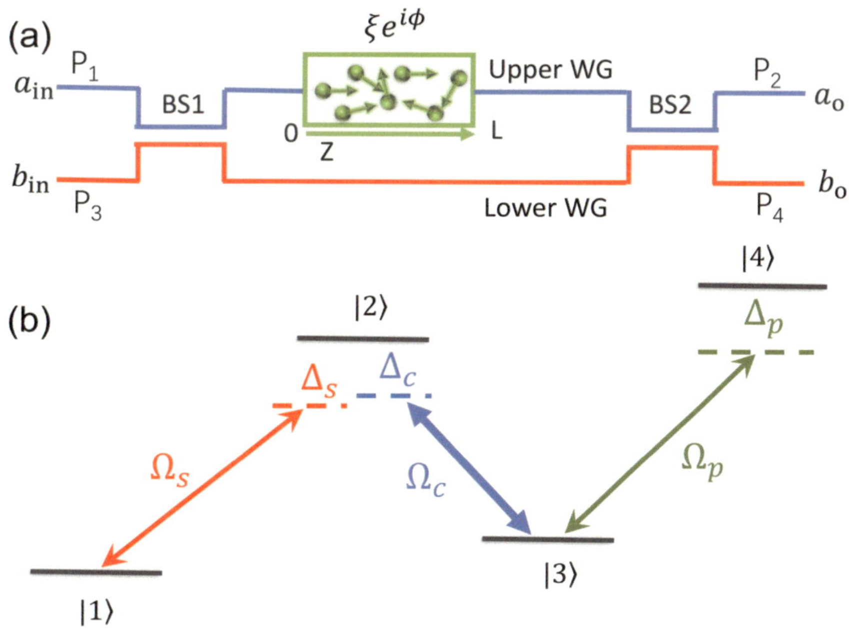

Figure 10.
(a) Schematic of the realization of optical isolator and circulator by using chiral cross-Kerr nonlinearity. To realize an optical isolator, we use only the upper waveguide (WG) embedded with a cloud of N-type atoms. The photon passing through the atoms suffers an amplitude transmission of ξ and a phase shift ϕ, which are dependent on its propagation direction. To achieve optical circulator, the lower waveguide is added to form a Mach-Zehnder interferometer with the upper one by using two beam splitters BS1 and BS2. (b) Energy-level diagram of N-type atoms. The switching (carrier frequency Ω_s), coupling (Ω_c), and probe (Ω_p) fields couple to transition $|1\rangle \leftrightarrow |2\rangle$, $|3\rangle \leftrightarrow |2\rangle$, and $|3\rangle \leftrightarrow |4\rangle$, with detunings Δ_s, Δ_c, and Δ_p, respectively. Reproduced with permission from [20].

thermal motion. The switching (coupling, probe) laser beam has the carrier frequency Ω_s (Ω_c, Ω_p), corresponding to the wave vector k_s (k_c, k_p). At room temperature, the inevitable random thermal motion of the jth atom moving with velocity v_j induces the "microscopic" Doppler shifts $k_s v_j$, $k_c v_j$, and $k_p v_j$ in the corresponding atomic transitions, respectively. The strength of the nonlinearity is strongly dependent on the effective detunings, and thus the Doppler shifts. As a result, these frequency shifts change the optical nonlinearity in a way strongly dependent on the propagation direction of the probe field with respect to the switching and coupling fields, leading to the chiral XKerr nonlinearity. Both the switching and coupling laser beams are left-moving and $k_s v_j = k_c v_j$ is assumed. Thus, the backward-moving (forward-moving) probe field "sees" the same (opposite) Doppler shift as the switching and coupling ones. Compared with the backward input case, where the Doppler broadening significantly reduces the total XKerr nonlinearity, the Doppler shift "seen" by the forward-moving probe field is partly compensated, and subsequently the nonlinearity remains large [20].

For a centimeter-scale medium, e.g., $L = 2$ cm, the medium is absorptive, and the forward and backward transmissions are very different, as shown in **Figure 11a**. As the probe detuning increases, the forward transmission T_{12} rapidly increases to 0.80 at $\Delta_p = 35.6\gamma_0$, corresponding to an insertion loss of 1 dB. As a result of Doppler broadening, the backward transmission T_{21} is much smaller than T_{12}, when $35.6\gamma_0 < \Delta_p < 60.6\gamma_0$. In this region, the insertion loss is smaller than 1 dB, while the isolation ratio is larger than 15 dB. The isolation ratio can be considerably improved with a large forward transmission by using a longer medium or, equivalently, increasing the density of the atoms. For $L = 4$ cm, the isolation rate can reach more than 30 dB in the range of $50\gamma_0 < \Delta_p < 60\gamma_0$, yielding an isolation bandwidth of $2\pi \times 60$ MHz. At the same time, the insertion loss is less than 1 dB. As a consequence, an isolation can be achieved by using this medium.

By carefully choosing the density and length of the atomic vapor, and properly arranging the switching and coupling fields, a phase shift difference, $\Delta\phi = \phi_f - \phi_b$, can approach π with high transmissions ξ_f and ξ_b. It can realize a four-port optical circulator by adding a lower waveguide to form a Mach-Zehnder interferometer (MZI), as seen in **Figure 10a**.

For a short medium ($L = 3.33$ mm), the transmission of the forward- and backward-moving probes can be comparably high, but the phase shift ϕ_b is always small, specifically about 0.011π at $\Delta_p = 7.77\gamma_0$, as shown in **Figure 11b**. In contrast, at the optimal point $\Delta_p^{\text{opt}} = 7.77\gamma_0$, the difference of the phase shift, $\phi_f - \phi_b$, reaches

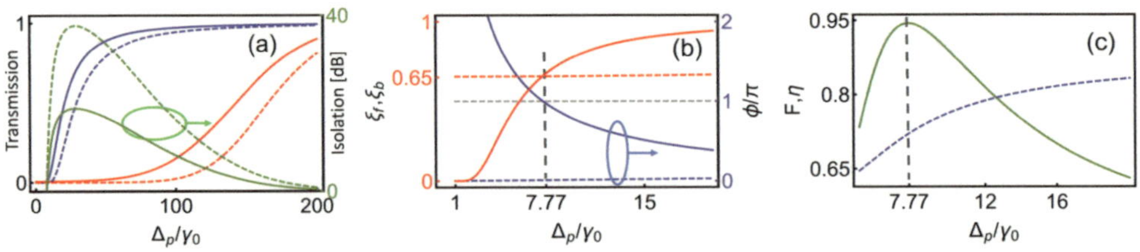

Figure 11.
(a) The transmission of the isolator for forward-moving (blue curves) and backward-moving (red curves) probe fields as a function of the probe detuning Δ_p. Green curves are for the isolations. Solid (dashed) curves are for the length of medium L = 2(4) cm. (b) Amplitude transmissions (red curves) and phase shifts (blue curves) for forward-moving (solid curves) and backward-moving (dashed curves) probe fields as a function of Δ_p. (c) Green curves are for fidelities, and blue dashed curves are for average insertion loss as a function of Δ_p. The vertical black dashed lines in the two figures show the optimal detuning $\Delta_p^{\text{opt}} = 7.77\gamma_0$. The length of medium is 3.33 mm. Other parameters $N_a = 5 \times 10^{12} cm^{-3}$, $\Gamma_3 = 0.1\gamma_0$, $\Omega_c = 20\gamma_0$, $\Omega_s = 4\gamma_0$, and $\delta = 0$ are fixed. Reproduced with permission from [20].

the optimal value of π. At the same time, $\xi_f^{\rm opt} \approx \xi_b^{\rm opt} \approx 0.66$. As a result, a high-performance circulator can be realized by inserting this nonlinear medium into a MZI composed of unbalanced BSs. In the lower waveguide, a phase shift $\vartheta = 0.01\pi$ is added to compensate the phase shift of the backward-moving photon in the upper one. As shown in **Figure 11c**, when the detuning Δ_p varies from $6\gamma_0$ to $20\gamma_0$, the fidelity $\mathcal{F}$ first rises up rapidly, reaches the maximum 0.944 at $\Delta_p^{\rm opt} = 7.77\gamma_0$, and then decreases. At the same time, the average photon survival probability η increases from 0.68 to 0.83. Although the photons have a larger probability to survive at a large detuning, the fidelity is low. Thus, there is a trade-off between the fidelity and the survival probability. The circulator operating within the frequency range $6.6\gamma_0 < \Delta_p < 9.7\gamma_0$ can achieve a fidelity larger than 0.9 at the expense of $\eta > 0.69$. The corresponding working window is about $2\pi \times 20$ MHz, and the average insertion loss is about 1.6 dB. At the $\Delta_p^{\rm opt}$, it obtains a fidelity $\mathcal{F} = 0.944$ and a survival probability $\eta = 0.72$, yielding an insertion loss of 1.42 dB. The circulator can also be quantified by the isolations $\{\mathcal{F}_i\} = \{41.7, 13.8, 13.8, 8.2\}$ dB with $i = \{1, 2, 3, 4\}$ (see Eq. (7)), implying nonreciprocal photon circulator along $1 \to 2 \to 3 \to 4 \to 1$.

The proposal can achieve the nonlinear optical isolation without dynamic reciprocity [36], because the XKerr nonlinearity itself is chiral and the isolation is based on linear equations [20]. According to this proposed method, the device that uses XKerr nonlinearity to achieve cavity-free optical isolator and circulator at ultralow light level has been demonstrated experimentally [21].

5. Conclusions

In this chapter, we introduce the optical chirality of light confined around nanophotonic structures and the chiral optical XKerr nonlinearity induced in atoms. Based on optical chirality, we propose single-photon isolators and circulators with chiral light-emitter interaction. These concepts have been demonstrated experimentally. Then we showed approaches to achieve an optical isolator and a circulator by using the chiral XKerr nonlinearity. All of these approaches can realize chip-comparable optical isolations with low insertion loss and high isolation performance. The methods also work at ultralow light level and even single-photon level. These optical isolators and circulators may pave the way for photon routing and information processing in a nonreciprocal way in integrated optical circuits and quantum networks.

Acknowledgements

K. X. thanks the support of the National Key R&D Program of China (Grant No. 2017YFA0303703) and the National Natural Science Foundation of China (Grants Nos. 11874212 and 61435007). He also thanks his co-workers, in particular, Prof. Jason Twamley, Prof. Yong Zhang, Prof. Min Xiao, and Prof. Franco Nori for their essential contribution to the original works.

Abbreviations

OC	optical chirality
WGM	whispering-gallery mode

QD	quantum dot
OSE	optical Stark effect
CCW	counterclockwise
CW	clockwise
FDTD	finite-difference time-domain
XKerr	cross-Kerr
MZI	Mach-Zehnder interferometer
BS	beam splitter

Author details

Lei Tang[1,2,3*†] and Keyu Xia[1,2,3†]

1 College of Engineering and Applied Sciences, Nanjing University, Nanjing, China

2 National Laboratory of Solid State Microstructures, Collaborative Innovation Center of Advanced Microstructures, Nanjing University, Nanjing, China

3 Jiangsu Key Laboratory of Artificial Functional Materials, and Key Laboratory of Intelligent Optical Sensing and Manipulation, Ministry of Education, Nanjing University, Nanjing, China

*Address all correspondence to: tanglei@smail.nju.edu.cn

† These authors contributed equally.

References

[1] Cirac JI, Zoller P, Kimble HJ, Mabuchi H. Quantum state transfer and entanglement distribution among distant nodes in a quantum network. Physical Review Letters. 1997;**78**(16):3221-3224. DOI: 10.1103/PhysRevLett.78.3221

[2] Kimble HJ. The quantum internet. Nature. 2008;**453**(7198):1023-1030. DOI: 10.1038/nature07127

[3] Hacker B, Welte S, Rempe G, Ritter S. A photon–photon quantum gate based on a single atom in an optical resonator. Nature. 2016;**536**(7615): 193-196. DOI: 10.1038/nature18592

[4] Riedinger R, Hong S, Norte RA, Slater JA, Shang J, Krause AG, et al. Non-classical correlations between single photons and phonons from a mechanical oscillator. Nature. 2016; **530**(7590):313-316. DOI: 10.1038/nature16536

[5] Sathyamoorthy SR, Tornberg L, Kockum AF, Baragiola BQ, Combes J, Wilson CM, et al. Quantum nondemolition detection of a propagating microwave photon. Physical Review Letters. 2014;**112**(9): 093601. DOI: 10.1103/PhysRevLett.112.093601

[6] Bi L, Hu J, Jiang P, Kim DH, Dionne GF, Kimerling LC, et al. On-chip optical isolation in monolithically integrated non-reciprocal optical resonators. Nature Photonics. 2011; **5**(12):758-762. DOI: 10.1038/NPHOTON.2011.270

[7] Tien MC, Mizumoto T, Pintus P, Kromer H, Bowers JE. Silicon ring isolators with bonded nonreciprocal magneto-optic garnets. Optics Express. 2011;**19**(12):11740-11745. DOI: 10.1364/OE.19.011740

[8] Fan L, Wang J, Varghese LT, Shen H, Niu B, Xuan Y, et al. An all-silicon passive optical diode. Science. 2012; **335**(6067):447-450. DOI: 10.1126/science.1214383

[9] Peng B, Özdemir Ş K, Lei F, Monifi F, Gianfreda M, Long GL, et al. Parity–time-symmetric whispering-gallery microcavities. Nature Physics. 2014; **10**(5):394-398. DOI: 10.1038/NPHYS2927

[10] Chang L, Jiang X, Hua S, Yang C, Wen J, Jiang L, et al. Parity–time symmetry and variable optical isolation in active–passive-coupled microresonators. Nature Photonics. 2014;**8**(7):524-529. DOI: 10.1038/NPHOTON.2014.133

[11] Ruesink F, Miri MA, Alu A, Verhagen E. Nonreciprocity and magnetic-free isolation based on optomechanical interactions. Nature Communications. 2016;7:13662. DOI: 10.1038/ncomms13662

[12] Shen Z, Zhang YL, Chen Y, Zou CL, Xiao YF, Zou XB, et al. Experimental realization of optomechanically induced non-reciprocity. Nature Photonics. 2016;**10**(10):657-661. DOI: 10.1038/NPHOTON.2016.161

[13] Fang K, Luo J, Metelmann A, Matheny MH, Marquardt F, Clerk AA, et al. Generalized non-reciprocity in an optomechanical circuit via synthetic magnetism and reservoir engineering. Nature Physics. 2017;**13**(5):465-471. DOI: 10.1038/NPHYS4009

[14] Dong MX, Yu YC, Ye YH, Zhang WH, Li EZ, Zeng L, et al. Experimental realization of quantum non-reciprocity based on cold atomic ensembles. arXiv:1908.09242v1. 2019. https://arxiv.org/abs/1908.09242v1

[15] Lodahl P, Mahmoodian S, Stobbe S, Rauschenbeutel A, Schneeweiss P, Volz J, et al. Chiral quantum optics. Nature. 2017;**541**(7638):473-480. DOI: 10.1038/nature21037

[16] Xia K, Lu G, Lin G, Cheng Y, Niu Y, Gong S, et al. Reversible nonmagnetic single-photon isolation using unbalanced quantum coupling. Physical Review A. 2014;**90**(4):043802. DOI: 10.1103/PhysRevA.90.043802

[17] Tang L, Tang J, Zhang W, Lu G, Zhang H, Zhang Y, et al. On-chip chiral single-photon interface: Isolation and unidirectional emission. Physical Review A. 2019;**99**(4):043833. DOI: 10.1103/PhysRevA.99.043833

[18] Sayrin C, Junge C, Mitsch R, Albrecht B, O'Shea D, Schneeweiss P, et al. Nanophotonic optical isolator controlled by the internal state of cold atoms. Physical Review X. 2015;**5**(4): 041036. DOI: 10.1103/PhysRevX.5.041036

[19] Scheucher M, Hilico A, Will E, Volz J, Rauschenbeutel A. Quantum optical circulator controlled by a single chirally coupled atom. Science. 2016; **354**(6319):1577-1580. DOI: 10.1126/science.aaj2118

[20] Xia K, Nori F, Xiao M. Cavity-free optical isolators and circulators using a chiral cross-Kerr nonlinearity. Physical Review Letters. 2018;**121**(20):203602. DOI: 10.1103/PhysRevLett.121.203602

[21] Li EZ, Ding DS, Yu YC, Dong MX, Zeng L, Zhang WH, et al. Experimental demonstration of cavity-free optical isolators and optical circulators. arXiv: 1908.07210v1. 2019. https://arxiv.org/abs/1908.07210v1

[22] Mahmoodian S, Prindal-Nielsen K, Sölner I, Stobbe S, Lodahl P. Engineering chiral light–matter interaction in photonic crystal waveguides with slow light. Optical Materials Express. 2017;**7**(1):43-51. DOI: 10.1364/OME.7.000043

[23] Shen Y, Bradford M, Shen JT. Single-photon diode by exploiting the photon polarization in a waveguide. Physical Review Letters. 2011;**107**(17): 173902. DOI: 10.1103/PhysRevLett.107.173902

[24] Shen JT, Fan S. Coherent photon transport from spontaneous emission in one-dimensional waveguides. Optics Letters. 2005;**30**(15):2001-2003. DOI: 10.1364/OL.30.002001

[25] Turchette QA, Hood CJ, Lange W, Mabuchi H, Kimble HJ. Measurement of conditional phase shifts for quantum logic. Physical Review Letters. 1995; **75**(25):4710. DOI: 10.1103/PhysRevLett.75.4710

[26] Junge C, O'shea D, Volz J, Rauschenbeutel A. Strong coupling between single atoms and nontransversal photons. Physical Review Letters. 2013;**110**(21):213604. DOI: 10.1103/PhysRevLett.110.213604

[27] Xu X, Sun B, Berman PR, Steel DG, Bracker AS, Gammon D, et al. Coherent population trapping of an electron spin in a single negatively charged quantum dot. Nature Physics. 2008;**4**(9):692-695. DOI: 10.1038/nphys1054

[28] Vetsch E, Reitz D, Sagué G, Schmidt R, Dawkins ST, Rauschenbeutel A. Optical interface created by laser-cooled atoms trapped in the evanescent field surrounding an optical nanofiber. Physical Review Letters. 2010;**104**(20):203603. DOI: 10.1103/PhysRevLett.104.203603

[29] Choi BH, Park CM, Song SH, Son MH, Hwang SW, Ahn D, et al. Selective growth of InAs self-assembled quantum dots on nanopatterned SiO_2/Si substrate. Applied Physics Letters. 2001; **78**(10):1403-1405. DOI: 10.1063/1.1352049

[30] Atatüre M, Dreiser J, Badolato A, Högele A, Karrai K, Imamoglu A. Quantum-dot spin-state preparation with near-unity fidelity. Science. 2006; **312**(5773):551-553. DOI: 10.1126/science.1126074

[31] Vora PM, Bracker AS, Carter SG, Sweeney TM, Kim M, Kim CS, et al. Spin–cavity interactions between a quantum dot molecule and a photonic crystal cavity. Nature Communications. 2015;**6**:7665. DOI: 10.1038/ncomms8665

[32] Yong CK, Horng J, Shen Y, Cai H, Wang A, Yang CS, et al. Biexcitonic optical stark effects in monolayer molybdenum diselenide. Nature Physics. 2018;**14**(11):1092-1096. DOI: 10.1038/s41567-018-0216-7

[33] Htoon H, Takagahara T, Kulik D, Baklenov O, Holmes AL Jr, Shih CK. Interplay of Rabi oscillations and quantum interference in semiconductor quantum dots. Physical Review Letters. 2002;**88**(8):087401. DOI: 10.1103/PhysRevLett.88.087401

[34] Shen JT, Fan S. Theory of single-photon transport in a single-mode waveguide. II. Coupling to a whispering-gallery resonator containing a two-level atom. Physical Review A. 2009;**79**(2):023838. DOI: 10.1103/PhysRevA.79.023838

[35] Söllner I, Mahmoodian S, Hansen SL, Midolo L, Javadi A, Kiršanskė G, et al. Deterministic photon–emitter coupling in chiral photonic circuits. Nature Nanotechnology. 2015;**10**(9):775-778. DOI: 10.1038/NNANO.2015.159

[36] Shi Y, Yu Z, Fan S. Limitations of nonlinear optical isolators due to dynamic reciprocity. Nature Photonics. 2015;**9**(6):388-392. DOI: 10.1038/NPHOTON.2015.79